CB

FORGIVE US OUR SPINS

FORGIVE US OUR SPINS

MICHAEL MOORE AND THE
FUTURE OF THE LEFT

JESSE LARNER

WILEY

John Wiley & Sons, Inc.

Published by John Wiley & Sons, Inc., Hoboken, New Jersey
Published simultaneously in Canada

For general information about our other products and services, please contact our Customer Care Department within the United States at (800) 762-2974, outside the United States at (317) 572-3993 or fax (317) 572-4002.

Wiley also publishes its books in a variety of electronic formats. Some content that appears in print may not be available in electronic books. For more information about Wiley products, visit our web site at www.wiley.com.

Library of Congress Cataloging-in-Publication Data:

Larner, Jesse.
   Forgive us our spins : Michael Moore and the future of the Left / Jesse Larner.
      p. cm.
   Includes bibliographical references and index.
   ISBN-13 978-0-471-79306-9 (cloth)
   ISBN-10 0-471-79306-X (cloth)
  1. Moore, Michael, 1954 Apr. 23—Criticism and interpretation. 2. Motion pictures—Political aspects—United States. I. Title.
   PN1998.3.M665L37 2006
   791.4302'33092—dc22

                                         2005036099

Printed in the United States of America

10 9 8 7 6 5 4 3 2 1

For Constance

CONTENTS

ACKNOWLEDGMENTS

I am very grateful to the many people who contributed to this project. I would especially like to thank my editors for the British and American editions respectively, Albert Depetrillo and Eric Nelson, both of whom kept the focus on the real story. This book would not be what it is without the hard work of editorial assistant Connie Santisteban, production editor Lisa Burstiner, copy editor Amy Handy, and proofreader Rima Dudko.

I owe many thanks and much appreciation to my agent, Sydelle Kramer, and to Maura Spiegel, who gave me the reference; to my dear friend Nathan Thompson, with whom I took a memorable trip to Washington, D.C.; and most of all to my wife, Constance Morrill, whose patience and wisdom have helped me more than I can say.

INTRODUCTION

At two in the afternoon on November 3, 2004, John Kerry gave his concession speech at Boston's Faneuil Hall: "It is now clear that even when all the provisional ballots are counted, which they will be, there won't be enough outstanding votes for us to be able to win Ohio. And therefore we cannot win this election."[1]

It wasn't supposed to be like this. Another four years of faith-based foreign policy, carried out by ideologues with no interest in facts or in the lessons of history. Another four years of attacks on the poor, of privatization of social goods, of gifts to the rich. Another four years of creeping theocracy and contempt for the Constitution. Another four years in which to nurture a rogue sense of national sovereignty.

It must have been a really bad day for Michael Moore. He'd had a hit movie, *Fahrenheit 9/11*, that was designed to drop-kick George W. Bush into the dustbin of history. His ego as bloated as his bank account, Moore probably believed that he was the kingmaker. He'd staked a lot of personal credibility on the election, and had confidently predicted victory for the team. At the Republican National Convention in New York City in late August of that year, he'd held up two fingers to show the conventioneers that Bush had two months left before his defeat.

But Moore's movie didn't make a difference. Where does that leave him?

■ ■ ■

1

Many of those who were delighted at George W. Bush's victory didn't make much of a distinction between Moore and the general opposition to Bush—that 48 percent of the American voters who voted for Kerry. Republicans were quite strategically brilliant in accepting, at face value, Moore's idea of himself as the preeminent voice of American liberalism and leftism, such as it is. The right-wing commentator James K. Glassman, writing about *Fahrenheit 9/11*, said, "The sad truth is that the left is so intellectually bereft at this point in its history that the buffoonery of Michael Moore is about all they've got."[2] The popular radical-right Web site www.freerepublic.com positively buzzed with delight at what its members saw as the unitary comeuppance of Moore, the Democratic Party, and the left in general. The right-wing commentator David Bossie wrote, "Mr. Moore and these left-wing, Bush-hating groups tried every trick in the book to energize voters with their anger and venom, painting the picture of a divided and pessimistic America. But thanks to their over-the-top rhetoric and scare tactics, it backfired and actually helped the American people see clearly."[3] Melanie Morgan, a former television news correspondent who has a right-wing radio show in San Francisco and is now a vice chair of Move America Forward, a "support the troops" outfit that also works to expel the United States from the United Nations and the United Nations from New York, told me, "I thank God that [Moore] decided to get as politically active as he did. I am grateful to him beyond measure for creating *Fahrenheit 9/11*, because by doing so, with such a lack of scholarship, he ended up motivating our base in a way that nothing else could have. Between the Swift Boat Veterans for Truth and Michael Moore and *Fahrenheit 9/11*, people got motivated on my side of the political fence in a way that I haven't seen before."

Michael Moore thought himself a kingmaker, and he turned out to be only a filmmaker. Contrary to a cherished belief of the right, any claim he may make to represent the broad-based opposition to the Bush agenda is dubious at best. But it is true that Moore, that ostentatiously working-class guy from Flint, Michigan, remains a political phenomenon in North America and Europe. His polemics reside on the bestseller lists. His Web site is visited by millions. His film *Bowling for Columbine* won the Academy Award for Best Documentary of 2002, and *Fahrenheit 9/11*—love it or hate it—needs no introduction.

Moore is a popular speaker, pulling in big crowds at home and in Europe who come to hear him rail against the imperial ambitions of the U.S. government.

However mainstream Democrats feel about him, however many on the left are embarrassed by him, Moore has become associated in the public mind with opposition to the Bush administration. His style of antiestablishment humor has been compared to that of the Yippies[4] of the late 1960s, but there are differences, differences that are important to the way Moore's work is received.

The Yippies were performance art anarchists who never would have campaigned within "the system." In their eyes, any electoral participation was a sellout, so Yippie impresarios Jerry Rubin and Abbie Hoffman ran a pig for president. It is unlikely that the pig—given the name Pigasus the Immortal—met the age requirements for the office, although he was certainly native-born. At the subsequent trial of the radical Chicago Seven, who included Rubin, Hoffman, and the folksinger Phil Ochs, who had purchased the pig, the radical lawyer William Kunstler asked Ochs, "Were you informed by an officer that the pig had squealed on you?"[5]

Moore's pranks are usually less abstract. He does not reject the political process, as the Yippies did, but he delivers a much more radical message than any serious American political party does. Corporations loot and pollute. Racism is a ubiquitous, defining reality of American life. Government—and, especially, American government—is a conspiracy of oppression and war. Authority is the enemy. Working people are never wrong. Those in power are never right.

Like all reductionist creeds, this one is not without some tiny truth at its core, and it is not particularly relevant to real life. It is not taken seriously in American politics, for good reason. The fact that it has a speaker and an audience now has been a tremendous help to the ideologues of the Republican Party, who enjoy nothing more than painting Democrats as a bunch of hippies who hate America. If the Democrats were somehow insane enough to nominate Michael Moore for the presidency, no one would be happier than Bush consigliere Karl Rove.

So why has Moore found an audience? Although his political ideas aren't necessarily more complicated than those of the hippies and the Yippies, his presentation is much better. He has a sly sense of humor.

He knows how to work with others when he wants to, and he knows how to use the machinery of capitalism to make contacts, contracts, and deals. He is tireless, often working on several projects at once and cross-pollinating them. He is genuinely fired up by issues of social justice. He is imaginative. And—one big difference between Moore and the campus radicals of the 1960s, the paradoxical conceptual weakness at the heart of his populist strength—he goes about his mission with ordinary, nonpolitical, working Americans in mind: people who want to be entertained, not lectured.

Moore became famous as something new on the left, someone who defied its stereotypes. Not a hippie, not a dour sloganeer, not a humorless disciple of political correctness, not a public executive like Ralph Nader or Marian Wright Edelman. He is an improviser. It's hard to mock him because, in a sense, he presents his work as a joke—a serious joke. He invokes the jester's privilege of saying serious things that wouldn't get heard if serious people said them. Part of Moore's charm—and a big part of his effectiveness—is that he is capable of self-mockery.

■   ■   ■

Moore is not running for any office; he doesn't *want* to hold any office. He reports to no editor, director, or foundation, and thus has no accountability. He's a true independent operator, and if you think about it, there aren't that many of them on the scene. Moore's only job is politics, one-man politics. Short of the law and the market, there are no restraints.

We all know by now what a Michael Moore/Dog Eat Dog production will look like. We know it will be funny and irreverent. That it will perhaps include a cartoon. That Moore himself will shuffle through the proceedings, making a point of dressing like a slob; that he will skewer important people on basic questions and make them look like fools. There will be pranks on bad guys, and there will be plenty of bad guys. There will be facts, or, just as often, highly debatable suggestions that imply facts.

Moore's career has received a boost from a particular conjunction of phenomena that have tended to discourage subtlety in American political discourse and to call forth the broad strokes of populist activism. The two most obvious are closely linked. There is the arrogance and ambition of the political right, put in power by appeals to popular indignation among those whom right-wing politicians do not represent, resemble, or respect, but whom, thanks to shrewd market research, they have come to understand quite well. At the same time—and by no means coincidentally—the American news media have been increasingly dominated over the last thirty years by the views of the extreme right.

The disgraceful attempt to impeach President Bill Clinton put these phenomena in focus. The stolen election of 2000 made them almost impossible to bear. The war in Iraq (more correctly, not the war itself, which many thoughtful liberals can and do support, but the arrogance and incompetence of the conduct of the war) made it clear that the stakes are very high.

It has not been easy for American liberals to hear the language of social justice being used to explain tax cuts for millionaires and the degradation of the poor, and to see how effective this strategy has been. It is not surprising that when Moore champions a more reasonable set of priorities, his arguments, even when they are sloppy and demagogic, are heard with delight.

But why is it that only Moore is saying these things in a way that gets attention? There should be many contenders for the role of liberal populist. There are more registered Democrats than Republicans in the United States, but since 1994 an increasingly conservative Republican Party has outmaneuvered Democrats and captured both houses of Congress, the presidency, and much of the judiciary. The American left has been on a long, long march from its heyday in the time of the New Deal—not through American institutions, as the right would have it, but into obscurity. It now has no one in mainstream politics, certainly no one among the moderate centrists and right-centrists, who are the only type of Democrat in Congress. John Kerry's miserable 2004 presidential campaign ended any possibility of Kerry taking a national leadership role.

The late Paul Wellstone of Minnesota was the last Democrat who might have been the next liberal hero, a man of passion, intelligence, and eloquence who had a sense of mission. He died in an airplane accident while campaigning for reelection in 2002, a tragedy that, no doubt, encouraged the contemporary notion that God loves conservatives.

Liberals, to say nothing of Democrats, have failed to present a coherent and effective alternative to Republican policies. There are some liberals in America, but there are no liberal politics in the sense of having an agenda and a party. There is no party in American contemporary life that is committed to a national, single-payer health-care system. Or that advocates a steeply graduated income tax as a matter of both good policy (to pay for the war on terror, and to buy back all that debt that the Chinese now hold) and as a matter of social justice in its own right. Or that proposes full civil rights for gay people. Or that treats global warming and AIDS as the threats to national security that they are. Or that stands proudly with unions and working people. Or that insists that we are a secular Republic and refuses to pander to flat-earth creationists. The death of left- and center-liberalism has created a hole at the heart of American politics, and our political discourse is suffering for it, on both ends of the political spectrum. The left suffers for the obvious reasons, but the right suffers too: in the absence of any coherent popular and intellectual challenge, it has descended into a lazy and bullying triumphalism.

So long as this is true, Michael Moore will be seen by many on the left as a necessary corrective. What George W. Bush has done to reward the rich and to destroy the established international order has brought centrist liberals and the radical left closer together, and drawn these groups closer to marginal protest groups that do not look to mainstream political leaders. A political clown with an edge, someone who is very calculatedly not careful with his words, is seen in many quarters as a great relief. There are liberals and leftists who are looking for a spokesperson who will paint the picture with the broadest possible strokes and offend the greatest number on the right. Damn the torpedoes!

But it is not only the right that sees Moore's weaknesses. Moore is a disturbing public leader for many liberals. He is good at mobilizing outrage, but his presentation of the issues is highly opinionated, usually easy to challenge, occasionally paranoid, and hardly of any depth. Most seriously, his belief in the ultimate truth of his political positions is so strong that he is willing to use dishonest arguments in their defense.

Moore is not the intellectual heir to the democratic left's glory days of *Partisan Review* or *Dissent*. There are plenty of reasons to doubt him, and even to despise him. Yet it is true that he has brought important issues of social justice to the attention of people who would otherwise not know of them. In his days as a regional journalist he agitated for, and often achieved on a local level, significant and positive changes in social policy. He's also hurt some good people on his way to a national stage.

This book is a detailed look at how Michael Moore's political style influences American culture in a reactionary age. It will require a few excursions into the context of some of the major political issues that span Moore's career, and have defined it, to understand why he has become a phenomenon. Why Moore? Why now? And where next?

PART ONE

CLASS STILL MATTERS

ROOTS

Moore" is the ninth most common surname in the United States, and its etymology is simple: it is derived from "moor," meaning "a fen" or "a bog," and it implies that the ancestors of the person carrying the name were poor and powerless, confined to the marginal land that the rich folk didn't want. To the extent that the United States is an Anglo-Saxon country, the prevalence of this name says a lot about the roots of its people and about the role of class (along with its American concomitant, the denial of class) in its sociology. An American, regardless of origin, is more likely to identify with the working man than with the aristocrat, yet—paradoxically—to insist, against all the evidence, that the accident of birth played no role in his personal fate.

Michael Moore is an anomaly in this latter regard. His identity seems to be drawn from folk memories of the New Deal 1930s, a much more radical time when working people were developing a self-conscious culture. Moore knows that class is important, if not determinative, in life prospects. He presents himself as just an ordinary working stiff who could have ended up as a factory worker, who dropped out of college and doesn't have any fancy degrees, yet who's managed to figure it all out. He's the descendant of Irish immigrants, the son of an auto worker and a clerk, who grew up near Flint, Michigan.

■ ■ ■

Michael Moore, with humor and a certain antistyle, exists to make it clear that class does matter. There's some history here, some background, and even if Moore himself is now a multimillionaire who never actually worked on a production line—well, class is more than a matter of income, more even than a matter of occupation. It's a matter of background, consciousness, and identity.

Moore's parents, Frank and Veronica, and his older sisters, Anne and Veronica, were not deeply involved in politics, but the family was devout in the religion of the Irish-descended American working class. Frank and Veronica went to Mass every day and raised their children in the faith, and they were one of the founding families of a new neighborhood Catholic church. They came from a socially progressive, blue-collar Catholic tradition that found inspiration in the social justice encyclicals of Pope Leo XIII and Pope Pius XI, and this gave them an awareness of class and the importance of union solidarity. They were almost certainly aware of, and influenced by, Dorothy Day and Peter Maurin's Catholic Worker movement. The family took up collections for César Chávez and the United Farm Workers and for Daniel and Philip Berrigan and their religiously inspired, nonviolent, anti–Vietnam War protests.

Michael himself attended a training seminary while he was in high school, and for a brief period he seriously considered entering the priesthood. Years later, he proposed a segment for his *TV Nation* television show in which a correspondent goes to confessionals in twenty different Catholic churches and ranks the punishments meted out, calling the results "A Consumer's Guide to the Confessional." But even then he was still enough of a Catholic to have doubts about this very funny and sharp idea. Moore and his wife, Kathleen Glynn, would later write, "When the segment was finished, Mike was confident he would burn in eternal Hell if this segment ever ran, so he spiked it."[1]

Although Moore didn't join the priesthood, he had a sense of mission from a very young age and was an enthusiastic agitator long before Flint's decline. Although he has wrapped himself in Flint's labor history, he didn't actually grow up there; he was raised in Davison, a bedroom community just to the east of Flint proper, an open and sunny place that bills itself as the "City of Flags" and the hometown of Ken Morrow, a member of the 1980 U.S. Olympic champion hockey team. There is no public mention of a much more famous native son. As a matter of fact, Moore is in the unusual position of being a worldwide celebrity who is apparently banned from his hometown high school's Hall of Fame. His candidacy has been vetoed by Davison school board members who believe it would cost the district private donations.

Moore's critics have made much of the fact that Davison is white, comfortable, and clean, with many more white-collar workers (middle managers at General Motors) than gritty, working-class Flint. All of this is true, yet the criticism is still a little off. Davison was an adjunct of Flint, and it was no playground of the leisure class. Its modest suburban charms were well within the reach of the line workers at GM's plants in Flint, among them Moore's father, who made spark plugs for thirty years. Davison—nearly mall-less and mostly undeveloped in Moore's youth—has come up considerably since that time, while Flint has gone down precipitously. If Davison has a higher average income than Flint, dramatically lower unemployment, and is almost entirely white, at least part of this is due to the aftershocks of GM's withdrawal from Flint, starting in the late 1970s, which separated those who could afford to leave Flint from those who could not. Moore's father had his place in Davison long before this happened. Moore himself had left Davison long before this happened.

In high school, Moore had already established a penchant for outspoken politics that predicted much that was to follow. Coming up at a time in which the Vietnam War was boiling through American political life, he was always an agitator. He started his first anti-establishment news sheets in grade school, while in high school he won a public-speaking contest with a speech condemning the local Elks lodge for barring black people from membership. He started a campaign to ban the Homecoming Queen contest, which he considered silly and sexist.

When the voting and office-holding age was lowered in 1972 from twenty-one to eighteen, Moore ran for the Davison school board and won, becoming the board's youngest member. From this position, he set about lobbying the board to fire the principal and vice principal, whom he clearly despised. The two submitted their resignations soon after Moore's election to the school board, and he would later take credit for forcing them out. It's not at all clear why Moore was so intent on getting rid of these men. Moore writes of feeling oppressed by deadening routine—not a remarkable memory of high school. In his own words, he has only nice things to say of the principal whose removal he sought:

> I had known this man, the principal, for many years. When I was eight years old, he used to let me and my friends skate and play hockey on this little pond beside his house. He was kind and generous, and always left the door to his house open in case any of us needed to change into our skates or if we got cold and just wanted to get warm. Years later, I was asked to play bass in a band that was forming, but I didn't own a bass. He let me borrow his son's.[2]

This passage has understandably been seized upon by right-wing critics of Moore; there's something shocking and unseemly about it, for Moore himself is writing that his antiauthoritarianism trumps any consideration of loyalty or human feeling or the character of his targets. The reader is left to assume that, to Moore, anyone in a position of authority—or who can be presented as being in a position of authority—is an enemy. Even politics at the school board level was for Moore a zero-sum game: teachers (except for the popular antiestablishment ones) were the enemy, students the victims of an oppressive system. Moore's instincts were to trust the students always to know what was in their own interests. He did not get along well with the other board members and did not hesitate to invoke the legal system, at one point threatening to sue the board for the right to tape-record board meetings, an issue that was, typically, couched in the highest language of public accountability. His confrontational style led to a recall effort, which failed.

The Davison school board was too small a stage for a talented social activist, and Moore soon expanded his work. He and his friend Jeff Gibbs started the Hotline Center, an emergency phone line that took calls and made referrals for unwanted pregnancies, drug overdoses, and suicide attempts, and they soon branched out into broader social issues like police brutality. The hotline led to a community newspaper named, in best early-1970s style, *Free to Be*. The pompous sense of self-importance of Moore and his young staff was written in the wet cement of the sidewalk they installed outside the hotline's office in the Flint suburb of Burton: WE SHALL STAY FREE! followed by Article I of the First Amendment.

Free to Be was mimeographed and distributed free, and its title was hand drawn, but there was some real journalistic competence behind it. Moore had been a socially conscious writer and investigator throughout his school years, winning an Eagle Scout badge for a slide-show exposé of polluting industries in the Flint area, and *Free to Be* took on some fine-grained but serious issues, mostly having to do with the politics of the school board and student rights. As Moore gained confidence, *Free to Be* began to address larger matters, such as the case of Ray Fulgham, a black man who Moore decided had been railroaded on a burglary charge and whom he made into a cause célèbre of local progressives.

Free to Be soon evolved into Moore's next project, the *Flint Voice*, which first appeared in 1977, after Moore dropped out of the University of Michigan. While at U of M, he had been majoring, presciently, in political science and theater.

In that year, Moore had a stroke of luck when he went to a Harry Chapin concert in Detroit and managed to talk his way into the singer's dressing room, where he told Chapin about the hotline. Chapin, then a big star known for his 1974 hit "Cat's in the Cradle," agreed to do a benefit in Flint and ended up doing eleven benefits over the years for the hotline and the *Voice*. He netted half a million dollars for Moore, which meant that Moore could buy some professional equipment and, with a little discipline, put out a serious monthly paper.

The *Flint Voice* was a bit ragged, but it became more and more professional over the years that it was published, 1977 to 1982. In its pages, Moore produced some excellent investigative journalism, as well as sponsored that of other writers. The *Voice* really dug deep into local and state stories and looked at things that the conservative *Flint Journal* would never touch. Not bound to any particular news format, the *Voice* could publish in a wide range of styles and tones, and many of the articles were written by Moore himself. He was relentless, and everywhere. He rooted out municipal and police corruption. He highlighted GM's demands for local and regional tax breaks with the implied threat of plant closings if it did not get them, a race to the bottom with other towns and counties that carried more than a hint of corporate blackmail. He found cover-ups of corporate chemical dumping. He ran pieces investigating illegal police surveillance and racial discrimination in municipal zoning. He caught Genesee County commissioners going on "working trips" to Hawaii while the county was $4 million in debt and laying off hundreds of workers.

Subjects that the *Voice* revisited several times were corruption in local government and illegal use of municipal employees in political campaigns. In late 1979, Moore ran stories alleging that the office of Flint mayor Jim Rutherford was coercing federally funded city employees to campaign for him on publicly paid time; that Rutherford had irregularly approved liquor licenses; that he had improperly billed the city for services in 1973, when he was the police chief; and that he and Flint Township police chief Herbert Adams were part owners of a bar (Michigan law prohibited law-enforcement officers from owning bars). In response to the *Voice* stories, City Ombudsman Joe Dupcza began an investigation into Rutherford's administration, and Moore somehow got hold of and published his report before the official release date.

Six months later, after Dupcza tried to have Flint police chief Max Durbin fired, Flint police obtained a warrant to search the offices of the printing contractor for the *Voice*. The *Voice* later wrote that the police were looking for evidence that Dupcza was the source of the leaked report;[3] if he had shown it to the press before its public release, Dupcza, who had caused both Rutherford and Durbin grief, could himself be fired. Moore made brilliant use of the raid, announcing plans to file a huge lawsuit against the city. He attracted the support of the American Civil Liberties Union, the American Society of Newspaper Editors, and the Reporters' Committee for Freedom of the Press, and he got national exposure for his paper and his issues. He also provocatively reran all the negative articles about Rutherford.

Rutherford is an interesting guy, a career policeman who joined the force in 1948, got a college degree, and rose through the civil service to become deputy mayor and chief of police. When Flint changed its city charter from the city manager to the strong mayoral system in 1975, he retired from the police force to run for mayor. He barely won in 1975 but did better in 1979. When I asked him about the *Flint Voice* raid, he seemed honestly unable to remember it. He did recall, however, that Moore had a problem with authority: "He was pretty much critical of most politicians. I can't think of any he would say were worth anything, and maybe he was right. . . . What he focuses on is what's wrong and what's going to be wrong. In my elections, Moore was trying to find out anything and everything that I had done wrong. This was his usual use of confrontation."

It's also what good muckrakers do, and Moore was a good muck-raker. "Moore is very smart," said Albert Price, a professor of political science at the University of Michigan at Flint who worked with Moore on several projects, including a local TV show called *Roadkill Politics*. "He was always very focused on class issues, and he's tried to bring political discourse around to social class and the distribution of wealth in our society. He reported on stuff that was serious, and he did it at a serious level. The *Flint Voice* was a far more legitimate source of information than the conservative, establishment *Flint Journal*. Moore simply provided much, much more information."

He was playful, too. The informality of the paper meant that he could run satirical social criticism like the diary of "Brian," an individual telling his story from sperm to adult, at first full of optimism, hope, love, and humanity, but increasingly distorted through mind-numbing schooling and soul-crushing factory work into a redneck racist slob who hated the world.[4] This story reveals quite a bit about Moore's view of human nature: that we are born good, trusting, and communitarian, and that it is only exposure to a warped, capitalist value system that trains us to be suspicious, greedy, and hateful. This is, of course, classic left-wing romanticism, the counterpart of which is the right-wing romanticism of the sacred, selfish individual. It is a shame that politics, philosophy, and economics have all greatly suffered from the persistence in Western intellectual life of both kinds of romantic theories of human nature. Jean-Jacques Rousseau, Friedrich Hayek, Karl Marx, and Ayn Rand can share the blame equally.

Moore's complete commitment to his causes made him some enemies at GM and in the city administration, but it won over many working-class people. Fran Cleaves, an auto worker, die-hard unionist, and activist, ran into him frequently at picket lines and community meetings, and they became close friends. Cleaves was much older, and unlike some in the black community, she trusted and welcomed this like-minded white boy. Cleaves grew up in Detroit but moved to Flint in 1964, when Moore was eleven, to work for GM. She laughed when I asked if she worked on the line or in an office. On the line. She was first assigned to "the hole"—Chevrolet Manufacturing Plant Number Six— where she put in her time hanging doors. Later she moved to oil pans and rocker arms, then the motor line in Plant Number Four, one of the plants that took part in the historic sit-down strike of 1937.

Cleaves has paid a very high personal price for being on the wrong side of the American socioeconomic divide. Her son Herbert was shot and killed in a drive-by shooting in a rough neighborhood in Flint shortly before the release of Moore's first film, *Roger & Me*. If you watch the credits roll at the end of the film, there's a dedication to him that warms the heart of his mother.

Cleaves saw Moore as a dedicated and effective activist long before he had any hope of money or fame. She told me:

> He was at everything. You couldn't hardly be involved in any social issues here and not meet him. He was always respected as a speaker; wherever he was speaking would be packed, and it would be packed with people who had everyday struggles, survival issues, especially people who worked in the plants and the hospitals, homeless people. There was a movement from Tent City; Michael was very involved with that. I can remember picketing one of the banks—just Michael, myself, and two or three other people, who picketed Citizens' Bank here to support the people who were trying to organize a union. I remember it well because Michael was covered in snow. He could always be counted on to come up with the right position that would help you teach and educate people. He seemed to have a thick skin and a sense of humor, never retreating from his position but being able to not take it personally.
>
> There was one case in particular, a kid named Billy Taylor who was killed by the police, and they tried to cover it up. They said that he was in the middle of a theft—which he was—but Michael was able to show that the boy's hands were up when he was killed by the police. There was a case in

which even a black policewoman was shot down and left to die. There was all kinds of evidence, even on the police recorder, where they were making jokes about leaving her dead. Michael exposed all of that in his paper. He got in trouble with some of the leaders of the black community, who would identify him as this kid from Davison who needed to go back where he came from, but Michael had enough support from people in the black community who knew him. . . . He wouldn't debate that kind of stuff; he just kept on doing the work he was doing.

Moore does seem to have been both careful and sincere in his racial politics throughout his career, to the extent—as some black associates of his have noted—of being unable or unwilling to call out black people on antisocial behavior. Sometimes his attitudes have earned him ridicule from the right, as when he has intentionally downplayed the effects of black street crime so as to focus on white corporate crime (indeed, one whole chapter in his book *Stupid White Men* is about the evil that specifically white people do). He has nurtured the essentialist view of race in America to the point that he is able to blame the nation's problem with guns in large part on what he sees as a racially hysterical news media.

Once, during a question-and-answer session with a sympathetic crowd in California, I saw a black man stand up to thank him personally for his films and for saying in an interview that he would never dream of undertaking any project without having black people involved at every level. Moore's sincerity, however, may be only rhetorical; as Peter Schweizer discovered when he looked into the matter, Moore's practice falls far short of his ideals in this regard.[5]

The questioner asked Moore how he had come by this attitude, which he considered rare in white people. Moore sat thoughtfully for a moment (although I would have bet that he had encountered this question before and knew exactly what he was going to say) before answering:

I was thirteen years old. It was Holy Thursday. We were coming out of Mass; it was kind of cold. Someone turned a radio on in his car in the parking lot. He called out, "They just shot

Martin Luther King!" And—a cheer arose from those people coming out of the church. It was one of those moments in which things suddenly become very clear: "Okay, fuck this. I don't want to live in this kind of world. These people have to change. . . ." And that's sort of been my motivation in what I say and do when it comes to race in America.

Sam Riddle is a friend of Moore's and a professional associate with whom he has retained a close bond over the years. Listed on the masthead as a "founding member" of the *Flint Voice*, Riddle has been an important figure in Flint, Michigan state, and national politics since the early 1970s. A high school dropout who did a stint in the army before getting a college and legal degree, Riddle now operates in the same territory that Moore does, although from a slightly different perspective: the intersection of politics and image, news and entertainment.

Riddle has political clients all over the country. He has represented politicians in Detroit, Flint, Colorado, and many other places; he has worked with Al Sharpton and the Word television network, the largest media operation for black ministers in the country; he's worked with Ralph Nader, Jesse Jackson, the eccentric Michigan politician Geoffrey Fieger, and several of the people who have been featured in Michael Moore's films. If there's a racial aspect to be worked, he will work it—not in the cynical spirit of shakedown but because of the plain fact that justice in America is still racial and that, if you expect to get justice where race is involved, you can't ignore race.

Riddle has known Moore since his early political days on the Davison school board. In his last year of law school, Riddle was working for Genesee County district attorney Robert F. Leonard when the recall movement against Moore was under-way. Leonard—an unusual district attorney for that time and place—was concerned that the recall movement was using illegal intimidation tactics against Moore and sent Riddle to investigate. Moore and Riddle have been friends ever since, and they learned to organize together in Flint.

Riddle points out that Moore did it the hard way, at the grassroots level, where he earned his beliefs about class and politics, all the while with his eye on a larger stage. He told me:

In 1983, he and I decided we were going to change the mayor of Flint. At that time, the mayor was the former police chief, Jim Rutherford, who had authorized those raids on the *Voice* offices—real Gestapo tactics. November 1983, there's an underdog black candidate, Jim Sharp, a former marine who doesn't have a prayer against this right-wing Jim Rutherford. I said we had to do something to get out the black vote. The *Voice* sponsored a get-out-the-vote rally in Whiting Auditorium in Flint, the same place we would later do Ralph Nader, where we outdrew Bill Clinton. So I fly down to Washington and negotiate a deal where, the day Jesse Jackson announced he was running for president—just before the Flint election—his first stop as a major black presidential candidate would be Flint, Michigan. Then, to ensure Jesse would be there, I get the jet that Lee Iacocca uses—if you got the money, you can charter anything. We go down and pick up Jesse the day he's scheduled to announce. Except that, when me and Michael get there, Jesse's with Marion Barry at a press conference and Jesse's about to back out; the party doesn't want him to announce. He's trying to make up his mind about whether or not he's going to run.

I went in and told him—and Michael's all embarrassed about the language I was using—"Look, you motherfuckers, you can do what you want, but I've got two, three thousand people waiting up in Flint, waiting for you to come there. That's your first stop. That's the deal we negotiated." Jesse glares at me, but he makes his announcement and he gets on the jet. And we get to Whiting Auditorium and they're just rocking. They've been there for three hours, but they're still there! The rally is a humongous success. It motivates the voters to get out. There's a big upset victory, Jim Sharp wins and Rutherford, who raided the offices of the *Flint Voice*, is out.

Jesse leaves Flint. He takes the jet and doesn't bring it back! He went down to Georgia and Alabama. Michael's thing is that Jesse is this great black leader. My thing is that he can help us get out the vote, and then get his ass out of town. Sharp won and Michael and I got our picture on the front page, side by side, and Michael said, "This is the kind of thing Sam and I do." With me and him, it's always been action. We *do* shit.

The celebrity weirdness, the secret weaknesses of powerful people, the power of the common people—it's a very American story. It's worth noting, too, that twenty years later Riddle and Rutherford are good friends and speak of each other with respect.

Speaking of a recent scandal involving Al Sharpton's personal life, Riddle offers an insight into the culture of American politics that is as profound as any I've heard:

Our personal lives are what do us in. They're also the foundation for our accomplishments in this nation, depending on the value systems that are implanted in us by our parents. Michael Moore knows how to play golf! He was an Eagle Scout! His family were all very kind. His mother was a great woman. She and his father gave him a value system that is, I think, an inner strength. Some call it stubbornness, some call it bullheadedness, but thank God for his parents or we don't know what he would be, because in many ways Michael could put the "Mac" in *Machiavellian*. He's a strange character, a very complex person. He's driven to get things done, by any means necessary, and I don't hold that against him.

Michael knows the streets. He helped John Conyers out a lot when Conyers ran for mayor of Detroit. He's worked with a number of black candidates. The difference between Michael and most other Hollywood politicals is that Michael has more field experience of hard-core grassroots politics than the rest of Hollywood combined. He was raised on black issues. He's been around. He knows what it is to work from the ground up. Michael has always had his fingers in the pot of politics, from high school to now.

The *Flint Voice* was committed to working-class cultural expression in every dimension, and it had a full slate of literary and cultural reviews. It let the "shop rats" speak. Michael Moore, by his own admission, called in sick on his first and only day on the line at GM, but he encouraged and developed some real talent at the *Voice*.

Moore's big find was Ben Hamper, who was everything that Moore was not, everything he aspired to be as a son of the working class. Hamper was fully conscious of the irony of giving up one's soul just because the blue-collar wages and benefits couldn't be beat. He wrote with a gritty poetry of the nihilistic—no, the *surrealistic*— emptiness of a life lived in the plant, of the frustrations of the workers who, in Hamper's time, were never asked to do anything creative.

Hamper is a fourth-generation shop rat; his great-grandfather made motorized buggies in Flint, and his bloodline carries a faint trace of the days before the Industrial Revolution, some genetic memory of the skilled artisans who were fed into the manufactories. His Catholic parents produced eight children, of whom he was the first. His father drank when he wasn't on the line; his mother worked as a medical secretary. Hamper knocked up his girlfriend and married her, and he saw his marriage starting to fall apart before he was even a year out of high school. He sought stability in GM's hefty paychecks and benefits, the fate he'd feared all his life but also, with three generations behind him, secretly considered inevitable. Why fight it?

Hamper's twelve years on the line were punctuated by four spells of layoffs to accommodate the vicissitudes of the market, a common feature of Flint life and of the auto industry in general. It was during a period of low-market idleness that Hamper fired off his first piece for the *Voice*, a record review. Hamper says of Moore:

> We hit it off well, both being natural smart-asses who didn't care at all for being told what to do. I'd heard of him before we met. He was always popping up in the local paper or on TV creating some nuisance with authority. I was aware that he'd been the youngest elected official in Michigan when he was on the school board in Davison. None of this really mattered to me. I didn't take a keen interest in him until I began reading his newspaper, the *Flint Voice*. Most of the writing in there was pretty bad, ranting hippie shit, but Mike's stuff was usually good. I realized that this was a place where I could get published. The standards appeared quite low, at least on a literary level.

The standard of Hamper's work was higher. Moore was impressed and asked him for more.

At first, Hamper wrote bar and music reviews and was defensive about documenting the life that unfolded before him on the line. He was persuaded to write about his other job after a bad bar review led to a lawsuit; in a memorable and very characteristic turn of phrase, Hamper had written of a brawler heaven called the Good Times Lounge, "What this place lacks in ambience it makes up in ambulance."[6] The owners took offense at this and at the headline under which it ran: FLINT'S MOST DANGEROUS BAR.

After the legal action fell through, Moore finally persuaded Hamper to write about the line and the characters he hung out with there. Hamper recalls:

> Once we began talking about the factory, we pretty much stuck to that. The yarns were plentiful, and Mike had a real curiosity about the way things went down inside a GM plant. He was like a voyeur. . . . The factory stuff was in his blood, his lineage. I always felt there was a small part of Mike that really wanted to give it all up and become a shop rat, surrender to the birthright, like I had. Then again, I don't think he'd have lasted long. The factory was hell on people who thought too much or tried to make some sense of it all.

Hamper began writing a regular column for the *Voice* called "Revenge of the Rivethead."

Hamper was inspired and angry, and he wrote beautifully. In one of his most famous columns, he describes his seven-year-old self visiting his GM-lifer father at the plant on "family day" and discovering that his father didn't actually "make cars"—entire cars—for a living, but only attached windshields:

> Car, windshield. Drudgery piled atop drudgery. Cigarette to cigarette. Decades rolling through the rafters, bones turning to dust, stubborn clocks gagging down flesh, another windshield, another cigarette, wars blinking on and off, thunderstorms muttering the alphabet, crows on power lines asleep or dead, that mechanical octopus squirming against nothing,

nothing, NOTHINGNESS. I wanted to shout at my father, "Do something else!" Do something else or come home with us or flee to the nearest watering hole. DO SOMETHING ELSE! Car, windshield. Car, windshield. Christ, no.[7]

In *Rivethead*, a collection of Hamper's best writing that originally appeared in the *Flint Voice*, *Mother Jones*, and the *Detroit Free Press*, Michael Moore emerges as more than a hobbyist provocateur. Hamper shows him as a man of tremendous energy who loved his work and had a lot of fun with it, and who was interested in people, really interested in what made them tick, although often reductionist in his Manichaean conclusions about the inherent characters of industrial workers versus those of industrial managers. (Hamper himself had no such delusions. He knew a bullying, soul-corroded burnout when he saw one, regardless of social background.) Hamper describes Moore coming with him to cover the "Toughman Contest," a legal, anything-goes fight put on by the bar crawlers of Flint for twisted entertainment. After the combatants mauled each other, Moore sent Hamper to talk to the fighters and get their stories. Hamper was appalled by this degrading spectacle, and for all the right reasons. Moore, however, was excited for all the right reasons: these were people with real stories; they had something to say for themselves. They might surprise you.

Moore was serious, but he was also playful. When General Motors started to send a giant cartoon mascot called Howie Makem, the Quality Cat, around to talk to workers on the line, Moore thought it absolutely hysterical. He tried hard to get Hamper to interview the cat. Hamper refused this humiliating concession to the infantile weirdness of GM's corporate imagination.

By 1986, Hamper's work for the *Flint Voice* and the *Detroit Free Press* was getting some attention, and he was featured in a *Wall Street Journal* article by Alex Kotlowitz on blue-collar writers, with a line drawing of his face on the front page. Television shows were calling him. But Hamper was the real thing: he struggled every day against the deadening absurdity of his line job, but it gave his life meaning. He couldn't escape the feeling that he was a line worker who wrote, not a writer who worked the line:

I was amused by the attention because I realized it was just as much a novelty as anything else: "Look at the shop rat. He can actually spin sentences together!" For me, it was more something to do, something to occupy the time. Moore was the big catalyst. He was the first to suggest that I start to document these stories about the shop. Until then I was just floundering around, searching for an inspiration or niche. There were times when I entertained the idea of being a full-time writer, but I pretty much realized that it was the factory that provided the spark, the adversary, that I needed.

Hamper stayed on with GM until 1988, when his job was moved to Pontiac and the accumulating stress of a dozen years on the line got to him. He started to have incapacitating panic attacks.

If Moore got Hamper some national attention, Hamper also helped Moore. There were truths in Hamper's work that lived on long after everyone had stopped caring about the union campaigns and corrupt local politics that filled the *Voice*'s reporting. Because his work was so good, and because it got noticed, Hamper brought national attention to the *Voice* and its editor, who soon found himself in contention for the editorship of a magazine with a national circulation.

The *Flint Voice* looks like it was a lot of fun to do, and it must have been run by true believers since it couldn't have made much money and was seriously dependent on Harry Chapin and his benefit concerts. This well tragically ran dry when Chapin was killed in a car crash in 1981, and contributions from Stewart Mott—an heir to the Charles Stewart Mott fortune who was incongruously sympathetic to left-wing causes, and was a friend of Moore—didn't quite take up the slack. As a free alternative monthly paper, the *Voice* struggled, although it did acquire some advertising and respect.

The *Flint Voice*'s successor, the *Michigan Voice*, was published between 1982 and 1985 and did eventually sell for money. It was glossier and more commercial, ran nationally syndicated columnists, and sold all over the state, although it remained true to its counterculture roots. Its first issue proclaimed that it would not accept advertising that was "racist or sexist in nature, or from the Armed Forces."

Reading the *Michigan Voice*, one gets the feeling that Michael

Moore was already a little bored. He'd been doing alternative journalism for years before the *Michigan Voice* even got started. He had a reputation and had branched out a bit, landing a gig as an occasional commentator on National Public Radio by 1985, but he was still doing more of the same and just getting by. Moore claims that until he was thirty-five—until a few years after he left the *Voice*—he'd never made more than $15,000 a year. And his tactless, antiauthority impulsiveness could hurt him: according to NPR's news director at the time, Robert Siegel, he lost the NPR position when, in a segment on child abuse, he suggested that it was the fault of parents who taught their children to obey.[8]

Reading the *Voice* now, almost twenty years after it closed up shop, one can clearly see the outline of Michael Moore's future career. All the elements are there: the playfulness, the humor, the unorthodox approach to public policy reporting, the polemics, the sense that political action is worth doing only as a crusade, and also the assumption that issues are black and white, the good guys against the bad guys, workers against parasites. The naïveté is sometimes inspiring and sometimes irritating, but, although the language is often inflected with the boomer anger of the 1960s and 1970s, the style is not a hippie style; Flint is a blue-collar town and the *Voice* was very deeply a blue-collar publication. In its attitude if not always its language, it is almost an early-twentieth-century socialist style with its belief in the essential perfectibility of human relations, if only all of that corrupting nonsense of industrial, capitalist life—bosses, police, destruction of individual potential through existential drudgery—could be swept away.

But, again in line with the idealists of the early twentieth century, getting to this happy place required some uncompromising militancy. The *Voice* published a lot of innovative and probing journalism. In poring over many, many issues, I never found a retraction or correction. If Moore was ever wrong, he wasn't likely to admit to it, and perhaps never believed it. And that, too, predicted the style of his future career.

2

NEW VISTAS, NEW CONFLICTS

n 1986, a distant age before the Internet and online communities and bloggers, *Mother Jones* magazine was the foremost journal of progressive American politics. The magazine was named for Mary Harris Jones, the Irish immigrant who became a formidable labor activist, feminist, organizer for the United Mine Workers, and all-around radical in her fifties. Based in San Francisco, it was, and is, a publication of the Foundation for National Progress. The foundation is funded in large part by the family money of Adam Hochschild, who was its chairman in the mid-1980s. This family money is a legacy of the AMAX mining corporation, which made its fortune in colonial-era Africa. Hochschild started the magazine, together with Richard Parker and Paul Jacobs, after the three of them left the radical magazine *Ramparts*.

Mother Jones had some significant investigative coups in the 1970s, reporting on things like the tendency of the Ford Pinto to explode when rear-ended, on how the A. H. Robins pharmaceutical company put the Dalkon Shield method of birth control on the market when it hadn't been properly tested, and on how the Nestlé corporation pushed infant formula as a replacement for breast milk in the Third World. In 1980 its circulation was almost 240,000, the largest of any liberal political monthly in the country, but in the early Reagan years this had declined to about 140,000. The magazine's reputation as a hard-hitting muckraking enterprise had also declined. Although *Mother Jones* was slowly making a comeback, there was a sense among its staff that new blood and a new direction were needed.

By 1986, the editor for the previous six years, Deirdre English, had decided that she wanted to move on to new projects, so the magazine was looking for a successor. Michael Moore's work at the *Voice* had brought him to the attention of the board members and the magazine staff. Mark Dowie, a seasoned journalist who was at that time the chief investigative reporter for *Mother Jones*, was assigned to do some background research on Moore, to talk to people who knew him, to check out the "references that weren't on the résumé." Dowie felt he had a very good sense of working-class values and habits of thought, and of how they differed from those of the educated liberals on the board of *Mother Jones*. He had grown up close to his grandparents, who were working-class immigrants from Scotland. His grandfather was a traveling apothecary and his mother an industrial worker and union activist who had organized the Edinburgh streetcar workers. He says, "She wouldn't have called herself a socialist, but the first book she ever gave me to read was the letters of Antonio Gramsci."

Dowie's research turned up some early warning signs. He told me:

> *Mother Jones* at the time was quite democratically managed, and we wanted someone who would fit that culture. [Moore] assured us that he would, but that flew in the face of everything I learned about him. People who had worked at the *Voice* told me that he was very difficult, not very well liked, and not very respected after a while. I collected all these impressions and I took them back to the magazine. I said, "*Mother Jones* is badly in need of working-class sensibilities, and it would be great to have a working-class editor on the board," which had been almost entirely comprised of Ivy League liberals. I recommended that they hire Michael but that they didn't give him the top job. By this time I had talked to him, too, and I got the impression that he really wanted a national audience. I think that if he had been told that he

could be the blue-collar editor and express working-class sensibilities in the magazine, he would have taken that job.

I liked Michael. I thought he was very amusing, very articulate. I was impressed with his politics. He's a very personable guy—when he wants to be. He's funny and self-effacing and all the things that you look for in a brilliant, modest person. And he *is* brilliant. But he's not modest.

Moore was hired as the new editor in April 1986 and moved to San Francisco to take up his duties, reluctantly leaving Flint behind. Five months later he was fired. His actions in the office—and, even more so, the manner of his leaving it—explain much about how he rose to become one of the most distinct and recognized voices on the American political scene and about why that is problematic.

Moore's tenure at *Mother Jones* was an odd one. The picture that emerges from the accounts of his coworkers is that he was impossible as a colleague: moody, abusive, unprofessional. He went on a publicity tour of the Midwest with Ben Hamper and didn't call the office or return calls for more than a week. He had no clue as to how to run a four-color magazine with a print deadline, and no interest in acquiring one. He was a terrible manager of people. In his first meeting as editor in chief, he told the assembled staff, "The magazine you've been publishing is shit, and we're going to change that." This is not a good way to build staff morale.

Sometimes Moore was just bizarre. This was San Francisco in 1986, when the AIDS crisis was in full bloom and hitting public consciousness very hard. A staffer pitched a proposal to him for an article about the various conspiracy theories that had sprung up regarding the origins of the disease: a CIA genocide of gay people, a white supremacist plot to wipe out Africans, a government germ-warfare experiment gone awry, and so on. How do these things get started? Why do people believe them?

Moore's astonishing response: "You want a story about AIDS? Here's the story we should do about AIDS: we should find a cure and publish it in this magazine." He didn't appear to be joking.

He also showed signs of what people who observed him in later years would call manic depression. A senior staffer who worked closely with Moore told me:

We had a staff picnic in August. Now, if you're the editor of a magazine that has a staff picnic, you go to the picnic and you lead; you have fun. Moore went to this picnic and he found a table in the picnic area off to the side and sat there by himself, staring into space for five hours with this really morose look on his face. He wouldn't talk to anybody. It was the weirdest thing, really bizarre. People were wondering, "What the hell? This is our editor? Our leader?" It was at that point that most people realized, "This guy can't run this magazine; he can't lead us." Some of this stuff would even be excusable if he was coming in on Monday with thirty great ideas, twenty great writers, but that wasn't happening at all. As a matter of fact, he was blowing us away with how stupid he was at running the magazine.

Moore's virtue as an editor—indeed, the reason he was hired— was that he would bring working-class perspectives to the scene. Deirdre English put it like this:

Moore's presentation is, "I'm a real man. I love baseball, I love hunting, I'm not working out, I'm not drinking lattes and I'm not drinking chardonnay. I'm the real deal; I'm a working-class guy who wants to raise wages. I'm against going to war. I'm for people power." I think everyone is so nostalgic for that, so bereft of it. And frankly, the liberal elite *is* so out of touch with working-class people that, when one rises up in this way and presents himself as this kind of archetype, he's embraced, for reasons I have a lot of sympathy for.

But none of this made Moore a competent executive. English recalled:

It was a daring but, in retrospect, crazy risk. We had the assumption that Moore was someone who was going to work well with people. He was going to bring this bracing blast of fresh air from the working-class Midwest into our office, but we also thought that he was going to be collegial and congenial and that he would turn to the professionals at *Mother*

Jones to find out how things were done there—not anything that I'd imposed on the culture but how you put out a magazine. We had all kinds of calendars and methods and protocols for how you do things that had been developed over time by me and others. There was a strong feeling of collectivity at *Mother Jones*. There was the belief that we'd be able to educate Moore as to these things that we had learned, and that he would be an inspirational leader. We didn't expect him to tear up the rules.

If some of the staff didn't know exactly what to make of Moore, Chris Lehmann—who has since become an author, an editor, and a contributor to publications such as *New York* magazine and the *Washington Post*—was one of the few people there who felt some cultural solidarity with him. At that time straight out of college, Lehmann came from Davenport, Iowa, a dying industrial town that, like Moore's Flint, was once voted "worst place to live in the USA" by *Money* magazine. "The *Mother Jones* chapter of Michael's career is very rich and very interesting," he recalls, "and if you talk to people there you'll get very different points of view—a real *Rashomon* situation. I was one of the few who didn't end up disliking him intensely. We bonded in an odd way: at one of the staff meetings, Michael said, 'Anyone who still smokes pot, raise your hand,' and everyone's hands went up—except for his and mine. It was a cultural marker of sorts, a left-coast/heartland kind of thing." When Lehmann told me this story, it occurred to me that Moore was setting a kind of trap and that, in falling into it, the staff—with the exception of Lehmann—had handed him psychological power over them. This is perhaps a clue as to why Moore was widely disliked at *Mother Jones*.

There were less complicated indiscretions. Lehmann remembers Moore circulating a handwritten memo describing how he and Hamper, on that publicity tour from which they had refused to phone home, had thrown burned pizza out of a hotel window. This didn't go over well with the senior staff, who quite reasonably worried about this childishness reflecting on the magazine. Lehmann recalls:

It was conduct unbecoming an editor. He was perceived as other than professional.

It was a clash of cultural sensibilities. Michael is very confrontational, and *Mother Jones*'s culture was very retiring and genteel. Adam Hochschild and Michael are as unalike as two people can get on the planet. Being editor of *Mother Jones* is a very difficult position to fill. Hochschild is on the masthead as a contributing editor, but he has hiring and firing power, and if you don't please him—as Michael very much did not—you're not going to get along. If you're talking about "the board," you're talking about Adam. The relationship between Adam and the editor was the central relationship there and, I think, the reason why Michael was fired.

Moore's introductory column as the new editor appeared in the September 1986 issue and was a very powerful, intelligent, well-written piece on the terrorism that Ronald Reagan was then inflicting on the people of Nicaragua.[1] By the time his second column was in print in October—this was the piece in which new editor Moore laid out his vision for the magazine[2]—he had already been relieved of his duties.

Why was he fired? At the time, Moore said it was because of a disagreement over an article by Paul Berman that was somewhat critical of the Sandinista government of Nicaragua. But he has said lots of other things, too. Some at *Mother Jones* noticed that, in the years following his abrupt departure, he tended to tailor his explanation of this event to suit the audience he was addressing. "If he was talking to New York subway workers, for example, he'd say, 'I was fired because I wanted to do an article about how dangerous the subways are, and they wouldn't let me.' Or, if he was talking to the Arab American Antidiscrimination Committee, he'd say, 'I was fired because I wanted to do an article on the Palestinians and they wouldn't let me.'"

Here is a no doubt partial list of the reasons that Moore has offered, at different times and in different forums, for why he was fired from *Mother Jones*:

- He wouldn't run an article critical of the Nicaraguan Sandinista government (UPI, September 6, 1986).

- He had put Ben Hamper's picture on the front cover, and management objected (claim made in *Roger & Me*).[3]

- Adam Hochschild refused to let him run Ben Hamper's column, calling it "smut" (Moore's introduction to Hamper's book, *Rivethead*).

- Adam Hochschild wanted a "yes man" so that he wouldn't have to show up for work (*San Francisco Chronicle*, September 13, 1986).

- He was planning a critical cover story on Governor Mario Cuomo of New York—whom he described as a "sacred cow" for *Mother Jones*'s "yuppie left"—and because he was planning a series of articles that were critical of the Israeli occupation of the West Bank and the Gaza Strip[4] (*San Francisco Examiner*, September 15, 1986).

- He objected to the dismissal of Richard Schauffler, an advertising salesman for *Mother Jones* who claimed that he lost his job because he had failed to disclose his affiliation with the radical Democratic Workers' Party (*New York Times*, September 27, 1986).

- Deirdre English had taken his criticisms of the magazine personally and Adam Hochschild "wanted me gone because I didn't kiss her ass" (*Media File*, October–November 1986).

- He had refused to participate in "management's numerous violations of its contract with the unionized staff of *Mother Jones*" (Moore, writing in the *Village Voice*, October 14, 1986).

- He had made plans to bring the Palestinian issue into the magazine (awards ceremony speech to the Arab American Anti-discrimination Committee, April 4, 1987).

- A number of female employees had complained to him that the then publisher of *Mother Jones*, Don Hazen, was treating them in a sexist manner (letter from Moore to *Michigan Voice* subscribers, December 28, 1987).

- Adam Hochschild wanted him to run an article on herbal teas (*San Francisco Weekly*, January 10, 1990).

- Management wanted him to put movie stars on the cover and make it "a *People* magazine of the left" (*Metro*, January 11–17, 1990).

- He had interrupted a discussion about hiring more women and minorities to suggest that *Mother Jones* hire an actual proletarian (*International Herald Tribune*, January 17, 1990).

- "The guy who owned the magazine [*sic*] was ordering me to run stories that I didn't think were right or weren't true or whatever. I figured I don't want anything to do with this. He thought that was a good idea so he showed me the door." (Commentary on DVD release of *Roger & Me*)

On September 2, Hochschild suggested to Moore that he ought to depart, and that if he didn't, the foundation board would most likely vote to dismiss him. Moore demanded a formal meeting of the board, which he got, and the board voted to fire him on the unanimous advice of the magazine's senior staff. Moore immediately went to the San Francisco papers, the *Chronicle* and the *Examiner*. In a dramatic press conference on the steps of City Hall, he explained that he'd been fired because he wouldn't publish "lies" about Nicaragua. "I thought, What are we doing, writing Reagan's next speech for him?"[5] He filed a wrongful dismissal suit and vowed to collect a $2 million settlement.

The suit became bitter and complicated. Moore's own carelessness and his litigious bent created even more trouble for the magazine, and, ultimately, for Moore himself. Two bizarre incidents in particular reveal him casting about in his attempts to rationalize his situation to himself and others.

In his depositions in support of his case against the magazine, he claimed that *Mother Jones* was so badly run, so corrupt, that a young freelancer named Laura Fraser supplied drugs to editors. Even today, almost twenty years later, a note of restrained anger comes into Fraser's voice as she describes the accusation and how it arose:

I had never met Michael Moore. I was a freelance writer, and I did occasional pieces for the magazine. In his lawsuit, Moore was basically trying to prove that the editors were so high on drugs that they didn't recognize his talent. It was just one of his many tactics to try to argue wrongful dismissal. It was completely ridiculous.

What actually happened was this. I came to the office to

deliver a manuscript to my editor. At *Mother Jones*, they would announce the writers over the intercom when they came in. Moore was with my editor when my name was announced, and he asked, "Who's that?" And I think because it was obvious that I was a freelance writer, and particularly because I had been published in the magazine many times and perhaps Moore should have known that I was a free-lancer, my editor joked, "Oh, she's my dealer" or "She's my connection." Moore used that in his fantasy of what had happened in his wrongful dismissal suit.

I was twenty-five years old at the time, and I was a really easy target. I've never sold drugs to anyone at *Mother Jones*; I've never sold drugs, period. So the whole thing was just unbelievably ridiculous, and incredibly hypocritical. Moore was so critical of the Reagan administration's "Just Say No to Drugs" campaign, and there he was using the same kind of smear tactics against an innocent bystander, someone who had no power in this situation. Then Alexander Cockburn was criticizing me for an article I had written about Moore and *Mother Jones* for Media File, and implied in the *Nation* that I was critical of Moore [after his falling-out with the magazine] in order to get assignments for *Mother Jones*. It was just astonishing to me that neither Cockburn nor Moore—nor, for that matter, the *Nation*—ever bothered to call me to ask what the real story was. The fact that he would go so far as to accuse me of a felony in a deposition, something that was completely fabricated, is astonishing. The deposition is in the public record. If I ever ran for judge, if I ever tried to get a security clearance, I could be told that there's this stain on my record. This was really an example to me of how he will go to any means to get his ends.

With equal nastiness but no more plausibility, Moore had let slip to several reporters—among them Paul Farhi, the reporter who wrote the September 15 *Examiner* piece on Moore and the magazine—not only that he was fired because he wanted to tackle the Palestinian issue but also that there was a bias among the Jews, including Hochschild himself and several others at the magazine, against any article sympathetic to the Palestinians.

Farhi, as any good reporter would, asked Hochschild about this for a story he was writing on Moore's dismissal, and Hochschild then publicly debunked the idea in the column he wrote for *Mother Jones* that dealt with Moore's departure: "[Moore told] several reporters that he had been blocked from doing hard-hitting reporting on the Middle East because of 'Jewish' or 'Zionist' influence at the magazine. (This might come as a surprise to readers of a number of *Mother Jones* articles over the years, such as Victor Perera's report on Israeli foreign arms sales, 'Uzi Diplomacy,' July '85.)"[6] Hochschild, who had several times said on National Public Radio that he considered the Israeli occupation of the Palestinian territories to be a crime, was understandably unhappy with being called a censor on behalf of Zionism.

When Hochschild's column came out, Moore was furious. He felt that Hochschild was accusing him of anti-Semitic statements, and sued. He and his wife, Kathleen Glynn, added charges of libel to his wrongful-dismissal suit against Hochschild and the Foundation for National Progress.

Farhi, who is now a reporter for the *Washington Post*, told me:

I was drawn into his lawsuit, and I didn't like that too much. They wanted me to come in and give a deposition about what I was told. Which seems in some ways to violate the whole spirit of journalism, asking reporters to give up their sources and their private conversations. I'm sure Michael Moore would have a problem with that if he were on the receiving end of it. I found that sort of odd at the time.

There was a sense of resentment at *Mother Jones* about Moore's accusations. It was, "You've got to be kidding, this is not about any particular issue, it's about the guy's work habits, he's never here, he's completely disorganized. . . ." [Moore saw it] as a political difference, whereas the *Mother Jones* people saw it as, "This guy can't run a magazine." It's really mundane to argue that someone is just a sloppy manager. It's much sexier to present it as an ideological dispute.

It's impossible to know what Moore was really thinking in his statements to Farhi, but it's hard not to notice that Farhi could easily be assumed to be an Arab or Persian name. Could it be that Moore was once again pitching the story of his firing to his audience of the moment? When I asked Farhi about this, I was a little surprised to hear that this had never occurred to him. He laughed and pointed out that his name is not of Arabic origin. "The name thing is really interesting. I don't know, I've never thought about it; I have no idea whether he thought he was being extremely clever with me. This may be naïve, but I took him at his word, that this was what he said it was, and not some crap he was putting together so that he could file a lawsuit. He really did seem to believe what he was saying."

This brought Farhi to an interesting observation about Moore as a journalist, and as a personality:

> It's funny about him, isn't it? He's almost naïve that way. To be what he is, to be as ideologically "pure" as he is, you really would have to believe certain things wholeheartedly. When you work for the mainstream press, everything's gray: one side says one thing, one side says the other; you don't try to make decisions in the way Moore does: "I'm going to focus on everything that supports my side and ignore or even attack everything that doesn't support my view of the world." So in some ways that would fit together: "I believe I'm the victim of a conspiracy by Jews who run this magazine and now I'm seeing red because I believe that." He wasn't saying anything anti-Semitic, but he was creating this notion that he was being perceived as anti-Semitic, and was defending himself against a contrived charge. Maybe he honestly saw the world that way.

Most likely, Moore himself truly never knew or allowed himself to understand why he was fired, and all of the explanations he offered over time seemed equally plausible to him—although it appears vanishingly improbable that they could *all* have been true. As he does in his movies, he seems to have been lashing out in all directions in the hope that one of his swings would hit its mark.

He missed with the charge that he'd been slandered as an anti-Semite. When Farhi was deposed, he said that Moore had indeed told him that there was a Jewish bias at *Mother Jones* and that he, Farhi, had asked Hochschild for his response to this idea.[7] Moore dropped the libel part of his lawsuit.

■   ■   ■

In conversations with people who worked with Moore, I came to think that the real reason he was fired was simply that he was out of his depth as the editor of a national magazine, in terms of both professional skills and political sophistication, and that he could not inspire or get along with the staff. To the extent that the Nicaragua piece played a role, it was because his handling of that matter exemplified these other problems with his work.

But the fact that Moore often put the particular issue of Nicaragua at the center of the dispute is central to the way he has cast his cultural role and image. In order to understand what this means, and why Nicaragua stirred such passions, it is important to put Moore's explanation in its historical and political context and to understand what Nicaragua meant to the left at the time.

Feelings were intense on both the left and the right about Ronald Reagan's wars in Central America in the 1980s, of which the conflict in Nicaragua was the most prominent and the most controversial. It was a different world then. Even after Gorbachev and Reykjavik, the Cold War had thawed only a degree or two since the early 1960s. The Soviet Union and the threat that it represented was thought to be a permanent fact of life, and the proxy struggle between it and the United States that was being waged all over the world was used by the political right as justification for every bloodily insane atrocity, every jackboot in the face of democracy and human rights, that was struck by "our" proxies against "their" proxies. Jeane Kirkpatrick had famously written in Norman Podhoretz's *Commentary* magazine that there was a meaningful difference between "totalitarian" left-wing opponents and "authoritarian" right-wing allies, and on the strength of such opportunistic strategic thinking, Reagan had given her the post of ambassador to the United Nations.[8]

Central America in the 1980s was one of the saddest examples of this sort of political cynicism and one of the bitterest betrayals of everything Americans claimed to stand for. In the name of anticommunism,

Reagan was supporting a tiny Guatemalan elite, the landowners of European background, that was waging a frankly genocidal war against the Maya majority seeking the most basic human rights. Reagan was much more concerned with blocking a communist insurgency in El Salvador than he was with the human rights violations of the Salvadoran army and the death squads associated with it in the early eighties, which used torture, rape, and massacre as political tools (which is not to say that he was entirely unconcerned with Salvadoran human rights; to be fair, there was a marked improvement in the Salvadoran human rights record after 1984, partially in response to U.S. pressure). He was turning a blind eye to Honduran human rights violations because he needed to keep the cooperation of the Honduran government in the conflict with Nicaragua. He was training officers of many Latin American armies at the School of the Americas, where they were taught how to torture captured leftist insurgents.

In Nicaragua, Reagan was supporting a fractious group of rebels known as Contras who were attempting to overthrow the government of Nicaragua. That government, dominated by a militant Marxist organization, the Frente Sandinista de Liberación Nacional, had itself thrown out a brutal dictator and American ally, Anastasio Somoza Debayle, in a 1979 revolution. The Contras' often brutal tactics, and Reagan's transparent concern for business interests over social justice, meant that his Central American policies were widely despised on the left. I can remember the white-hot fury I would feel on hearing one of his deeply unreal addresses on the subject of Latin America and democracy. But for many on the left, that didn't mean that we had to be blind to the problems of an uncritical view of the Sandinistas.

For the Sandinistas were far from perfect social democrats. Ominously, there was no meaningful distinction in revolutionary Nicaragua between the Sandinistas (the FSLN as a political party), the government, the civil service, and the armed forces. The Sandinistas made no secret of the fact that they considered themselves to have a monopoly on legitimate political expression, and they had a dangerous and self-serving belief in what they presented as direct popular democracy, a belief that legitimized, in their own eyes, their reluctance to hold elections.[9]

Worse, the Sandinistas mounted a major forced relocation campaign against peasants who were resisting their control, a colossal

mistake that, along with rationing and confiscatory agricultural policies, fueled recruitment to the Contra forces. One of the largest
sources of Contra recruitment was not, as many leftists throughout
the world understood it to be, former Somocistas and National
Guardsmen, but the indigenous Chibcha peasants of the central high-
lands, who saw themselves as continuing a struggle against domination that had been going on for a thousand years, first against the
lowland Nahua and the distant Aztec Empire, then against the
Spaniards, a battle that continued into modern times. Ironically,
the previous generation of Chibcha had fought with Augusto Sandino,
the Sandinista namesake and political icon, for their freedom and
independence. The Sandinistas also targeted the rebellious Miskito
Indians of the Atlantic coast, creating a dedicated ethnic focus of
resistance.[10]

Yet much of the antidemocratic character of the Sandinistas and
popular resistance to them was not known to the American left, or
was dismissed as right-wing propaganda. Reagan's hostility toward
working people at home was obvious, and he supported freedom
struggles abroad only when they were directed against communist
states; otherwise he suppressed them. Reagan's loyalty was to ideology, not to freedom—South African apartheid never seemed to
bother him[11]—and it was perfectly clear that his priorities in Latin
America had nothing to do with democracy or human rights. And
although the 1984 election had not been fairly organized, it was true
that 75 percent of the population had voted and that the Sandinistas
had won 67 percent of that vote; international observers had found
few irregularities in the conduct of the vote itself. These results were
not really surprising, both because the Sandinistas controlled almost
all Nicaraguan media and because until late in their administration,
when war and economic sanctions had brought the entire country to
a state of deep misery, they really did retain significant popular support. Somoza, whom the Sandinistas had deposed, was widely hated,
and the Contras had a very dubious human rights record. Some of
their leaders indeed had been associated with Somoza's old National
Guard, and this made their own commitment to democracy highly
suspect.

For these reasons, the great majority of the American left generally supported revolutionary Nicaragua against Reagan's obsessions.

But in addition to, and quite distinct from, this general support, there were some on the left who felt that there was no legitimate criticism of the Sandinistas. These were generally the same people who had nothing bad to say about Cuba, about North Korea, about Vietnam, about Mao's China, about the Soviet Union. Either out of a fear of inadvertently aiding the right or out of a conviction that leftist revolutionaries truly could do no wrong, these people would not speak up for democracy and human rights in Nicaragua when the Sandinistas attacked these things, and they feuded with those on the left who did.

The argument about whether the left should acknowledge any wrongdoing by the Sandinistas was playing out at *Mother Jones* during Michael Moore's first few months there. Paul Berman had been commissioned by Deirdre English more than a year before Moore's arrival at the magazine to write a two-part piece about Sandinista Nicaragua. *Mother Jones* had committed to publishing it before Moore took up his duties.

For English, publishing pieces like Berman's that might rouse debate were what should define a vigorous, courageous, liberal magazine. She told me:

> *Mother Jones* had the largest circulation of any left-wing magazine in the country, and I thought we needed to have room for a variety of different kinds of opinion on the liberal spectrum. I didn't believe in a party line; yes, a liberal point of view, but an attempt to question our own thinking and bring in writers who would do that. [Berman's piece] was very much an attempt to say, "Let's not look like knee-jerk Sandinista supporters. Of course we're critical of the role that the U.S. has played, and of course we're critical of the U.S. support of the former Somoza dictatorship, and we have an interest in seeing a good socialist party in Nicaragua emerge, but that doesn't mean that we can't be critical of it, just as we would be critical of Carter, of Clinton." Later, when Moore killed Berman's article, I thought it was a violation of an important principle: you didn't have to agree with Berman, but his piece belonged in the magazine. It was a good article, and the left needed to be thinking more critically about revolutionary nationalist organizations like the Sandinistas.

Berman had learned Spanish for the assignment and spent a lot of time in Nicaragua at all levels of society. The first part of his piece ran in the February 1986 edition of *Mother Jones*. The second part—the part that Moore balked at publishing—was on the whole favorable to the Nicaraguan revolution but did not ignore its defects. Berman noted that the Sandinista tendency toward Leninist discipline was necessary to make a revolution but problematic in building a truly free and egalitarian society. He was sharp and saw through to the heart of the matter:

> The Sandinistas have made clear that, in their eyes, the San-
> dinista vanguard is the Revolution, is the Nicaraguan people,
> is the government. The health of the Revolution and the
> power of the party are to them inseparable. . . . They consider
> that they have fought and died for that idea and not merely
> for the land reform and the medical campaign and the dig-
> nity of Nicaragua. . . . No one seriously believes the Sandin-
> istas mean to go so far with democracy as actually to engage
> in some form of significant power sharing, not even if the
> country and the Revolution would be better off for it.[12]

One type of leftist might or might not argue with Berman's inter-
pretation of the Sandinistas' position. An entirely different type of leftist might agree with this interpretation but argue that the Sandinistas had a right to claim political legitimacy in this manner.

Berman's piece was initially accepted by new editor Michael Moore and the editorial board. Moore later asked Berman to cut much of the critical section, then rejected it outright. What had hap-
pened? One thing that seems clear is that Moore had fallen under the influence of Alexander Cockburn, a leftist hard-liner whom Moore had recruited to write for *Mother Jones*. Cockburn is among those who are reluctant to criticize even the most brutal socialist governments. For him the romance of the struggle takes on a life of its own, a life that demands that one choose sides at every point or face con-
demnation as a traitor.

Cockburn has recently gone so far as to attack George Orwell because in 1949 (a particularly grim time in the history of the Cold War when the totalitarian nature and ambitions of the Soviet Union were, or should have been, quite clear in the West), Orwell warned the British Foreign Office against allowing those he suspected of being Soviet sympathizers to undertake sensitive work. Cockburn said of Orwell, "The man of conscience turns out to be a whiner, and of course a snitch."[13] Cockburn's contempt for Orwell—a dedicated, democratic socialist who was consistently vigilant against the totalitarian tendencies of both the left and the right—is a bit shocking, and it says a lot about Cockburn's ideological approach.

Cockburn has rarely met a left revolutionary despot or government he didn't like or for whom he couldn't find an excuse.[14] Indeed, in a column in the *Nation* that appeared soon after Moore was fired from *Mother Jones*, he defended his earlier criticism of the tortured and imprisoned Cuban dissident Armando Valladares with this rather amazing statement: "I don't think Cuba today has thousands of political prisoners being tortured. . . . I do not think there is institutionalized torture in Cuba. . . . I don't think that any evidence has been advanced to show that there is."[15]

Moore's editorial memoranda to Cockburn suggest that he was quite overawed by the radical journalist, so authentically uncompromising in his revolutionary sympathies, such an inspiration. And Cockburn hated the Nicaragua piece, thinking the criticisms of the Sandinistas unfair and inaccurate, a betrayal by a pampered American liberal of a genuine leftist revolution.

What Moore probably did not know at the time was that Cockburn and Berman despised each other and had been writing nasty things about each other in their respective columns for years. This is one situation in which Moore clearly comes off as a bit of a naïf. The irony is so obvious as to be hardly worth mentioning: in an argument about the Sandinistas, Cockburn and Moore rushed to enforce the style of authoritarian orthodoxy that they denied the Sandinistas practiced.

Hochschild and the board stood by Berman and his article. Cockburn remained adamant. Moore rather pathetically appealed to his mentor: "I was wrong—Dracula lives! Did I not drive the stake through at sunrise?? The Paul Berman piece lives. Adam and I in a row. Need your help in building an argument."[16] Hochschild and the board worked out an arrangement whereby Moore would run the piece, in a slightly edited form, and publish it side by side with a rebuttal by Cockburn or Moore himself. But this wasn't good enough for Moore.

Moore was unwilling to see any blemishes on the face of the Sandinista revolution. There have always been those on the left who have been uncomfortable at any whiff of the authoritarian, those who see the point of the game as expanding human freedom and opportunity, not as an affirmation of the One True Path that offers a political tribal identity. Moore, apparently, was not among them—or, at the very best, his ability to sense the authoritarian taint was underdeveloped. He had been to Nicaragua in 1983 and never remarked on any of the undemocratic practices that Berman saw. Berman, for his part, continued to write about Nicaragua throughout the 1990s, and later came to a more hard-edged criticism of the Sandinistas' penchant for Leninist, undemocratic rule—as would several of the former Sandinista ministers.[17] After Moore was fired from *Mother Jones*, Berman was ostracized by many colleagues on the left who, incited by Moore's and Cockburn's position, felt that he had betrayed the Nicaraguan revolution—the last flawed adventure of the Cold War, the last chance for American romantics to throw in their lot with genuine Third World revolutionaries before the world became both simpler and more complex. It was hard to forgive.

■   ■   ■

In the long run, the debacle at *Mother Jones* could not have turned out better for Moore. As Chris Lehmann put it, "In a way, it was the best thing that ever happened to him. He was motivated almost entirely by revenge, and he went forward and made *Roger & Me* and moved on to better things." Moore seems to have instinctively known how to set up a narrative of his departure on his own mythic terms: the poor boy from Flint against the publishing Goliath with its sinister colonialist roots. Cockburn was an enormously helpful ally in this, writing in the *Nation*, "Michael Moore . . . is learning to his cost the old rule that the rich are different. They think they can get away with anything. Hochschild is heir to the AMAX mining fortune, and although he has devoted substantial amounts of the family income—originally generated by African wage-slaves—to finance the quasi-liberal periodical *Mother Jones*, he can still behave like a 19th-century mill owner." Cockburn goes on to contrast Hochschild's industrialist background with that of Michael Moore, the working-class boy from Flint whose uncle took part in one of the great strikes in American labor history.[18]

The almost autonomic reversion to the logic of class as the determinant of political outlook and legitimacy owes more to Lenin than to Marx. There are those who have never had any trouble explaining, say, Franklin Roosevelt as a tool of the capitalist class. Real life, in the case of FDR and others, is usually more complicated, and in real life Adam Hochschild is a man who has devoted enormous effort and resources to advancing the causes of human rights and to unearthing the brutal truths of colonialism.[19] Cockburn's unanswerable ideological device enables him to be as *inherently* right as Hochschild is undeniably rich, to bury any of the real issues. Certainly to bury any of the ambivalence that thoughtful leftists might feel about the Sandinistas. Moore's own behavior as editor and day-to-day manager of a business is, in this approach, completely beside the point: Moore is poor, Hochschild a rich colonial!

It was a trick that Moore already knew well, and one that he has used throughout his career whenever his biography came up: the little guy against the Man; the unpretentious working-class stiff against the fey habits of decadent, too-comfortable "quasi-liberals" (as Cockburn put it) or outright reactionaries. There's a scene in *Roger & Me* in which Moore, briefly describing his time at the magazine, jokingly shows his own puzzlement and dismay at the enormous list of specialized beverages available in a San Francisco coffeehouse. That's it! He was too *real* for *Mother Jones*! It's interesting how, in hindsight, Moore's attack on the sophisticates who gave him a chance at the big time anticipated the now-ubiquitous attack tic of the right: the depiction of anyone on the left as an elitist, out-of-touch, latte-sipping snob. Simplistic and deceptive though this story line might be, it was useful for Moore and enabled him to burnish his iconic image when he launched his next project, *Roger & Me*, a movie that he was able to begin thanks to the $58,000 settlement of his wrongful-dismissal suit, which he used as seed money.

There's an interesting story here, too. *Mother Jones* was usually represented in its legal affairs by the corporate law firm of Pillsbury, Madison, and Sutro—the very name reeks of a world Moore despises—but the board members felt that, even if they won, taking on Moore with such a firm could be fatal to the magazine's credibility as a voice for the progressive left. Instead, they hired left-wing civil-rights and employment-law attorney Guy Saperstein for one of only a very few occasions in Saperstein's entire career that he has repre-sented the employer in an employment law case. Saperstein was ini-tially suspicious and told Hochschild and publisher Don Hazen that if his investigation determined that the magazine was at fault, he wanted the authority to settle, which Hochschild and Hazen gave him willingly. They assured Saperstein that, if they had done wrong, they would admit it.

When Saperstein deposed Moore, he had some sense of the difficulties the magazine had been having: "Michael showed up in baggy jeans, worn tennis shoes, a shirt hanging out of his jeans, and a baseball cap cocked at an angle on his head. . . . He certainly didn't look like the editor of a national magazine. Michael sat down, turned sideways, crossed his legs and gave the appearance of complete indifference."

Some of Saperstein's observations seem to foretell the reputation that Moore would later develop:

> He was often funny and had a bit of roguish Irish charm, but he was doing a terrible job of making a case for himself and his tenure as editor of *Mother Jones*. . . . He was full of bluster. . . . I deposed him for three days, and while he was one of the most entertaining witnesses I had ever deposed, he was also one of the worst. . . . His iconoclastic rebellious-ness, his obvious disdain for the opinions of others, his quick wit at the expense of thoughtful explanations would sink him in front of a jury.[20]

Although Moore complained of "emotional distress" that was causing physical symptoms, Saperstein concluded that he was incom-petent, that the firing was justified, and that the magazine should offer no settlement. This, too, is part of the legend. Some of Moore's fans believe that he had *Mother Jones* dead to rights, that the courts and *Mother Jones* itself had been forced to recognize this in the set-tlement, and that using the magazine's money to begin the filming of

Roger & Me and to crusade on behalf of the working class was poetic justice since *Mother Jones* was so corrupted, so effete, so . . . so . . . *liberal*!

In fact, *Mother Jones* never admitted any wrongdoing, and Saperstein insisted that no part of any settlement would come from the magazine. *Mother Jones*'s corporate insurer calculated the cost of fighting the suit up to the point at which it would inevitably be thrown out and offered Moore slightly less to go away. This amount turned out to be about what Hochschild had offered him as no-fault severance pay.

But doing it that way would have been no fun at all.

3

A NATIONAL STAGE

W hen he left *Mother Jones*, Michael Moore had no particular reason to be optimistic about his career. He'd had a national platform, and he'd been fired after holding it for only a few months. There was no more *Flint Voice*; that part of his life was over. For a little while he worked on seemingly transitional projects. He won grants from consumer advocate Ralph Nader's organization and from the J. Roderick MacArthur Foundation to publish *Moore's Weekly*, a small Washington, D.C.–based journal of labor and media matters. Moore put out about twenty-five issues before the journal petered out in late 1988. By that time, with his *Mother Jones* settlement money, some more grants from the MacArthur Foundation and from Nader, and some technical advice from the progressive filmmaker Kevin Rafferty, who just happens to be George H. W. Bush's cousin, he had begun work on a film.

Moore's entry into the new world of the feature film seems to have been almost haphazard, but he'd already worked in television and radio, and he wasn't shy of the technology of mass communication. He'd gotten to know Rafferty just before his stint in San Francisco, when Rafferty and his partners, the journalist James Ridgeway and the documentary filmmaker Anne Bohlen, had asked for his help in making *Blood in the Face*, their documentary on American white supremacists. Rafferty, Ridgeway, and Bohlen apparently thought that because Moore had run pieces in the *Voice* on the Klan, he could get them into a Klan meeting. Moore was game, and was even willing to show his face onscreen with the supremacists, something the other filmmakers were leery of doing. He appears in one scene of the film, in a shot taken from behind and over his shoulder as he interviews a pretty girl in full Nazi uniform. The costumes are somehow less chilling than the name tags worn by the neo-Nazis—"HELLO, my name is . . ."—through which they claim normalcy as they gather at a Michigan retreat to talk about "mud people" and white power.

The way Moore tells it in *Roger & Me*, he began to think about the film as soon as he returned to Flint from San Francisco, when his homecoming coincided with an announcement from General Motors that the company planned thousands of layoffs: in effect, the destruction of Flint. If any one project made Moore's career and established him as an important political voice, it was *Roger & Me*.

The film is all about Flint, Michigan, and to those who know American labor history, Flint is talismanic. Mentioning the town is a shorthand reference to a whole history of working-class achievements and, more recently, working-class humiliations. *Roger & Me* is an attempt to claim and capitalize on this legacy, and it makes little sense without some understanding of what Flint means.

Flint has been an American center of vehicle manufacturing since 1886, the year that local entrepreneur Billy Durant hitched a ride in a friend's horse-drawn carriage. Durant was so impressed with the suspension of the vehicle that he went to see its designers at their plant in Coldwater the next day and bought the rights to manufacture it. The carriage made him a millionaire—a billionaire many times over in today's money. The manufacture of horse-drawn carriages had some of the same industrial logic of motorcars, and in 1903 and 1904 Durant absorbed the Buick Motor Company and its supplier, Mott Axle, to create the nucleus of General Motors. In the next few years Durant acquired Pontiac, Cadillac, and Oldsmobile. By 1911 there was a Chevrolet division, named after Louis Chevrolet, a former race-car driver for Buick. With growth and prosperity, the company, as the town's virtually sole employer, became deeply involved in the politics and sociology of Flint.

Charles Stewart Mott, the owner of Mott Axle, accepted ten thousand shares of General Motors stock in payment of a debt from Durant, which eventually made him one of the richest men in the country. His charitable Mott Foundation became in many ways a surrogate government in Flint, picking up the slack when the real government's resources ran low. Mott money heavily subsidized Flint's public schools, and the Mott Foundation lobbied for and partially financed the Flint campus of the University of Michigan.

The Mott Foundation and GM were two of the three major nongovernmental powers in Flint. The third was the union. From the 1940s through the early 1980s, local and state politics were heavily determined by the policies and internal politics of the United Auto Workers.

There's some history behind this. It was in Flint that organized labor, through the UAW, won a significant victory in American society. In late 1936, the union targeted GM for a risky strike to assert important emerging principles of organized labor, such as the right to collective bargaining. The strike was organized by Walter Reuther and his brothers Victor and Roy, who were then emerging as leaders of the union. It began on January 1, 1937, and it was the kind of thing that, back when there was an industrial working-class culture in the United States, used to be commemorated in broadsides and ballads. UAW members seized the Fisher Body Number Two plant, which made bodies for Chevrolet, and refused to leave the shop floor. The company embargoed food supplies and brought in private and city police, who attacked the strikers and their sympathizers massed outside the plant with bullets and tear gas—an encounter that the workers called, with high-labor romance, "the Battle of the Running Bulls." When these attacks were repulsed, Governor Frank Murphy called in the National Guard.

The strike spread. One hundred and twenty-five thousand workers went out in solidarity with the Fisher workers, which forced GM to shut down fifty plants. When the strike reached Chevrolet Number Four—GM's main plant for Chevrolet engines—President Roosevelt personally pressured the company to negotiate, and the UAW won the right to collective bargaining. It was a groundbreaking victory, hard fought, and it had implications that reverberated through the country and inspired workers in many different industries to unionize. To this day, a monument to the strikers stands in the parking lot of the UAW local on Flint's West Atherton Road, with the original settlement text reproduced on the plaque.

The strike was one of the key events that would eventually bring some measure of autonomy and dignity to American industrial workers. For a long time, the UAW's influence and the deals it could broker benefited both GM and its workers, as GM became the world's largest corporation and one of the country's most profitable. The union quite reasonably demanded an ever-increasing share of profits in the form of wages and benefits for its members, but there were plenty of profits to go around. And the unions took care of their members, making sure that they had everything from decent vacation periods to prescription eyeglasses to funeral insurance—a mini-model of the welfare state.

This period of opportunity for the working class, as recalled fondly and frequently by Michael Moore, was a golden age in which his father could raise a family on an auto worker's salary and still maintain his hope for the future and his sense of himself as a human being, as something other than an underpaid, interchangeable, and expendable work unit tending the great conveyor belt of production. Moore's uncle Laverne was a 1937 striker. Moore says, "Because of what my uncle and others fought for over the years, families like mine were able to live in homes that we owned, go to a doctor whenever we were sick, get our teeth fixed whenever they needed it or go to college if we chose to—all thanks to the union."[1]

The subsequent shift in power relations between the unions and the auto manufacturers is the narrative at the core of Moore's activism. To the enormous detriment of the status of working Americans, social issues such as abortion and school prayer began, in the late 1970s, to overshadow economic issues. The efforts of the Republican Party, the conservative churches, and the right-wing media convinced many American workers that their economic interests were identical to those of their employers. This was happening despite the decline in the share of profits that went to labor as unions were crushed and taxes were lifted from the rich and from corporations. When Reagan fired striking unionized air traffic controllers in 1981 and got away with it, when Caterpillar broke a UAW strike in 1995 by hiring scabs and got away with it, the rights and prospects of all American workers were seriously damaged.

By the 1980s, the social orientation of the old UAW under Walter Reuther—which sought not only money and benefits for its workers but also strove to protect their autonomy and dignity—was gone. The mainstream UAW leadership was eager to salvage its privileges and its relationship with GM's management at the expense of its constituents. GM moved jobs to Mexico and laid off sixty-five thousand of the eighty thousand workers who had been employed in the Flint area in the late 1970s. The town descended into ruin, crime, joblessness, and despair. That, in brief, is the proposition behind *Roger & Me*.

∎ ∎ ∎

The film opens with archival footage of prosperous downtown Flint in the 1950s, full of businesses and shoppers, a bustling, healthy community. The scene is astonishing to anyone who has seen Flint as it is now. The town no longer looks like that. Flint was stunned and stonily unimaginative in the face of GM's pullout in the 1980s. Accustomed to automobile income, city officials and auto workers alike had long taken GM tax revenue for granted. Even as it was clear by the mid-1980s that the jobs were never coming back, Flint was still giving all the tax breaks it could afford to auto plants, meaning that it had little left over to encourage diversification into other industries. Crack dealers moved in to take advantage of the economic despair, and gangs and drug-related killings soon followed. At one point, Flint had the highest murder rate in the United States. By the 1990s, the town could not pay its fire department. In 2001, Flint's budget process was so abysmal that it was taken over by the state of Michigan. Mayor Woodrow Stanley was recalled because he could not find enough revenue to keep the city running.

Flint isn't ruined. There are some nice, quiet neighborhoods along its outer edges, comfortable houses on Chevrolet and Miller avenues with lawns and driveways, which were lit up in melancholic glory by the autumn leaves of the Great Lakes region during my visit. There is a very extensive arts, culture, and sciences complex on Kearsley Street, set up with funding by the Charles Stewart Mott

Foundation in the boom years of the 1950s. The auto companies and the Flint-Genesee County Economic Growth Alliance say that life is getting better in Flint, that it's on the way to recovery, and this is marginally true. The number of auto workers in Flint has now stabilized at around fifteen thousand, and GM has put almost $2 billion of new investment into its Flint plants in the last few years, indicating its intention to stick around at this reduced level. Flint proper has been losing population for years, however, partly from the industry shake-out and partly just as a result of national trends toward suburban residence that have left downtowns struggling all over the United States.

But if things are better now than they were a decade ago, Flint must have been a wasteland then. In 2003, unemployment in Flint was a whopping 16 percent against a Michigan rate of 7.3 percent and a national rate of 6 percent.[2] The northwest part of town—the black quadrant, laid out along the spine of the inevitable Martin Luther King Jr. Avenue—looks like a gray dream of the Apocalypse: rotting, boarded-up houses collapse into weed-strewn lots, the streets as pot-holed as those on Indian reservations. Along Saginaw, the main street of Flint, there are more empty shops than live ones, and there are lines outside the State of Michigan Employment Office. An abandoned storefront sports a glossy poster touting the town's "Business, Entertainment, and Loft District," but there's not much here at all.

On North Saginaw, the bones of former malls stare bleakly out from the littered expanses of their parking lots. The clerk at Brother's Beer, Wine, and Whisky dispenses alcohol and cigarettes from behind bulletproof Plexiglas, but businesses that cater to almost all other aspects of human life—hardware stores, bakeries, beauty salons, and, poignantly, auto-parts shops—are abandoned black holes. Even store-front churches and bars are boarded up, signs of a community that has fallen on hard times indeed.

As I drove around Flint in the autumn of 2004, I was surprised to hear a particular song constantly repeated on the radio, even though it was nowhere near the charts at the time. Reba McEntire's 1990s ballad "Fancy" is a song about a working-class girl whose family is in such desperate economic straits that her own mother has to push her into prostitution for her own survival. But Fancy is no victim; she gets her own in the end, dragging triumph out of humiliation. It's an aston-ishingly brave and gritty song for McEntire to sing, and it's profoundly unsentimental about class and the burdens of being born into the wrong one. Is it just coincidence that the song is big here? I'd like to think that it hangs on because somewhere, deep down, the working people of Flint know they're getting screwed and want to think of themselves as being strong and resourceful.

∎   ∎   ∎

Roger & Me is held together by Moore's klutzy, shuffling self as he seeks an audience with Roger Smith, chairman of General Motors, so that he can ask Smith to come to Flint and talk to some laid-off workers about the consequences of GM's corporate strategy. It's a playful hook that might owe something to Ben Hamper, who for several years had a running theme in his *Flint Voice* "Revenge of the Rivethead" column on his attempts to get Roger Smith to come bowling with him.

The film was made for a total of $260,000, including Moore's $58,000 settlement from *Mother Jones*. Moore introduces many memorable characters in his breakout hit: the cowardly and aloof Roger Smith, so addicted to corporate-speak that he uses a seasonal speech to talk about the "total experience" of Christmas; Deputy Fred Ross, evicting the families of laid-off auto workers from their homes; the buffoonish, insensitive rich people living it up at a 1920s theme party; Ben Hamper, shooting baskets and talking about cracking up on the line; the Auto World robot; the GM flacks Pat Boone and Anita Bryant, themselves robotically presenting cheerful American banality while insisting that if capitalism requires human sacrifice, this is all to the good; the "rabbit lady," Rhonda Britton, selling bunnies for "pets or meat" because her family is out of work. Britton is shown first cuddling a cute floppy-eared rabbit and then conking it on the head, tying it to a tree and skinning it, a scene that works as a metaphor for GM's relationship with its workers as presented in the film, for executives who talk about one big happy family when workers are needed and then turn them loose without a thought when they are not.[3]

Above all, there's Moore's own overweight, rumpled heroic self, stumbling and bumbling around town while delivering a narrative that just happens to have all the answers about what was going on in Flint in the late 1980s.

The lesson, I guess, is always to be suspicious of the guy who has all the answers.

I spoke with Michael Moore about what was happening in the auto industry in Flint twenty years ago. Not Michael Moore the film-maker. This Michael Moore is a professor of labor relations, management, and industrial production. He's a serious and impressive man who speaks with great courtesy and precision. His father owned an auto supply company, and he was born to the industry. He started his career at Ford in labor relations in Dearborn, right outside the place where the "battle of the Overpass" was fought, a famous union confrontation of the 1930s. He's an academic at the intersection of blue- and white-collar work, and after getting a doctorate in industrial relations and human resource management he became one of the first faculty members at Michigan State University's School of Labor and Industrial Relations. Since 1996 he's also been a consultant to General Motors on matters relating to the labor and human resources aspects of the industrial doctrine known as "lean manufacturing": the concept of making the most of space and human resources while keeping at-hand inventory to a minimum. This Michael Moore told me a story about Flint, about GM and the unions, and about the reinvention of the auto industry in the 1980s that is remarkable, both because there truly was a lot going on here while the filmmaker Michael Moore was making *Roger & Me*, and because the filmmaker missed most of it.

By 1982, the domestic auto industry had lost 25 percent of its capacity to Japan. That doesn't necessarily mean that GM was losing a lot of money; the corporation had concentrated on making fewer, bigger, more expensive cars with a higher profit margin, the lessons of the 1970s oil shocks already receding. But GM was hard pressed to figure out Japan's production dominance. Roger Smith had a deep belief that the Japanese had a secret technology, machines that allowed them to make good cars at a tremendous cost advantage. After losing so much of the market, GM decided—way too late—to do something different.

In 1984, GM looked at auto plants around the world and tried to decide what was the best way to build a car. They picked the Volvo method, something radically new in the automobile industry. Since the 1920s, much of industrial theory had accepted Frederick Taylor's thesis that the worker must accommodate the machine, an idea that has had an enormous impact on the development of American technology, production, and sociology. The Volvo method took the opposite approach. It was anti-Taylorism.

At Volvo's plants, workers didn't work on assembly lines. Instead, cars were placed on platforms and moved from one group of workers to another. Workers also did large modules of work, such as a two-hour task with twenty people working on a car, putting on the power train or most of the interior trim. They weren't just doing the same thing over and over, like Ben Hamper's father had; they were actually encouraged to think and to solve problems. They were trusted.

GM adopted this idea from Volvo for their new Saturn model. "After years of kicking the union in the teeth, GM now embraced the union," Moore told me. "They had union partners in everything they did, including dealings with suppliers, purchasing, retailers, and shop-floor management. Foremen were removed; supervisors became group leaders with less authority but more diplomatic skills. Workers took charge of schedules, quality, timing, and output, and they interviewed new members for their teams. It was a tremendous investment in good union-management relations." There was also meaningful profit-sharing; four years after GM's Saturn plant in Tennessee opened, each worker received a $10,000 bonus.

But Saturn was still never as efficient as the Japanese. Not even close. In fact, it wasn't very efficient at all. Neither was Volvo. The productivity difference was so staggering that GM was forced to try again. Team bonding was not the answer.

The company responded by building "Poletown," a factory in the Polish settlement of Hamtramck in Detroit. This section of Hamtramck was old Polish, deep Polish, with lots of old churches and a traditional cultural life, and Detroit mayor Coleman Young found a way to tear it down so that GM could build a plant within the city limits. This plant made Cadillacs, and it operated on a completely different theory from that of the Saturn factory. It was to be the most automated auto plant in the world, and it was not supposed to need workers for much more than turning on machinery. Trouble with the UAW was supposed to be a thing of the past. No workers would mean no hefty benefits packages, no grievances, no strikes. Problem solved! The thoroughgoing commitment to automation at the Poletown plant invites recollection of an exchange between a Ford executive and the

UAW leader Walter Reuther that captures some of the dead-end quality of this kind of thinking. While giving Reuther a tour through an automated plant, the executive observed with satisfaction, "You know, not one of these machines pays dues to the UAW." Reuther replied, "And not one of them buys new Ford cars either."[4]

The plant was a disaster. The machines painted each other, attacked each other, broke down, and missed quota more often than the most goldbricking shop rat. Automation was not the answer.

So Roger Smith, the stolid bureaucrat-plutocrat of *Roger & Me*, did yet a third big thing in the 1980s, conducting another billion-dollar experiment: he learned how the Japanese did it.

In 1983, holding its corporate nose, GM went into partnership with Toyota, which was a little company then (it's now bigger than Ford). The two companies set up a joint venture called New United Motor Manufacturing, Inc., or NUMMI. To further this experiment, GM gave Toyota one of its plants. Its worst plant, actually.

The GM facility in Fremont, California, had been closed for two years. It had twenty-five thousand unanswered union grievances when it closed, along with a history of low-quality work and low productivity, extremely adversarial union-management relations, and a very personal anger between foremen and workers. It was a nightmare. It made no sense to make a car in that plant. That was how much GM wanted the Japanese experiment to succeed. Toyota did not want to hire a unionized workforce, but GM insisted that they rehire the old workers. Toyota gave in and took most of them, refusing only the ones who had actually been convicted of things like sabotage. But Toyota was absolutely adamant that no GM manager would be in that plant. The Japanese would manage it. They installed lean-manufacturing principles and management techniques that were similar to the Saturn team approach, with the workers' input valued and creativity encouraged. But while labor-management relations were less hierarchical than they had been at the plant under GM, there was also less emphasis on the union as a partner.

Within two years, the plant began to win awards: Best Plant in North America; Second-Best Plant in North America. The workers showed levels of productivity and quality comparable to Takaoka, one of the best plants in Japan. It seemed that the right management system really did make a difference.

That's where GM finally got wise that the Japanese didn't have secret machines; they had what the management manuals call "people skills." They treated workers with respect and gave them training in many areas. They gave them a career path. The workers felt as though they had a stake in what they were doing. That made them very productive.

Give Roger Smith credit as a manager—if not as a sensitive human being concerned about his employees—for asking the question three different ways. Within five years he tried embracing workers: *We love the union, the union is our strategic partner*. That was Saturn. He tried: *We hate unions, we don't need workers* and *We're going to build it all ourselves using technology*. That was Poletown. And he tried the Toyota production system, which uses some technology and some team approaches: *We love workers, we love efficiency, we'll work with the union on wages and benefits, but we won't compromise on production methods*.

The Toyota system won. Today, every American automobile manufacturer uses it, with greater and lesser degrees of success. GM has it down the best. As the investment analyst Maryann Keller has written of GM in this period, the company wasted a lot of money looking for quick fixes to problems that were structural, institutional, and "sociological," but under Roger Smith's leadership it was able to keep looking for solutions and, in the end, was able to see the solution to a problem when one of its experiments paid off.[5]

Not everyone took such a sanguine view of the various new management models that GM tried. David Yettaw, the former president of UAW Local 599 at Buick in Flint, led 599 into a loose alliance of hardline union locals known as "New Directions" that fought for the rights of auto workers in this new world of pressure from the bosses and from international competition—and, often, from entrenched union accommodationists who wanted nothing better than to go along and get along with the bosses. From Yettaw's point of view, traditional union contracts and rights were being shredded at Saturn, where workers got only 80 percent of a formerly guaranteed pay scale, the rest being in incentive pay. Yettaw saw management and "mainstream" union officers colluding to support the accommodationist consensus, through the use of a mandatory employee contribution fund that was funneled to the accommodationists' campaigns for union offices:

Michael was doing exactly the right thing. He was exposing what GM was doing to us as a community. The UAW had already agreed to help management downsize, so they were very distant from Michael. They took the status quo line, used very disparaging remarks about him, and me as well. Michael was only sounding the alarm about what was going to happen to the rest of the auto industry in this country. In the Flint area you had the Flint *Journal* that's always been controlled by the City Club as well as the Chamber of Commerce; the Chamber of Commerce in Flint is controlled by General Motors. They were constantly bashing Michael Moore: "Look how he's portraying our city to the nation! We're not like that!" Well, there were people in Flint who were devastated.

The response of the auto workers to *Roger & Me* was tremendous. They felt Michael Moore was on their side, and he was telling their story. He was especially telling the story of what we call "automotive gypsies." GM was saying, "If your factory closes, we have a right to force you to drive sixty-five miles to another job." In some situations they moved people from Flint to Tarrytown, New York. People were living in vans, four or five of them in an apartment. The other kind of people who were most effectively portrayed by Michael Moore were not auto workers, but their livelihood depended on auto workers. It was very disturbing to anyone with a conscience, a moral, social conscience. He told a powerful story about those people. It was just a tornado of economic dislocation for people who couldn't hold on.

The voices of those like Yettaw, who didn't think there was much to be gained by accommodating management, were eventually silenced. Buick informed its workers that it would close its plant in Flint if Yettaw retained his presidency of Local 599. Yettaw was voted out. Within three years, Buick closed its plant anyway. It was a lesson in where the power lay.

Ben Hamper is also skeptical about the new management style:

I think the Pontiac East plant that I transferred to in the late eighties qualifies as one of these [new-style, lean-manufacturing]

plants. It opened the year I transferred there. I didn't see anything that went on there that suggested an effort to treat workers better. In fact, the place was much worse for the
workers—a real Gestapo atmosphere with overloaded job
duties and very weak union representation. They had a program there, as they do in many other plants, called "Team
Concept," but all it seemed to boil down to was an attempt to
get the workforce to police itself via fears of job security and
rewards to ass-kissers. From what I hear from former line
mates, the plants as a whole are a lot more rigid. The union
has really lost a lot of its clout, both at the bargaining table
and on the shop floor.

Still, the overall picture was complex. The enormous changes in
the auto industry, in its sociology as well as its technology and economics, were not of interest to Michael Moore. He saw only the reality of lost jobs and martyred workers.

These were important realities. The old-style Flint workers had
no reason to love GM and many to fight it. As they saw it, no matter
how much GM paid the line workers, GM executives and stockholders were profiting from their labor. The hard battles for unionization,
the sit-downs, and the company goons were all remembered in Flint,
a town that was proud of its union history. The alienation of the shop
rat that Moore and Hamper idealized was indeed in some sense
heroic.

Here's Hamper on an employee-motivation session in his ancien
régime plant: "Hardly anyone tuned in for the technical presentation.
It was one long lullaby of foreign terminology, slides, numerology, and
assorted high-tech masturbation. Why would any of us give a shit
about the specifics of the great master plan? We knew what holes our
screws went in. That was truth enough. Point us toward our air guns
and welders and drill presses and save all the particulars for the
antheads in the smocks and bifocals."[6]

The measure of how little the old GM valued its workers' skills or
made use of their full abilities can be seen in how easy it was for Hamper and his line buddy to mine potential for efficiency unrecognized
by the company—not in the service of corporate profits, but in the
service of their own freedom as they "doubled up" on shifts, each

pushing his limits to do his own job as well as that of the other guy for half the shift and spending the other half in one of the many bars near the plant, getting slammed and getting paid for a full shift. The shop rats were brilliant and hard-working in their own interests, but the company wasn't getting the benefit of any of that brilliance and wasn't asking for it.

■　■　■

Auto plants don't work like that anymore; they really *do* demand both more creativity and more responsibility from their workers, which means that workers are both more and less powerful than they used to be in the old-style, smart-enough-to-be-too-dumb-to-care mode. This was just starting to happen when Michael Moore was making *Roger & Me*, but it's so antithetical to his thesis that he could never have been interested in it.

There is also the cold, hard reality of GM's unwillingness to invest billions in a community that took adversarial labor relations as a historic point of honor. Moore never acknowledges that not all the jobs that GM pulled out of Flint went to low-wage Mexico or Brazil. Some of these jobs went to Lansing, some went to Saginaw, and some—like Hamper's—went to Pontiac. They went to places where GM managers thought that new manufacturing concepts would be welcomed, where they wouldn't have to fight the union every step of the way on every change. For the first time, jobs in the auto industry were transcending Hamper's descriptions of mechanical roles in which lives were wasted in dehumanizing drudgery. Changing this grim working relationship was, of course, the secret of the new approach to auto manufacture, but that was entirely beyond the sphere of Michael Moore's consciousness.

What Moore really wants of Roger Smith—what he won't forgive GM for not providing—is job security and high wages at the expense of GM's stockholders and market position. He wants a corporation that puts people before profits. This isn't such a bad idea. It has, in fact, worked to some extent in Japan, where corporate loyalty flows both ways and companies value the respect of their workers, and where there is (or used to be) a tradition that the highest-paid executives make no more than seven times the income of the lowest-paid line workers. This may well have been more symbolic than actual; undoubtedly the Japanese managers had other, nonsalary compensation. But it was important symbolism.

Unfortunately, Moore was selling this idea in 1989. His timing was poor. The American working class had been led to believe that socialism was synonymous with the crumbling totalitarian governments of Eastern Europe, that it was dead, and that capitalism was synonymous with freedom. Right-wing intellectuals were declaring Reaganism triumphant and capitalism the end of history, even as Reagan's recession, the result of the mountain of debt he had accumulated, was kicking in. Unions had been weakened by a lack of solidarity, global competition, and their manifold humiliations at Reagan's hands. Corporate responsibility in such an environment was a hard sell, even to workers. There were no sit-downs, no riots in Flint in the 1980s.

Moore is a traditionalist. He believes in the power of organized workers in high-paying industrial jobs. But, in a way, he also has little faith in the working people whose misfortunes he shows in his film, because outside of that scenario he sees working people as essentially lost. Without anything to keep the employer in town, without aggressive and militant backing from their union, Moore goes to some lengths to portray the people of Flint as passive victims with nothing else to do but invest themselves in sad schemes, pathetic in their delusional nature—the "color consultant"—or wait for the sheriff to put them out on the street.

■   ■   ■

Moore, his wife, and all of their friends who worked on the project had pretty much expected that he would take it around the country in a van and show it at union halls and working-class recreation centers. It didn't happen quite like that.

John Pierson, the producer's rep who brokered Moore's distribution deal, told Moore that, based on production costs and the money-making potential of comparable films, he might get $200,000 for the film. Moore shrugged off this prediction. He was right to do so: after the film screened to rapturous receptions at the Toronto, Telluride, and New York film festivals and got fantastic reviews from Gene

Siskel, Roger Ebert, and Vincent Canby, the film's market value dras-
tically changed. Nowadays, political films with the candid, improvised
flavor of *Roger & Me* and the imaginative use of stock footage mixed
with new material are not so unusual, but this is partly because Moore
invented a style that has been widely imitated. At the time—and in
the context of the late-eighties reaction to the economic folly and
class warfare of the Reagan years—the film was enormously exciting
and satisfying, thrilling and original. Susan Dalsimer of Warner Bros.
films saw the first New York Film Festival screening at Alice Tully
Hall, which garnered a seven-minute standing ovation. She immediately called Lucy Fisher, Warner's executive vice president for worldwide production, and told her, "I've just seen the film that drives a
stake through the heart of Reagan's America, and we should find a
way to be involved."[7]

The competition for the film was intense, which meant that
Moore could be a hard bargainer, and he showed a great deal of professional savvy and insight in playing the studios and the independent
distributors against each other. He went about this with an aggressive
theatricality.

He also made some astonishing errors in his approach. Pierson
describes Moore's conference with Disney vice president Andrew
Hersh, in which Moore complained about members of Disney's board
who also sat on the board of General Motors, and suggested that GM
was working through Disney to buy the rights to the film and keep it
out of circulation. It's impossible to tell whether this self-sabotaging
behavior stemmed from the purest idealism or the most pathological
paranoia. There is also Moore's odd behavior in the aftermath of the
1989 Loma Prieta earthquake, which struck while he was in California.
The quake was centered on northern California, but its shocks were
felt as far south as Hollywood. Sixty-seven people died, three thousand
were injured, five hundred thousand were affected, and there were
billions of dollars in damages. Moore couldn't figure out why the studio executives he was meeting with were fixated on the earthquake
coverage on TV rather than paying attention to the deal for his film.

Moore pushed for some very unusual items in the distribution
contract. He offered to promote the film in twice as many markets as
usual, but insisted that he would not fly on union-busting Continen-
tal Airlines. Any distributor had to employ five associates from Flint as

a field promotion team. The film could never be shown on the Public Broadcasting Service. Moore also wanted twenty-five thousand free tickets for unemployed auto workers, $25,000 for the families shown getting evicted in the movie, a seat reserved for Roger Smith at each screening, and no distribution in Israel or South Africa (although he had no qualms about taking the film to a festival in Leipzig, then still part of East Germany).

In the end, after wide-ranging negotiations with many studios and independent outlets, Warner Bros. picked it up, paying around $3 million for distribution rights. This was a stunning amount to pay for a first film, and unprecedented for a documentary.

Roger & Me more than met the studios' expectations. In the four and a half months that the movie ran in commercial release it grossed $7 million, making it the top-grossing nonconcert documentary ever made up to that time, and it was made by someone who was essentially an amateur, an unknown who had no major studio connections. Since then it has probably doubled its gross theater takings in cable, video, and DVD releases. Part of the film's success was undoubtedly due to the fact that Moore promoted it tirelessly, especially in the blue-collar Midwest, logging thousands of travel miles to areas that were certainly not on the usual film-promotion circuit. *Roger & Me* opened in Burton, a suburb of Flint (Flint itself was so economically devastated that it had no movie theater), and Moore did things like debating Flint's mayor on the merits of the film and GM's corporate citizenship.

Moore was a local hero in Flint. His appearance of stubborn authenticity was known and respected. Dave Barber, the host of Flint Supertalk Radio AM 1570, who says he has interviewed Moore over a hundred times, told me of seeing Moore in his beat-up old Honda—a car that could get its driver's ass kicked in Flint—by the county courthouse soon after he closed his deal with Warner Bros. "I said, 'Michael. Jesus Christ, man, three million dollars. What are you going to do now?' And he said, 'Well, I know some things I *won't* do. If you ever see me sitting in a hot tub sipping champagne, hit me with a baseball bat.' He's done very well now, of course, but I think fundamentally, philosophically, you have the same guy. I see the same passion."

■   ■   ■

For a while, *Roger & Me* was touted as Oscar material. GM pulled its ads from any TV or print production mentioning the film, which must have thrilled Moore. The movie won him a national reputation as the friend of the working man, the guy who would stand up to GM and tell it like it is. More or less adoring reviews appeared in national newspapers, *Time*, *Newsweek*, and *Rolling Stone* (this must have been especially sweet for Moore, a Van Halen fan), and Moore embarked on a major U.S. speaking tour.

Not everyone was willing to go along with the idea that *Roger & Me* was a straight documentary. Starting with work by John Foren in the *Flint Journal*, analysts began to notice that some of what Moore presents as cause and effect doesn't hold true. In a major development for the fate of the film, the critic Harlan Jacobson became uncomfortable with the film as a documentary. Although Jacobson liked much of the film—he wrote that Moore was "glitteringly smart in his analysis and arrestingly right in essence"[8]—he felt that being right "in essence" wasn't enough; he worried about the particulars.

Jacobson confronted Moore in an interview in *Film Comment* with the misleading use of sequence: twenty thousand of the thirty thousand layoffs Moore cites had happened over a decade, not all at once after 1986 as he implies when he opens this segment of the film with "I wasn't back in Flint more than a few days when the bad news hit" and follows this with GM's 1986 announcement.[9] A visit from televangelist Robert Schuller, which Moore presents as a response to the layoffs, occurred in 1982; the plans for reviving the city's economy that Moore pokes fun at, also presented as a response to GM's retreat, including an overinvestment in a convention center and the ridiculous Auto World amusement park, had been planned since the mid-1970s and had closed or gone bankrupt before 1986.

As Jacobson himself points out in their interview, Moore is correct about the overall effect of the layoffs on Flint. It's not illegitimate to view the layoffs of the mid-1970s through the mid-1980s as part of a single process that generated the silly responses Moore shows. But there's a reason why newspapers care about whether a witness's first name is John or Jon: credibility matters, and sloppiness puts credibility in doubt. If the facts are wrong, or if broad generalizations are presented as specific fact, the entire documentary nature of the project—and therefore the point that Moore was trying to make about GM's corporate responsibility—can be lost. The interview includes this very revealing exchange:

HJ: That's what happens when one manipulates sequence . . . and that's the core credibility of the documentary.

MM: All art, listen, every piece of journalism manipulates sequence and things. Just the fact that you edit, that certain things get taken out or put back in. That's just a ridiculous statement.

HJ: It goes back to the issue of the belief in the integrity of the information.

MM: Uh-huh. Yeah, sure.

HJ: Do you see a problem with the inclusion of the Reverend Schuller footage, which happened in 1982, and the impression you give that it was done post-1986?

MM: I didn't say it was done post-1986 . . . it happened during the same decade, when after thousands of people were laid off, they brought in Reverend Schuller. You are trying to hold me to a different standard than you would another film . . . as if I were writing some kind of college essay. . . .

HJ: No. I hold you to documentary-film standards.

MM: Because you see this primarily as a documentary.[10]

Moore often protested that giving the context behind his editing would make the film unmanageably long. Perhaps in reaction to the criticism this aspect of the film received, Moore's voice-over commentary for the special features section of the 2003 DVD release includes this caveat: "This film covers essentially the entire decade of the 1980s. It's meant to present this mosaic of what happened in Flint during the 1980s, so we'll be going back and forth—there are no dates in the film. I thought I should point that out just so you know where you're at here." If he had only had this voice-over in the original release, or scrolled it at some point, or even presented it onscreen at the beginning of the film, he could have saved himself a lot of trouble. It takes exactly twenty seconds for him to say this on the DVD.

There were things that Jacobson didn't catch but others did. In the segment that purports to show laid-off GM workers talking about meeting with Ronald Reagan at a restaurant in Flint in 1980, Moore starts with an actual interview about this event and then splices in footage shot at an entirely different event, which is why the comments in these clips are vague and never mention GM or Flint. Although he never states that the second set of clips relates to the restaurant meeting, the direct segue leaves the viewer to assume that they do. In the segment in which Moore goes looking for Roger Smith's home, at least some of the big houses of the rich that Moore describes as being in the wealthy enclaves around Flint (he lists Grosse Pointe Woods, Grosse Pointe Park, Grosse Pointe Farms, Grosse Pointe Shores, and Bloomfield Hills) are actually in Flint itself (Moore disingenuously responded to this by writing that the critics' problem was that "the houses were shot on a different street than stated,"[11] which misses the point he was making in his own film, which, it is fairly obvious, had to do with the isolation of the rich in privileged enclaves). The rats that Moore shows taking over Flint were from Detroit.

Perhaps all of this criticism was trivial. But more seriously for the logic of *Roger & Me*, Ralph Nader has said that he saw Moore interviewing Roger Smith on camera in 1988 at the Waldorf-Astoria in New York, refuting Moore's contention that Smith had refused to have any contact with him—which is, after all, the organizing theme of the film.[12] Nader and his associates James Musselman and Michael Westfall also say that, in May 1987, while he was working on *Roger & Me*, Moore filmed a GM shareholders' meeting during which he questioned Roger Smith on the tax abatements granted by the city of Flint to GM. Nader actually supplied a transcript of this meeting to *Premiere* magazine, and in the published version Smith responds to Moore's questions for half a small-print page.[13] This never made it into the film; all we see in *Roger & Me* are the GM corporate flacks shutting down a shareholders' meeting as Moore approaches the microphone, and Roger Smith, finally cornered at a Christmas party, refusing to come to Flint to meet the families of former GM workers being evicted from their homes. Smith actually taking questions did not fit into Moore's plan. Moore had cast him as a stonewaller.

■   ■   ■

Some film critics took Moore's side, agreeing that as a filmmaker he was entitled to play with things like sequence in support of his larger goals. As Roger Ebert wrote,

> I would no more go to *Roger & Me* for a factual analysis of GM and Flint than I would turn to the pages of *Spy* magazine for a dispassionate study of the world of Donald Trump. What *Roger & Me* supplies about General Motors, Flint and big corporations is both more important and more rare than facts. It supplies poetry, a viewpoint, indignation, opinion, anger and humor. When Michael Moore waves his sheaf of *New York Times* clippings in the air and defends the facts in his film, he's missing his own point.[14]

But Ebert is missing Jacobson's. If a film claims legitimacy as a documentary, "poetry" can't trump sequence.

Jacobson's criticisms of Moore's veracity were picked up by Pauline Kael, the influential film critic for the *New Yorker*, who slammed the film on journalistic, aesthetic, and political grounds, branding it "a piece of gonzo demagoguery that made me feel cheap for laughing." She went on to say that Moore had improvised history and that his approach meant that "members of the audience can laugh at ordinary working people and still feel that they are taking a politically correct position."[15] Moore responded that Kael wrote a spiteful review because he hadn't allowed Warner Bros. to provide a videocassette for her private viewing.[16]

Moore never conceded a thing to his critics. At the time, and in many restatements since, he insisted that everything he showed was true if you use a longer time scale: GM indeed had eliminated thirty thousand jobs in Flint and the town was ruined; twenty thousand workers had been laid off before Auto World opened; all the town's schemes were connected with bolstering the local economy, and it was a GM economy—what more do you want? Typically, he took all criticism personally, impugned the critics' integrity, and invoked conspiracy as an explanation for bad press: "*Film Comment* is a publication of the Film Society of Lincoln Center; Lincoln Center had received a $5 million gift from GM just prior to its publishing of the piece trashing *Roger & Me*. Coincidence? Or just five big ones well spent?"[17] This labored explanation was refuted by the facts, however. Jacobson was fired soon after his interview with Moore appeared in *Film Comment*. He did not attribute his firing to the interview, or at least not entirely, but he did say that "the interview was the last and most visible expression of an editorial policy that the Film Society did not like and could not support." For those so inclined, a different and opposite conspiracy theory is at least as plausible as Moore's in explaining why Jacobson was fired: the Film Society of Lincoln Center was a sponsor of the New York Film Festival, where *Roger & Me* was a big hit.

In an echo of the Paul Farhi incident at *Mother Jones*, Moore also claimed that Jacobson had flown into a rage during the interview and accused him of making an anti-Semitic film that would inspire pogroms against Jews (because, according to Jacobson according to Moore, the film contains a brief scene of the Palestinian intifada, and—even more far-fetched—because a blue-collar audience would assume that the Jews are behind America's industrial decline).[18] Jacobson denied that he said anything of the kind.

In his rebuttals, Moore clearly fails to grasp what's at stake. It's a cheap dodge to insist, as Moore does, that the movie is meant to inform by entertaining and to imply that its entertainment value justifies the fudging of facts. Why? He could have had both. It also seems almost gratuitously self-destructive.

As the editor of a small paper competing for the trust of a small town with the conservative *Flint Journal*, Moore could strike poses and write controversial editorials, but his reporting had to be pretty straight or people would notice—and it was. As Moore's work has become better known, as he has become more ambitious—more of a polemicist and less of a journalist—and as he has become a national figure without a local constituency that is invested in the issues to keep him in line, he has taken a frequently casual attitude toward the facts. This attitude was already starting to come out with *Roger & Me* and, perhaps even more so, in his response to criticism of his techniques.

Moore's persistent use of poetic license in areas where it is clearly not legitimate seems almost masochistic, a self-sabotaging habit; like the bank robber who returns again and again to hold up the same bank, you can speculate that he wants to be caught. Moore's enemies have never failed to hit him with charges of playing loose with the facts where it suits his editorial position, and he has given them many opportunities to discredit not only his material but also his theses. This has considerably dulled the effect of Moore's voice on American politics, and on much larger issues than the date on which Auto World closed.

If we can't trust Moore on Auto World, why should we trust him on the relationship of the Bushes with the Saudi royal family? If those big houses are actually in Flint rather than Grosse Pointe, isn't the class divide in America more complicated than Moore says it is? But this is not the way Moore wants viewers to approach his work, which is meant to be enjoyed, and believed, on its own terms. When his supporters insist that his films are designed to stimulate independent thought, they seriously misjudge what Moore does.

■　■　■

Roger & Me was widely hailed as a political breakthrough, and Moore as the authentic voice of a revived, scrappy working class. Not everyone agreed with this assessment. Dave Marsh has spent a lot of his working life in the company of rock stars—he's a co-founder of *Creem* magazine, a contributing editor for *Rolling Stone*, a biographer of Bruce Springsteen, and the founder of the seminal music/politics/culture newsletter *Rock & Roll Confidential* (now *Rock & Rap Confidential*)—but he's a genuine working-class guy from Michigan. His father was a railroad brakeman before he moved into the railroad's front office, and Marsh has well-developed ideas about the meaning of class in America. He's written extensively on the subject.

Marsh knows Moore from Moore's days on the *Flint Voice*, and the association wasn't a pleasant one for him. Moore wanted to run features from the weekly *Confidential* in his monthly *Voice*. They worked out a reprint arrangement that involved a tiny fee: if Moore used anything from *Confidential*, he owed the newsletter ten dollars a month. But there were problems. Marsh says, "If you want to talk about solidarity, one of the things that you're honor-bound to do is to keep your commitments to your comrades. Michael just persistently refused to pay us. Finally, we had to say, 'Hey, don't run our stuff anymore, you do not have permission.' We sent him a formal letter to that effect. We didn't really have a choice. Michael took this the way he takes most things that he doesn't like: as an affront. It's immoral to say no to him, is the way it works." When I expressed astonishment that Moore would be a deadbeat on such a paltry amount, Marsh remarked, "I'd worry about leaving a tip on the table in a diner if Michael hadn't stood up yet."

Whatever ill-feeling this episode created, Moore didn't hesitate to come to Marsh several years later, just after Moore had left *Moore's Weekly* and was working on *Roger & Me*. He was raising money to finish the film. Moore showed Marsh his work-in-progress. Marsh was not impressed.

> He came by on a Sunday afternoon. At the time the only VCR we had was in the bedroom; we had to sit on the edge of the bed. This was weird because I'm not comfortable with the guy even in a big open room. He shows me his film. Two things I remember were the lady who sells rabbits for pets or meat, and the sheriff who's evicting people. And I totally read this thing in terms of class condescension. First of all, the rabbit lady could be my mother, in certain ways. My mother doesn't look like that, but in other ways, yes. And it ain't far away—you couldn't walk from there to my mother's, but you wouldn't need more than a sixteenth of a tank of gas. And even the sheriff thing, I thought it was snotty, it was snide. Which leads to the question: whatever Michael's professed class allegiances are, what are his real class politics and how does that reflect how he really grew up?
>
> I will tell you this: I don't know anybody else who grew up in Michigan, the most class-conscious part of the United States, who has the particularly snide attitude about the working class that Michael has. I simply don't know any other working-class person who grew up between Lansing and the Ohio border who thinks like that. His consistent perspective on working people is that they're kind of dumb, very crude, and there to be made sport of by their superiors, the leading example of whom is Michael Moore. So that's what he shows me, and that's what I see. When it's over he asks me what I think. I'm pretty noncommittal, I wasn't really looking to

have a fight with him. I was looking to get this over with. So then he starts in about how he needs money for the film. I'm like, what does that have to do with me? I ain't writing you a check. Maybe I'll promise you one for ten dollars. He says, "Bruce Springsteen."

Marsh's wife, Barbara, was one of Springsteen's managers. But what Moore had perhaps forgotten was that during his time at *Mother Jones*, he'd published a piece by Ben Hamper on rock stars and class, in which Hamper wrote that Springsteen was a fake, a rich guy with a fashion-model wife, who impersonated working-class characters in his song-stories. Springsteen wasn't the only rock star Hamper took on, but the column was titled "Brucie Can You Hear Me?"[19]

So when Moore asked Marsh to try to get some of Springsteen's money for him, he was irritated. And it wasn't only money.

It's also possible that Michael wanted permission to use Springsteen's "My Hometown" in his film—anyway, he wanted Bruce. And Springsteen, at that time, I think he'd maybe only allowed one or two of his things to be used in films, for example in the John Sayles film *Baby, It's You*, so it would have been a coup. I said, "Yeah, my wife works with Bruce, but I can't go to them for you." He says, "Why can't you go to them?" I say, "Well, during your brief tenure of editing *Mother Jones*, you managed to run that idiotic piece by Ben Hamper that says that Springsteen wasn't for real, wasn't really working class"—this is the reason that Michael's class background is an issue, because he's *comfortable* telling somebody else they're not real. "They found that stupid and hurtful"—I don't know how hurtful they really found it, but I probably said that they did. "How am I supposed to go to them and tell them they should write a check to the guy who ran that piece, even if I thought they should write you a check, which I don't?" He knows exactly what I'm talking about. "That has nothing to do with me—what was I supposed to do, censor Ben?" I said, "Let me get this straight. You edit a magazine of media criticism, and you think that the editor of a magazine has no responsibility for what appears in his magazine? And you think it's unreasonable for other people to think that he does?" So he was jawing at me and I was jawing at him, and finally I picked his fat ass up by the collar, frog-walked him over to the goddamn door, and pushed him out and closed the door on him. It's not the way he tells the story. But my recollection of it is very clear.

Indeed, in Moore's telling, there's no mention of money, only of Moore asking Marsh to ask Springsteen for permission to use Springsteen's song, and Moore has Marsh grimly proclaiming, "Ben Hamper is my ideological enemy." It is noteworthy that just before describing this scene with Marsh, Moore gives yet another wildly implausible account of his firing from *Mother Jones*: Adam Hochschild fired him because he insisted on running Hamper's work, which Hochschild, Moore wants us to believe, called "smut."[20] Moore doesn't have the greatest record on consistent recollection. When I asked Marsh about the "enemy" comment, he replied, "I don't recall saying that Hamper was my 'ideological enemy,' but it's not impossible. I doubt I said it that way—that amount of pomposity. But Michael doesn't bring out the best in me, and it was a nasty little moment, so maybe I did." Marsh added, jokingly, "Come to think of it, maybe I said Michael was my ideological enemy—or maybe that's what I was trying to say. God knows, it's true enough."

■ ■ ■

In making *Roger & Me*, Moore was ruthless as well as stubborn. In Flint there are people who love him and people who don't much care for him, and not all of the latter are corporate fat cats or corrupt cops. Take Larry Stecco.

If you've seen the movie, you've seen Stecco. He's the guy at that Great Gatsby party for rich toffs, the one where black folk are paid to pose as props in period costume. Stecco is the guy who's so out of it that he talks about what a great place Flint is to live, even as working-class people are being thrown out of their homes; how there's ballet and hockey, how everything is great in his privileged little world.

Except that wasn't really Stecco's world and Moore knew it. He knew Stecco personally, if not well. He knew that Stecco wasn't part of the idle rich set and that, in fact, he was on the same side as Moore on many issues. Stecco had helped him out several times. And although Moore never mentions it, the Great Gatsby party was an annual charitable event that raised money for a shelter for battered women, a shelter that Moore himself had supported in editorials in the *Flint Voice*. The party was hardly a decadent gambol.

Almost twenty years after the unfortunate interview at the party, I met with Stecco and his lawyer, Glen Lenhoff, at a dark and comfortable bar in Flint. Stecco's a bit grayer, but still quite recognizable from the film. I was glad Lenhoff was there. He's a smart and interesting guy who had a lot to say.

Stecco is soft-spoken, thoughtful, and idealistic, someone who supports his town even when things go very bad. He's clearly very decent, clearly nothing like the shallow caricature of a rich jerk that he appears to be in *Roger & Me*. He's a former chairman of the Genesee County Democratic Club, a lawyer who has done a lot of pro bono civil rights work. He's a strong union supporter. Since 1997 he's been a judge in Michigan's 67th District Court, an elective office. Moore's friend and long-time associate Sam Riddle told me that Stecco is "a very fair-minded guy, a very fair-minded judge."

Stecco first met Moore during the time of the recall movement to get Moore removed from the Davison school board. Stecco's law partner's daughter worked on the hotline, and he'd helped with some legal issues there at her request. The county Democratic Party, under Stecco's leadership, had donated $1,000 to fight the recall, a lot of money at the time. Stecco himself gave regular if not large sums to the *Flint Voice*. He and Moore had mutual friends, and Stecco supported the idea of an alternative paper. At the time he felt that Moore "stirred things up" and that "there was a legitimate place for someone like that."

When Stecco ran into Moore at the Great Gatsby party, Moore told him that he was making a movie in response to *Money* magazine naming Flint as the "worst place to live" in the United States, that it was for local PBS channel 28 and was being produced in conjunction with the Junior League. Stecco knew enough about Moore to find the Junior League connection a bit ironic and thought that it would probably be hard for Moore to get responses. He agreed to help out by doing an interview for the movie:

In the film I look like an insensitive fool, babbling about hockey and ballet, but we were talking about raising kids here. I said that times were tough here, but it's still a good place to raise a family. Moore also set it up to make me and the party look racist. There were both African American and white actors hired to pose as human statues in period costume, but Moore shows only the black actors, making the whole scene look exploitative. The black actors sued him for the way they were portrayed.

So did Stecco. He took Moore to court for presenting his character in a false light, actionable under Michigan law. The trial dragged on for a long time, and it was very bitter. "He's a tough man to deal with personally," Lenhoff said. "He threatened to file a grievance against me with the Michigan bar—'You'd better get the papers out! It's coming!' he said. I was reminded of this when he threatened slander suits in connection with [*Fahrenheit 9/11*]."

The jury was persuaded that the reality of Stecco was nothing like the guy in the film and awarded him $6,250. Lenhoff explained that Moore had publicly claimed that he gave $25,000 to the four families shown being evicted so that they could buy houses—actually he negotiated this amount in his contract with Warner Bros.—which sounds like a pretty good sum, but in fact the amount was $25,000 in total, so each of the four families got $6,250. The jury thought Stecco should get as much. "What irks us no end," says Lenhoff, "is to see the scene that was pronounced illegal under Michigan law continue to appear in new releases of the film, to see Moore and his distributor continue to make money on a scene that a jury found to misrepresent its subject."

Stecco is particularly upset about Moore's effect on Flint's fortunes:

Roger & Me hurt the town of Flint. It hurt the job situation in Flint, which Michael Moore supposedly cared so much about. The only people in *Roger & Me* who looked like they knew what was going on are Michael and Deputy Fred Ross. He made everyone else look like an idiot. Woodrow Stanley, who later became the mayor, testified in our lawsuit that he knew of no other single thing that had so damaged Flint's reputation.

When I used to see that Moore was using found footage to make a point outside of the real context—like those laid-off workers supposedly meeting with Reagan in Flint—I used to think that he didn't have much money, that he was trying to make a point and he resorted to doing this. But he's still doing the same thing in his films, and he's got plenty of money now. I have to think that, in some strange way, he just enjoys the power he has to twist the truth. I believe he does it to further his own personal ends, not for the cause that he purports to represent. I think Moore trashed Flint, used it for his purposes, and then moved on.

Moore hasn't stopped using the Great Gatsby scene for his own purposes, in new ways that continue to distort reality. In his voice-over commentary for the DVD release special features, Moore asks, while Stecco is shown, "Why would they even let me into this place? . . . It's always better just to let them talk. . . . Just to let them, in their own words, say what they want to say . . . you learn a lot more letting the other side talk, letting the people who are in charge, in control, who've got some money, let them have their say." So Moore makes Larry Stecco—with whom he had been friendly if not friends, whom Moore knew to be a decent guy who'd supported his early causes— represent "them" and "the other side," one of the people who were "in control."

The story of Larry Stecco and his involuntary cameo in *Roger & Me* captures many of the contradictions of Moore's career and per-sonality. Moore is genuinely concerned with social justice; he doesn't think it's right that rich people should be partying while poor people struggle to get by on their leavings, and this is an admirable, even noble position; no doubt, in stating it frequently, Moore has changed the world for the better in certain ways.

But it's a *meta*-position, because the actual people and arguments that Moore uses to make this point are often manipulated and exploited. There are plenty of genuinely callow, shallow, selfish, igno-rant, passively racist rich people out there. Larry Stecco isn't one of them, and Moore knew it. His portrayal of Stecco in *Roger & Me* exhibits both a solid show-business instinct and a cold, hard core of relentless ideology, an attitude that, as with Leninists of yore, will always put the cause of increasing human well-being before the well-being of any particular human, and will put the meta-truth before the actual, immediate truth of any situation. Like the story of Moore's political attack on his high school principal, it recurs throughout his work.

PART TWO

ROADKILL POLITICS

4

FUN WITH A PURPOSE

ichael Moore has never been bound by any one medium. He's been working in print from his earliest school days, and he had a weekly radio show—*Radio Free Flint*—in high school. After *Roger & Me*, he came back to Flint and did a political show called *Roadkill Politics* for the local PBS station, in which he would research issues of public concern and present them as entertainment.

Television is a natural medium for Moore: ubiquitous, despised by intellectuals, susceptible to populist uses. By the 1990s, it was a medium with a particular appeal to someone of Moore's talents— "Ringmaster" Jerry Springer had already obliterated a lot of prissy old conventions—but before Moore there were few on the left who were willing to do a show that was both political and a circus (although Springer was once the mayor of Cincinnati).

This shortfall opened a certain cultural niche for Moore somewhere between the present-day *Fear* and *O'Reilly* factors, and his ability to fill this need has always been a key aspect of his success. He hates documentaries—or, at least, the sober PBS style of documentary. He likes to be playful. He needs a gimmick, a hook to draw in his audience—the more outrageous, the better. When he finds one, he can appeal to people who would be moved by the leftist conspiratorial arguments of, say, Noam Chomsky if they weren't too lazy to read him. Moore's diatribes are easy to absorb: precut, prechewed, and often highly entertaining.

Some of Moore's television ventures were poorly conceived, like the 1997 two-hour test for a show for Fox, in which Moore interviewed O.J. Simpson. According to witnesses, the studio audience reaction was not good; when they saw it really was Simpson, half the group walked out. A cameraman dropped his camera. The show never aired. Moore later declared himself agnostic on the question of O.J.'s guilt or innocence, but he developed an idiosyncratic theory of the public antipathy to O.J.: white America hadn't lifted a finger to help Nicole Brown Simpson when he was beating her, so the rush to judgment was misplaced guilt. Besides, white people believed that O.J. had betrayed their trust, and this was a kind of racism.

> [B]ecause we let him into white America, we let him on our boards of directors, we let him play at our country clubs, he tried very hard to be one of us, we even let him marry one of our own without any objection, then he had the arrogance and the audacity to go and kill her? After we let him in? Who does he think he is? I think this is really what's at the center, the racial element that white Americans don't want to acknowledge. Do you think if he'd killed the first wife, the black one, the overweight one, the ugly one, that there'd be one tenth the media coverage? No, I don't think so.[1]

Moore honed his skills in political satire on his 1990s cable TV shows *TV Nation* and *The Awful Truth*. In 1992, after the commercial success of *Roger & Me* became very clear, he was handed the opportunity to do *TV Nation* by NBC, whose executives were—in Moore's telling, at least—thrilled to have him work on a show that would be "a cross between *60 Minutes* and Fidel Castro on laughing gas" and that, Moore promised, would "go after [your advertisers] like a barracuda."[2] Just the kind of show a network could be expected to rush to sign up.

The negotiations for the show generated some serious connections for Moore and did a great deal to forward his career. At that time, Moore had been trying unsuccessfully to raise money for a fictional film with political overtones titled *Canadian Bacon*. The *TV Nation* pilot tested well with the network executives and in a screening in the blue-collar town of Scranton, Pennsylvania. The response wasn't strong enough to win network support.

But the pilot did win commitments from Alan Alda and John Candy to appear in *Canadian Bacon*, and getting the stars on board brought funding for the film. Eventually released in 1995, *Canadian Bacon* is in fact very much like an extended *TV Nation* segment. Evil elements in the U.S. government and in the arms industry conspire to set up the Canadians as a new mortal national enemy to keep the Cold War military contracts flowing and President Alan Alda popular. The film borrows liberally from Stanley Kubrick's Cold War classic *Dr. Strangelove* and anticipates elements of *Wag the Dog* and the *South Park* movie ("Blame Canada!"). But Moore is no Kubrick, and no Trey Parker or Matt Stone, for that matter. The satire is both broad and shallow, and the main lesson of the film (aside from the fact that Wallace Shawn, playing Canadian prime minister Clark MacDonald, bears a distinct resemblance to actual former Canadian prime minister Sir Wilfrid Laurier) is that this kind of thing might work in a ten-minute *TV Nation* episode but gets old somewhere around the eleven-minute mark. Commercial audiences agreed.

But the original *TV Nation* pilot was still making the rounds, and it was very helpful for Moore's career. In the U.K., the head of BBC2, Michael Jackson, liked it and offered to split the cost with NBC, and the show was back on track as a summer series. In a pep talk to the staff as they began shooting, Moore told them to assume that they would never work in television again, because any future résumé submissions were sure to be met with, "Oh, you worked on that show that pissed off all the sponsors."[3]

The show was truly groundbreaking, and nothing on TV since then, except for Moore's own *The Awful Truth*, looks anything like it. In several segments each week Moore would harass corporate evil-doers and poke fun at the conscience-impaired in high places, borrowing gimmicks from game shows and anticipating what is now called "reality TV." Moore bugs the hell out of receptionists and security guards, standing there with his crew and asking questions while the fifth "Sir, I'm asking you to remove yourself from the premises right now" rings in the audience's ears, pushing the envelope further than would seem possible (or indeed would be possible, one thinks, with no camera present). The viewer hardly notices that Moore usually does not get past the front desks of the evil corporations he confronts, or that the people whose day he ruins are those very receptionists and security guards, rarely their bosses—working-class people just like him, although making far less money.

But if Moore was obnoxious, he was also wildly imaginative. He sent a Mexican mariachi band and the cheerleading squad of historically black Spelman College to disrupt a Klan rally with chants promoting love between *all* people. He sent a multiracial chorus line to serenade the Aryan Nations with "Stop! In the Name of Love" and the Gay Men's Chorus to homophobic senator Jesse Helms's doorstep (the senator's wife thanked the singers graciously). He threw a concert—Corp Aid—to help big corporations facing lawsuits and scandal. He invented Crackers, the Corporate Crime-Fighting Chicken. When he discovered that Mississippi has never ratified the Thirteenth Amendment, he sent a black reporter to Jackson to purchase white people as slaves and lead them around in chains. He sent a former Soviet spy to find the heart and soul of the Democratic Party. He loaded up a tractor-trailer with Soviet memorabilia and Gus Hall—the American Communist Party's longtime leader—and took "Communism" on a farewell tour across the country. He went to the former Soviet Union on a mission to find the missile aimed at Flint.

To its credit, NBC (and Fox, a carrier in the second season) rarely stepped in to stop the mayhem. They censored or refused to run only five segments out of 105: a piece on a high school boy in Topeka, Kansas, who got extra school credit for picketing the funerals of gay people, carrying a placard bearing the legend THANK GOD FOR AIDS; one on a leader of the antiabortion movement; one that featured a reenactment of the 1992 Rodney King riots; one in which Ben Hamper searches drugstores for small-sized condoms; and one, oddly enough, on the savings-and-loan crisis of the 1980s. The networks had good reason to be indulgent of the show: it had captured the valuable eighteen- to thirty-four-year-old demographic. *TV Nation* won an Emmy in 1995.

The Awful Truth, which began running in 1998, continued where

TV Nation left off; the shows are hardly distinguishable, although *The Awful Truth* showed more confidence as Moore gained experience. As a cable production originally aired on Bravo and, in the United Kingdom, on the independent Channel Four, it had a bit more leeway than the original network show. Michael Jackson had recently become the chief executive of Channel Four, and he brought Moore along to the channel, with a package deal for a television series, a talk show (*Michael Moore Live*, which aired only in the United Kingdom, in 1999), and a feature film.

As with *TV Nation*, the targets that Moore chooses in *The Awful Truth* are, for the most part, genuinely despicable, and he's not restrained by any qualms about good taste. He sent a group costumed as seventeenth-century Puritans to harass Clinton-persecuting Special Prosecutor Kenneth Starr, and he dispatched Crackers, the Corporate Crime-Fighting Chicken, to lobby Mickey Mouse at Disney World on behalf of Disney's exploited cartoon-character actors. He sent a group of schoolchildren to harass an executive of a polluting corporation, and later in the show a group of lingerie-clad models is assigned the same task (you've never seen so many security guards drawn to the scene). He toured the South with a group of queens in a "sodomite bus," inducing predictable discomfort in the followers of the gay-hating fanatic Reverend Fred Phelps, whose modus operandi is sending groups to brutally taunt the mourners at funerals of gay people. He sent Adolf Hitler to Zurich to withdraw all the money the deceased Führer still has on deposit in Swiss banks, much of which came from the gold dental fillings of his victims.

Sometimes Moore's sense of social irony verged on cruelty, as when he ran segments called "Pie the Poor" (featuring real stockbrokers pushing pies in the faces of actors representing homeless people) and "Pin the Tail on the Illegal Immigrant." The show had a brief moment in the national political spotlight when Moore convinced Alan Keyes, one of the most conservative candidates for the Republican presidential nomination, to jump into a mosh pit in exchange for an *Awful Truth* political endorsement.

For many viewers, the show's most satisfying moment came when Moore surreptitiously stole DNA from Lucianne Goldberg, Linda Tripp's book agent, the woman who told Tripp to record her telephone calls with Monica Lewinsky, with results we now know all too well. "I had a ball doing it," said Goldberg of her role in the Lewinsky scandal, and Moore had a ball focusing a webcam on her bedroom window, calling her in the middle of the night, and otherwise violating her privacy. It's low, but it couldn't happen to a more deserving person. The only sad part is that Goldberg is too much of a narcissist to really get it. When the joke is sprung on her and she realizes that a large studio audience (and all those people in front of their TVs) are laughing at the idea that her bedroom window is under twenty-four-hour surveillance on the Internet, you can tell that she sort of relishes the attention. It's justice, but it's not the way to get someone like Goldberg to feel anything. "Why did I do it?" asks Goldberg. "I wanted to do it. I did it. It's done. Now, can we move on, as you people say?"

■ ■ ■

Behind the scenes at the television shows, it wasn't all laughs and going after the bad guys. Moore wasn't particularly considerate even of the needs of his corporate sponsors. He had no discipline with money, and the BBC had to send people to New York to keep an eye on his spending. It was more self-indulgence than artistic exuberance: Moore took a first-class seat on the Concorde when he went to London at BBC's expense, and when he got there he stayed in the best hotels.

Moore had a reputation for being hard on his staff. Alan Hayling is a documentary film specialist. Since 2004 he's been the head of documentaries at BBC Television, and he used to be a commissioning editor at Channel Four, where he worked with Moore as the commissioning editor responsible for *The Awful Truth*. Although commissioning editors aren't usually involved in day-to-day production issues, Hayling ended up spending a lot of time actively engaged in the series because the series producer became ill halfway through the season. He also worked with Moore in the early stages of *Bowling for Columbine*. He acknowledges that Moore could be difficult, but this didn't mean that working with him was unpleasant.

Michael was a mixture. He is a quite brilliant man—it's not instantly apparent, but it becomes rapidly clear when you work with him. He's very, very good in the cutting room. He's got a fantastic sense of how to make something work comically, but at the same time make very serious points. That is his particular genius. But there's another side to Michael. Like many authorial documentary filmmakers, he can be difficult. These are strong-willed people who are managing relationships with equally strong-willed producers and commissioning editors. Everybody has a strong view, and naturally, the directors want their views to prevail. Michael was absolutely delightful at times and the most generous person on the planet, and at other times he was very, very difficult. I think he would admit to that himself. I've worked with more difficult filmmakers than Michael, but not many; but I also haven't worked with many more gifted.

Not everyone agreed that working with Moore was a rewarding experience. A former Moore staffer told Larissa MacFarquhar of the *New Yorker*:

I have let go of Michael. I have not seen one of his products, his movies, his TV shows, his books. I'm sure they're all good. I'm sure they're spreading the message and enraging all the right people. But I can't accept him as a political person. I can't buy into this thing of Michael Moore being on your side. It's like trying to believe that Justin Timberlake is a soulful guy. It's a media product; he's just selling me something. For the preservation of my own soul, I have to consider him as just an entertainer, because otherwise he's a huge asshole. If you consider him an entertainer, then his acting like a selfish, self-absorbed, pouty, deeply conflicted, easily wounded child is run-of-the-mill, standard behavior; but if he's a political force, then he's a jerk and a hypocrite and he didn't treat us right.[4]

Writing in the online magazine *Salon*, Daniel Radosh reported that Moore, contrary to all his supposed class and union loyalties, actually intimidated staff writers at *TV Nation* in an attempt to keep them from unionizing. Moore hit back at Radosh in typically paranoid style: Moore had criticized the union policy of the book-store chain Borders, who sponsored *Salon*, so *Salon* was out to get him. David Talbot, *Salon*'s editor, had worked at *Mother Jones* and had protested against Moore getting the editor's job eleven years previously, so obviously Talbot was out to get him. Radosh had written for the *National Review*, the *Weekly Standard*, and *Playboy*, so Radosh was a conservative who was out to get him. Moore threatened to sue *Salon* for libel if the publishers didn't retract the story of his intimidation of the writers. "One writer remembered Moore telling him and a colleague that *TV Nation* could not afford two writers at Guild rates and that, 'If you want to be in this union, only one of you can work here,'" Radosh responded. "Once they did join the union, they had to constantly file complaints [with the Writers' Guild] about Moore's treatment of them."[5]

A former producer at *The Awful Truth* told me that Moore frequently took credit where it wasn't justified: "If he liked someone's idea, he would make it his own and might even say, several days later, that the person who had the idea had stolen it from him. And he seemed to deeply believe this. There's something wrong there."

Many employees initially felt a lot of respect for Moore and joined his shows with a feeling of idealism, only to find that Moore didn't live up to their expectations. A second producer at *The Awful Truth* told me, "My exposure to Moore was brief. I walked in there sort of wide-eyed, thinking, 'My God, here I am working with Michael Moore, there's no one in public life with whom I agree more politically, and more with his style and method of doing things.' Even today, with *Fahrenheit 9/11*, I applaud what he did there. But I cannot say that he's a benign character. There's a gap between who he pretends to be and who he really is. . . . He's the antithesis of the guy he portrays on film. He *is* General Motors."

This idea was echoed by several other people who worked closely with Moore. Kyra Vogt was a young hire at *The Awful Truth*. She signed on first as assistant to the senior producer, then became the office manager, and then—for one week, which was all she could stand—Moore's executive assistant. Vogt didn't want the executive assistant job and didn't see it as a promotion; she'd seen Moore go through two previous assistants and felt that he treated them with little respect. Once, returning from a trip, Moore had handed an assistant a bag full of his dirty underwear and told her to take it to the laundry. Vogt didn't want to have to put up with things like that, but Moore seemed to feel a special affinity for her:

> He thought that I was working class because I hadn't graduated college. I wouldn't exactly consider myself working class; my parents didn't have money, but they were hippies; they didn't come from a working-class background and they didn't live like working-class people; they didn't live in a working-class community and they didn't have working-class ideals. I think it was because I didn't graduate college and because my family didn't have a lot of money that he liked me, that this was why he wanted me to be his assistant.

Vogt observed that Moore often seemed to feel embattled even among his closest associates. "The people who work for him in general are college grads who want to work in TV and agree with Moore in general, but in my opinion he considers them the enemy, because he thinks that because they're not working class, they can't really understand him. He doesn't trust them because of their backgrounds." Moore's initial instructions to Vogt when she became his personal assistant reveal something of this paranoid attitude. "'You have to protect me from everyone else,' he told me. 'Everyone's always coming after me, they always want something, and you have to protect me from them.' . . . It was like I was his bodyguard. He wanted protection. I didn't understand how I was going to do that."

Moore seemed to expect that any sense of working-class solidarity among his staff would flow only one way—from them to him. He threw a Christmas party and invited only the producers and editors. Once, convinced that someone was sneaking into his office to read his e-mails, he had the locks changed; only he and Vogt were to have a key. This meant that the cleaning staff couldn't get in to clean his office. Moore informed Vogt that in addition to her other duties, she would have to clean his office. This irritated Vogt, but she did her best. She would put his wastebasket outside his office at night, so that the cleaners could empty it, and she would then put it back in his office before he returned the next day. Once Moore came in early, before Vogt, so the wastebasket was still outside his office.

When Vogt got to the office Moore told her, "My wastebasket wasn't there, so I spit my gum out where it usually is and now it's on the rug. Can you clean it up?"

Moore's work habits made everyone who worked on the show miserable. A producer described how much extra work Moore created for everyone: "The first staff meeting we had, he told everyone that he wanted them to have a life, to spend time with their families, not to give all their energy to the show. That he believed that happy employees were more productive employees. Well, that was the last time we heard that. He'd expect everyone to be at work at nine, but he himself would come in at three, four, five in the afternoon and work till three in the morning—and everyone else was expected to work with him, so they were working eighteen-hour days. He's an insomniac, and everyone had to adapt to his schedule." Moore took a two-week Christmas break, during which his staff would overnight him tapes of the rough cuts for his notes and approval, but he wouldn't screen them, or else wouldn't send his notes on the screenings. This drove everyone nuts and kept the whole staff working overtime, backed up on production, guessing what he wanted.

He also had some decidedly non-working-class tastes. You know his proud costume of jeans and flannel shirt and baseball cap, the getup that tells the world that he's the ordinary guy from Flint who's not going to change just because he's rich and famous? Those flannel shirts are custom-made, hand-tailored. His assistants would order takeout for him, under strict instructions that the different parts of a sandwich—the meat, the lettuce, the tomato, and the bread—had to be packed separately and could not touch one another. If the deli failed to follow this request perfectly, Moore would go into an embittered sulk, taking it out on his staff. Ordering meals on location, he would often order every dish he thought he might like, taste each one, take the one he wanted, and throw out the rest. Nor could a hungry staffer eat the rejected meals; that idea disturbed the fastidious Moore. Ivan Boesky, the disgraced billionaire Wall Street trader, used to do something similar: at the very expensive Café des Artistes, he would order eight entrées and choose the one he liked best.[6] Ivan Boesky is probably not a person to whom Michael Moore would like to be compared.

He was also not particularly considerate of some of the people who appeared on his show. An early episode of *The Awful Truth* tells the story of Chris Donahue, a south Florida man who needed a kidney and pancreas transplant to stay alive, but who had to sue his health insurance company, Humana, because it had refused to pay for the procedure (Humana would pay only for the kidney transplant). By stalking the corporate executives and demanding to know why they won't approve the transplant, even inviting them to a premature funeral for Donahue, Moore embarrasses Humana into funding Donahue's surgery. He also successfully highlights the cruel absurdities of for-profit medicine and the desperate need for a public, single-payer health care system like that of France or Canada, whose citizens enjoy much better health statistics than those of the United States. This is certainly a good deed, a constructive and imaginative activist approach that got results, and in fact apparently got Humana to change its policy for *all* such clients, not just for Donahue.[7]

Moore deserves a lot of credit for this. But he seems to have been more interested in Donahue as a political symbol than he was interested in him as a person with a serious problem. *The Awful Truth* paid to fly Donahue to Humana's corporate headquarters so that the show could film the encounter with the executives. Moore, however, had a chronic problem about making his flights, and he missed his flight for the rendezvous. Donahue was kept waiting for a whole day without access to the constant medical supervision he needed. Later, when the live introduction to the show was filmed in Chicago, Moore refused to pay for Donahue's airfare to attend. He was welcome to come, but at his own expense.

Likewise, the elderly former smokers who'd had laryngectomies, the ones who were brought in to sing Christmas carols to the folks at Philip Morris, were treated more like props than like people: they were given no meals and no comfortable dressing room, but sat in a fifteen-person van with only water and granola bars available, while called out to shoot the scene over and over and over again. Some of Moore's staff were distressed by this, and it illustrates again the problem of a bold and heroic commitment to a cause that is not tightly connected to the actual people it is meant to serve.

There was an incident that ironically turned Moore's mode of bulldog investigator against him. On *The Awful Truth*, Moore once made a big deal about how the millionaire industrialist Ira Rennert got a restraining order against him—he made it the focus of the segment, in fact, with Moore dramatically hiring a guard to ensure that he, Moore, did not yield to temptation and come closer than the marked-off, legally allowed distance. Moore shouted questions and answers up to Conan O'Brien's set at Rockefeller Center for an interview because O'Brien's show is in the same building as Rennert's offices. But when Moore fired a producer, Alan Edelstein, Edelstein wanted to know why and began to follow Moore around with a camera, trying to get an explanation on film. Moore didn't take kindly to this at all. Edelstein's action apparently greatly inflamed an apparent paranoid streak in Moore that had already been remarked upon by several people who worked with him.

A close associate at *The Awful Truth* told me that Moore went into a full-fledged panic over Edelstein. He would hold two-hour staff meetings about increasing security to respond to the threat. He was terrified of Edelstein's camera. What if the portable light was designed to blind him so that Edelstein could pull a gun? While taping the introduction to an *Awful Truth* segment in Chicago before a live audience, Moore learned that Edelstein had been spotted in the lobby, so he shut the show down while he called the police and made a report. Nine hundred people waited for Edelstein to be removed before the show could go on.

By the fall of 1999, Moore, possibly aware that the publicity could do him no good, seemed to have lost interest in the Edelstein case and dropped the matter.[8] He continued, however, to tell his friends and associates that there were FBI men on the roofs near his Manhattan apartment, watching his comings and goings.

■ ■ ■

Like Moore's past and future productions, his television work came in for a certain amount of criticism on grounds of fact. It was confusing to some critics because it sometimes did serious investigation in a humorous way, and sometimes pursued pure satire that was not intended to have any connection to literal truth. Alan Hayling believes that Moore was right to trust his viewers to understand the distinction. Of the purely imaginative pieces, he said:

In *The Awful Truth* and in *Bowling for Columbine* there were different kinds of humor at work. There were serious items like the HMO episode, and others that were surreal. We assumed that the audience was reasonably intelligent, and that they'd be able to understand that this guy who needs a pancreas transplant is a real guy who really needs a transplant, but that the idea that huts in Montana are a threat to civilization in the United States, or that kids should be taught better aim for school massacres, or that televisions should be dropped on Afghanistan to break the grip of the Taliban—those are not real situations or suggestions. They are nondocumentary elements, completely surreal, but they make a point. That last was an out-and-out attack on the Taliban, and quite right too in my view.

In practice, the distinction wasn't always so innocent or so clear. There were times when truth was lost to the cheap ideological shot and the quick emotional punch. There were episodes that were light, but they were deceptively light; just because Moore wasn't afraid to be goofy didn't mean that there wasn't a core of steel behind his attempts to stir outrage.

This sort of relentless ideological reductionism is best showcased in *The Awful Truth*'s segment on William Cohen, the moderate Maine Republican who was Bill Clinton's second secretary of defense. The segment starts off in a cheerful if slightly ironic tone, most of it spent satirically questioning Cohen's manhood. Moore recalls the sturdy, manly military men of yore: Patton, MacArthur, Schwarzkopf. Then he shows us Cohen, with his shy and genuine smile, the sign of a truly nice guy. We see Cohen dancing awkwardly and vaguely effeminately, handing flowers to a military aide in camouflage. It seems Cohen has written poetry, too. Terrible poetry. Terrible, sensitive poetry.

We see Cohen getting married—on Valentine's Day!—and dodging the kiss on the lips, going for the cheek. To top it all off, his middle name is Sebastian.

Moore builds his case against Cohen's manhood, deeply disturbed that America's enemies will have no cause to fear America with this guy in charge of its military. He gathers citizens of Iraq, Afghanistan, and North Korea—as well as a six-year-old girl—in front of the Department of Defense to shout insults. The North Korean uses a bullhorn to yell, "Your poetry is for wusses!"

But where's Moore really going with this? We find out at the very end of the segment, in a quick but densely packed forty seconds. He's going for the jugular.

After confronting Cohen in person and calling him a wuss—and getting brushed off in the nicest manner possible—Moore concludes that Cohen must have had a change of heart: "Like most pansies when pushed into a corner, he had to prove himself to be a man. And did he ever!" What follows is a quick list of U.S. military actions during Cohen's tenure as secretary of defense and their consequences, starting with the response to the East African embassy bombings in 1998 and moving on to actions against Saddam Hussein and the Yugoslav War in 1999:

> First he bombs Afghanistan. . . . Our guy knows how to take out tent-loads of innocent people. Still think Cohen's a gentle man, Mr. [Sudanese] Ambassador? Tell it to the people working at your medical facility. He doesn't get mad; he kills Sudanese civilians. Still think Cohen's weak? Well, he's tough enough to smart-bomb Iraqi apartment buildings full of women and children. Now he's blowing up Serbians on trains! And the occasional Chinese embassy! That'll show 'em!

All of this is accompanied by appropriately gruesome images of victims of war: bodies blown apart, paramedics carrying dazed victims—very ordinary people—on stretchers, buildings reduced to rubble. After the light satire of the preceding part, it's horrifying, and devastatingly effective. Cohen isn't a nice guy after all, screams Moore's technique. He's a murderer!

Never mind that each of these cases is much more complicated than Moore would have it. Never mind that Americans had been attacked in East Africa by agents trained in those Afghan camps; that Saddam had been firing on U.S. and British air patrols designed to protect Kurdish and Shi'ite civilians; that Yugoslavia's Slobodan

Milošević had been destabilizing his country and his region for a decade and had launched wars in which two hundred thousand people died, and that Clinton's decision—as executed by Cohen—set in motion a process that eventually ended Yugoslavia's outlaw status.

There are legitimate arguments against these U.S. military actions, but Moore's argument is not one of them. The United States did not bomb Afghanistan, Iraq, and Serbia because Cohen was freaked out about being a sissy.

So then what is Moore really trying to do here? When *Saturday Night Live* has actors portraying George W. Bush and Donald Rumsfeld going into a deep kiss—as the show has done—we're not really being told that the president and his secretary of defense are lovers, but in the Cohen segment Moore does seem to be saying that the United States *really did* kill people to protect Cohen's threatened sense of masculinity. At least if this *isn't* what he's saying, it's hard to find any point to the episode. Unlike the vulgar shock of the *Saturday Night Live* skit, Moore's segment on *The Awful Truth* is really not funny in its own right.

This is art meeting demagoguery, and meeting it brilliantly. Moore manages to make the real issues disappear under his cleverness, his easy style, the wit and humor of his montage. All that's left is a conviction that our leaders are out of control, that war is bad, and that it is the result of an overcompensating psychopathology. We don't have any real enemies. It's all about acting tough.

The sympathetic studio audience comes away believing that Moore's insight has revealed a profound truth, whereas in fact he hasn't approached any truth at all. Another word for this is *propaganda*, and Moore has never been more skillful at it—not in *Bowling for Columbine*, not in *Roger & Me*—than he is here. If this is what he does best, we should watch his movies very carefully and thoughtfully because, when you take away the fun and games and ideological agenda, the images aren't necessarily attached to anything in the real world.

5

TAKE THE GUNHEADS BOWLING

L et's talk about guns.

Guns are the pathological obsession of the right, and there's really nothing else in American culture that so combines romantic myth, ahistoricism, and terrible social policy.

To a great many people in the United States, guns are still symbols of individualism, independence, and rugged frontier character, and personal possession of them is still thought to be effective for crime control and resistance to state encroachments on liberty.

Americans also suffer, more than the citizens of most modern, secular states, from a bizarre philosophical affliction: belief in "natural law." This is the idea that human rights come from a mystical, supernatural absolute rather than from their actual source: human culture that creates human values and human law, and a human society presided over by human institutions capable of defending that law by force. Significant segments of the American conservative movement believe that the U.S. Constitution in fact creates no political or human rights, but merely recognizes the rights given by God. This delusion allows religious political activists both to sacralize the constitution and to claim the U.S. government as the instrument of God's

will. If this idea ever becomes widely accepted in American jurispru-
dence, we can tear up the actual Constitution because it will never be
the final word: lawyers and advocates can always invoke a "higher constitution" and turn the matter over to the religious authorities for
disposition.

There is one country in the world that has already pioneered this
form of democracy, but it's not the United States. It is Iran.

Sometimes the religious zeal with which gun fanatics defend the
Second Amendment is made explicit. Warren Cassidy, once head of
the Institute for Legislative Action—the National Rifle Association's
lobbying arm—put it like this: "You would get a far better understanding if you approached us as if you were approaching one of the
great religions of the world."[1]

Although gun hobbyists, ably represented by the former NRA
president Charlton Heston and the executive director Wayne
LaPierre and partisan scholars like John Lott (whose work is sponsored by the gun industry), may sincerely believe that all our liberties
rest on private ownership of firearms, and even that this is the meaning of the Second Amendment, this is a matter of some debate. Yes—
to refute an argument often made by the NRA—Hitler and Stalin
took away private guns. So do most of the European democracies.
There is an obvious difference in social organization between fascism
(of the left or the right) and European social-welfarism, and what
matters are not the similarities of regulation but the differences of
institutions. I've always thought that the tautological argument about
how tyranny is both a cause and an effect of gun control is deeply
insulting to the power and stability of culturally rooted, consensus-
derived government, conspicuous by its historical absence from any
of the lands that fell to tyranny in the twentieth century. People who
are governed by consent do not need to encounter their leaders on
the battlefield. And if we did, our leaders control machine guns,
tanks, chemical and biological weapons, cruise missiles, radar, sub-
marines, aircraft carriers, advanced jet fighters and bombers, and tactical and strategic nuclear weapons. Should all of these things be
available to private citizens, in the name of preserving an equalizer?

The founding fathers certainly didn't think so. The headquarters
of the NRA, in Washington, D.C., has half of the Second Amendment
engraved in stone by its entrance: . . . THE RIGHT OF THE PEOPLE TO

KEEP AND BEAR ARMS SHALL NOT BE INFRINGED. The association was honest enough to use the leading ellipses. Here's what the amendment actually says: "A well-regulated Militia being necessary to the security of a free State, the right of the people to keep and bear Arms shall not be infringed." Note the context: security of the state, not of the person. Not just a militia (which gun-rights advocates routinely interpret as "every able-bodied man") but a "well-regulated" militia, which implies officers trained, commissioned, and overseen by the state. What is there in this passage that suggests that the founders intended to endow an unbounded, individual right to firearms? As shown in their individual and collective writings and debates, the founders had an exceptionally nuanced and careful sense of the meaning of words. That first clause is there for a reason.[2]

In defending handguns, the NRA appeals to a strain of paranoia that seems to have developed only in the United States, which (with apologies to Richard Hofstadter) could be termed the paranoid style in American popular culture. It's no accident that *The Turner Diaries*—the white-racial-supremacy fantasy by neo-Nazi William Pierce[3] that inspired Oklahoma City bomber Timothy McVeigh—is a best seller at gun shows. This doesn't mean that most people who are regulars at gun shows are vicious racists, but if sales of Pierce's book are any indication it seems that most people who are regulars at gun shows have a paranoid streak, and this tale of secret armed resistance to sinister conspiracy naturally resonates with them.

In a not-so-very-different way, it shouldn't be surprising that a crusade against gun culture would resonate with Moore. It's no great revelation that people often react most strongly against belief systems that have points in common with their own, and the stereotypical gun-lover's creed[4]—distrust of government, faith in community and the people, a call to activism, a willingness to entertain grand conspiracy theories, a pugnacious and tenacious defense of perceived constitutional (or God-given) rights—has many similarities to Moore's own.

Before producing his Oscar-winning movie *Bowling for Columbine*, Moore had shown that he enjoyed taking on big targets in print, film, radio, or television, whether these were GM, the tobacco industry, Ted Turner, or major corporate polluters, and after *Columbine* he would take on the president of the United States. He

has always recognized that the political right is not only, or even primarily, a system of economic and political beliefs; it is a culture. Guns,
in the United States, are fundamental to that culture, because an
absolutist belief in the right to own them affirms one particular idea
of what makes America what it is and what makes it different from
other countries. What better subject for Moore's ambitious agenda?
Seen in this light, all of his work on television—his confrontational
ten-minute spots that attack the ironies and insecurities and brutal
contradictions at the edges of American social life—becomes a prepa-
ration for taking on this one particular idea.

It wasn't only the question of guns that made sure that Moore's
Bowling for Columbine would be a focal point for anger on both the
left and the right. There's the obvious fact that anything that involves
children and how they are raised and educated carries enormous
emotional power, and in choosing to look at a particularly horrible
recent phenomenon—high school mass murders—Moore was stoking
an ambient social anxiety that most Americans feel but express very
differently, depending on their political orientation. To some on both
sides of the gun issue, these kinds of crimes validate a set of internally
consistent, comfortable, prepackaged political beliefs. Columbine was
a symptom of the breakdown of the family, of a culture that devalues
personal responsibility, of lax institutional discipline, moral relativism,
parental abdication, lack of school prayer, perhaps even of evolution
and sex education on the public school curriculum—not enough guns
in private hands. Or perhaps it was a symptom of insufficient spending
on social services, mental health care, and law enforcement; of a culture that suppresses human dignity and worships casual violence in
movies and video games; or of the economic power of the weapons
industry—too many guns in private hands. Many or even most of these
diagnoses may not be contradictory, and many of them could be simultaneously true and still be insufficient to explain the phenomenon, but
they have different and bitterly disputed policy implications. That's
why people argue about *Columbine*.

∎ ∎ ∎

The movie begins with Moore at center stage, as he opens an account
at a Michigan bank and walks out with a rifle as a reward for his

business. After completing his transaction, Moore delivers the scene's punchline: "Do you think it's a little bit dangerous handing out guns at a bank?"

Is it? It is certainly bizarre and disturbing. But as Dave Kopel, research director for the right-wing libertarian Independence Institute, has pointed out, Moore had to display photo identification and submit to a background check before he received his gun, a process shown in the film. His face would have been captured on the bank's security cameras. And he didn't receive any ammunition. Sure, he could have brought some with him. But would anyone sane enough to complete and pass the required procedure use the gun he received to rob the bank? The odds of getting caught would be as certain as anything can be in life.

The scene is set up as candid camera investigative journalism. Its power is supposed to come from its ordinariness, from the suggestion that it is an everyday event in U.S. gun culture. The bank people don't find it odd that anyone can walk in off the street and walk out with a rifle. But Moore has changed the rules for his film.

Normally a customer would not receive his gun in the bank, but Moore's people had called in advance and arranged for the staff to have one on hand in the bank's vault; Moore was insistent that he had to get it right away if he was going to open his account. The staff were also told that he would be a major depositor, and for this reason they were willing to give him special treatment. When we hear in *Bowling for Columbine* that the bank has "five hundred guns in the vault," the tellers are referring to the bank's central storage vault, located miles away and not easily accessible, but Moore edits this out and allows us to believe that all those guns are right there on hand to distribute to walk-in customers. Moore wants credit for exposing, in gumshoe fashion, a surprising blank spot at the center of the bank's institutional gaze, but he's already using the tools of the editor's trade to violate the standards of the journalist's trade. His own filmed experience has little to do with what normally happens when a customer tries to get a gun from the bank.[5] The disconnect between images and reality continues throughout the film.

■   ■   ■

The Columbine killings struck very close to home in Moore's native Michigan. There is a long sequence in the film about a six-year-old boy in Flint who took a gun to school and shot a six-year-old girl, Kayla Rowland, on their way to the computer lab.[6] The boy had been left by his mother in the house of her brother, a crack dealer, and had found a stolen gun and taken it to school. The episode is central to the development of Moore's plans for his film.

I spoke with Art Busch, who is an old friend of Moore from their college days and who, as the district attorney of Genesee County, was the prosecutor in the Rowland case. He served as an adviser to Moore while he was making *Columbine*, and he's interviewed in the film. He told me why the film was so important to him, and, in doing so, suggested the larger social context that Moore was working in:

> I was so committed to what this film was about. The film really stood up for victims, and I think those that watched it are deeply moved by what the victims of crime are doing and what they're saying. Not so much about the NRA as about what's happening to the people of our country. . . . None of [the news coverage] was to the point. Why do we have kids in America today who are living in dope houses with teenage boys and who have to go begging for their food on the main street after they get out of school? I felt that many of the biggest issues in this case were just being ignored, that the problems behind the case were here today and would be here tomorrow after these people were gone. Even as we spoke, the factory down the road from where the shooting occurred, the Fisher Body plant, was being torn down.

Moore was determined to address pathologies that are very deeply rooted in American society. "Michael said he'd like to do something with this that has a lasting impact, something greater than the *60 Minutes* format. I talked to him for many hours. Just as we in trial practice begin to develop a theory of our case, he develops a theory of his movie, and his movie is, 'Why are Americans so violent? Why do Americans want to have guns? And what's behind all that?' He came to the conclusion that we are simply afraid of one another."

But, having stirred the pot, what does Moore put into the stew? This is where it gets interesting, and it's also where *Bowling for Columbine* begins to fall apart. Most people on both sides of the issue who saw the film came away from it thinking that Moore is in favor of gun control.

He's not—or, at least, not necessarily so. The right-wing talk radio host Larry Elder made a whole anti-Moore and pro-gun movie, *Michael & Me*, but he failed to grasp this essential point. Elder wastes a couple of hours attacking Moore for a position on gun control that Moore never took. In *Columbine*, Moore is after something bigger than guns, and Elder acts as his inadvertent foil. For Elder's work begs the question: if access to guns is not the reason for high levels of violence in America as compared to other democratic, industrial nations, what is? This is exactly the assumption that Moore makes, and the question that he asks.

In fact, he starts out in the film with a voice-over explaining that he's been around guns all his life and, as a boy, won a marksmanship award from the NRA. I once attended a Moore event where he said that he'd started out with the belief that stronger gun-control laws would save lives but that he'd begun to think about it differently when he learned that Canadians have even more guns in their homes than Americans[7] yet still don't go on murderous rampages. This is also famously true of the Swiss. "So it seems like the NRA has a point when they say, 'Guns don't kill people; people kill people,'" Moore said. "But it's really more like, '*Americans* kill people.'"

Moore disingenuously ignores a very major difference between American and Canadian guns: while there are many of them in circulation, Canadian guns are almost all long-barrel, single-shot hunting rifles. Canada does indeed have very tight legal restrictions on private ownership of handguns, the type of weapon suited to committing crimes and that is, overwhelmingly, the type of firearm that is used to commit crimes in the United States.[8]

Since his "Americans kill people" approach dismisses all actual gun-control arguments, Moore has to torture the facts for social explanations. We were bombing Serbia when the Columbine attacks took place. Nobody listened to the young killers. The Canadian welfare state builds social bonds that Americans lack. Littleton, Colorado, where the Columbine massacre happened, is the home of several major weapons contractors and a military monument. Moore tries hard to portray the entire area as permeated with the ideological stench of death and killing.

Not everyone in the film goes along with Moore's analysis. In one scene, a Lockheed spokesman objects to making a connection between parents who work at defense plants and children who commit violent crimes. He quite reasonably points out that in the real world, violence may sometimes be an unfortunate but legitimate aspect of national defense, but that it is never a legitimate way for individuals to handle disputes. Moore seems to consider this statement transparently delusional. Unfazed, he follows the Lockheed PR guy with footage recapitulating the litany of American-orchestrated international violence since World War II: the 1953 overthrow of the legally elected prime minister of Iran, Muhammad Moussadeq, and the installation of the Shah; the overthrow of the legally elected president of Guatemala, Jacobo Arbenz, in 1954, a turning point in Guatemalan history that led to a genocidal civil war and the deaths of hundreds of thousands; the assassination of President Ngo Dinh Diem of South Vietnam in 1963 and the expansion of the Vietnam War; the military coup that overthrew elected socialist president Salvador Allende of Chile in 1973, and so on and so on, right up to the first Gulf War of 1991, the bombing of Yugoslavia, and U.N.-imposed sanctions against Iraq, which are said, on the basis of a common belief but no real evidence, to have killed five hundred thousand children.

Now, some of these things—Iran, Guatemala, Chile—were indeed bad stuff. They were crimes of arrogance, brutality, and delusion, and they left the world with less rather than more democracy. Others—Vietnam, the Gulf War, the Iraq sanctions, Yugoslavia—are harder to make such one-dimensional judgments about. But contrary to Moore's apparent belief, this kind of history and sociology really doesn't have much power to explain the events at Columbine High School in 1999. Did state-sanctioned violence in Serbia really drive suburban kids to slaughter their classmates? Yes, Lockheed and Martin Marietta and Marathon have big weapons contracts and plants in the Littleton area—was it *that* that made Eric Harris and Dylan Klebold homicidal?

Perhaps it was the overthrow of the Iranian prime minister in 1953. No, it was the coup against Allende in 1973! To suggest these far-off events as *direct causes*—which Moore is smart enough not to do—is to realize the absurdity of the idea that they are even indirect causes.

If it's hard to take Moore's proffered theories seriously, it's even harder to know what to do with his pastiche touching on the arms industry, the war on terror, the military budget, Enron, and the Columbine killings, as if these things can all be tied up in one package of sinister cause and effect. Perhaps the terror war and the Enron collapse (both of which occurred *after* the Columbine killings) tainted the town retroactively by the violence and perverse priorities that brought them to completion. There's a pattern here, Moore is saying. But is there really? Others have found patterns that reflect the secret machinations of the Masons, the Jews, the Illuminati, and the Trilateral Commission. The emotional pull of a thesis doesn't mean that it explains anything.

■   ■   ■

But when it comes to hidden meanings, Moore is on a roll. He borrows from the University of Southern California sociologist Barry Glassner's book *The Culture of Fear* and expands on Glassner's thesis to argue that the racist media feeds on a racist society's racist assumptions to produce an environment of racial fear and hysteria in which people are trigger happy. Is slavery ultimately to blame for the massacre?

The film's sequence on racism and the media is particularly instructive as to Moore's methods. Here he shows clips from many cop reality shows in which black suspects in street crime are tackled by police and wonders why there aren't more white perps or, at least, more white-collar criminal arrests. It's all a racist media conspiracy. But, of course, street crime in many American urban areas *is* perpetrated predominantly by black individuals against black victims, for reasons that have nothing to do with the inherent proclivities of blacks or whites and everything to do with the historical echoes of crimes committed by whites against blacks.

But the police aren't social workers or historians. Neither are the television networks; they want entertainment value, not socially responsible narratives, and they'll take it where they find it. Despite

Moore's obsessions, it is an equal opportunity endeavor. A brief and unscientific survey of the cop reality shows confirms that their chases and arrests reflect the fact that American petty crime relates to class, not race (although for historical reasons the two are, of course, connected). The shows peek in on plenty of drug busts and domestic disputes involving poor whites in a manner that hardly shows them at their best. You wouldn't know this from the clips that Moore presents in this segment of his film, which show only black perps.

In *Columbine*, Moore interviews Dick Herlan, who produced *Cops* and *The World's Wildest Police Videos*. Throughout the interview, Herlan, who describes himself as a liberal, seems to have a much better idea of the social reality of the United States than does Moore. Herlan looks weary when Moore asks him why he doesn't show white-collar criminals being brought in: "I love the idea. . . . I just don't think it would make very interesting reality TV. If we can get those people to get in their SUV and drive really fast down the road away from the police . . . if you can get [a corporate criminal] to take his shirt off and throw his cellular phone at the police as they come through the door, and try to jump out that window . . . then we'd have a show."

It's a little surprising that Moore included this clip because Herlan has him here, and in an interesting way. The media angle is no help at all to Moore's racism argument because, in fact, it's not racial; one gets the impression that Herlan would show white people smoking crack, Jell-O wrestling with prostitutes, and carving their bloody initials on their own grandmothers if he could find the footage. But this media angle is actually a great help to Moore's anticapitalist argument, since it shows the utterly exploitative nature of profit-driven showbiz.

The problem for Moore is that he can't have it both ways. If it's racism—if Herlan could keep his ratings up by showing white-collar crime arrests but chooses not to—there's something else going on here besides the pursuit of profit. But if profit is all that matters, capitalism is motivated only by mindless, almost impersonal greed. This would normally be a tasty morsel for Moore, but he can't use it here without contradicting himself because it nullifies the racism argument. Moore resolves the paradox brilliantly by bounding to the higher generality of asking why Canada has a lower murder rate, somehow managing to *suggest* both theses simultaneously to the viewer without having to take responsibility for either one.

And yet the racism angle is not as completely far out as some on the right have insisted it is. Dave Kopel has gone to some lengths to pour scorn on Moore's linkage, in *Columbine*, of the origin, goals, and ideology of the NRA and the Ku Klux Klan,[9] and in the limited histor- ical circumstances Kopel addresses, he has a point. But listen to Art Busch, who was on the front line of law enforcement in Flint for a dozen years:

Shortly after [the Kayla Rowland shooting] started, I was all over the news media as a spokesman for our city. Michael and Kathleen were talking to me throughout this incident, and I was sharing with them the hate mail that I was receiving, which was bizarre. I had done an interview with Katie Couric in which I started to describe the boy who shot Kayla as a "lit- tle guy" and said that we needed to wrap our arms around him and love him and realize that he's a victim as well. That really stirred a lot of nutty people across our country; it stirred up the racist people because it didn't take them long to figure out that he was black and she was white, although no pictures of him were ever published, since he was a juvenile.

So the racist people of the world decided that they would begin to write me letters, notes, threats. What amazed me was the anger of these people as I began to talk about guns. You see, the context of Kayla Rowland was the assault- weapons ban in Congress, the 2000 election cycle, and the fact that we were having all these school shootings all at the same time. I pointed out that the gun used to shoot Kayla was stolen in a burglary, and I began to talk about how this was a huge problem, that guns were being stolen from people's houses and used in crimes. People get these guns and they think that they're safer, but just the opposite is true. Well, that stirred up the gun nuts. They were writing me letters comparing me to the prosecutor who was prosecuting Byron de la Beckwith[10] down in Mississippi. I didn't take the com- parison as an insult.

It was pretty disturbing to see people writing stuff like

that. My life doesn't involve gun nuts, usually, and I was struck by how these two—the racists and the gun nuts—came together in one package.

∎ ∎ ∎

In *Bowling for Columbine*, Moore has refined the technique of deceptive editing that he developed in *Roger & Me*. He cuts and edits short snippets from two different speeches given by Charlton Heston more than a year apart, and presents them in such a way that the viewer assumes they are part of the same speech—one given at Denver just days after the Columbine massacre. By using cutaway edits to distract from Heston's apparent mid-speech change of clothes, Moore suggests that Heston is a callous fool who doesn't care or doesn't realize that the people of Denver and its suburbs have just been traumatized by a terrible crime. So we see Heston saying, in the first speech, which was given at Charlotte, North Carolina, more than a year after the Columbine killings: ". . . from my cold, dead hands!" while brandishing a rifle over his head. Chilling and stupid, but not quite so much as it would have been in Denver only ten days after Columbine.

The second speech, the one that *was* given just after Columbine, shows Heston's response to Denver mayor Wellington Webb's request that the NRA not hold its convention there so soon after Columbine. "Don't come here? We're already here!" The speech—both the edited version that Moore shows and the full version—is as much pathetic and idiotic as it is offensive. Heston completely fails to understand why the people of Denver and Littleton might have good reason to resent the NRA in the aftermath of Columbine and completely fails to make the connection between guns and mayhem. Heston gives the speech with his resonant actor's voice. He seems to be in a different world, a delusional one.

But offensive as the speech is, Heston and the NRA were not completely insensitive. In fact, far from being blusteringly defiant, they canceled every event associated with their Denver meeting out of respect for the victims of Columbine, with the single exception of their officers' meeting, which had been planned two years previously and which, as a chartered association, they were legally obligated to hold at that time and place, unless they could notify their millions of members of a change in plan in the few days remaining before the scheduled meeting, clearly an impossibility. Moore doesn't mention any of this.

In a rebuttal to his critics, Moore acknowledges the proximity of the edited images but not the possibility that they were meant to be perceived as part of the same speech. For anyone who has seen the film, this is rather disingenuous. Moore's voice-over narration says, "Just ten days after the Columbine killings, despite the pleas of a community in mourning, Charlton Heston came to Denver and held a large pro-gun rally for the National Rifle Association" while the "cold, dead hands" scene is still playing, while Heston is still holding the rifle over his head. The viewer, cued by the voice-over, would have a hard time *not* thinking this took place right after Columbine. I certainly thought so when I saw the movie for the first time. Moore's technique has a built-in drawback: in allowing the gun nuts to focus on his editing, Moore has unwittingly handed them an opportunity to avoid confronting the more important question of the sociopathology of Heston and the NRA. They took him up on it.

When he calls on Heston, Moore does himself no honor. Heston invites Moore into his home and gives him a lengthy interview, eventually walking away when Moore starts to badger him for some expression of contrition for holding an NRA rally in Flint soon after the shooting of Kayla Rowland. Moore may have miscalculated here. Heston's a crackpot, but for most of a lengthy interview—an interview he had no reason to grant beyond personal politeness—he is gracious and hospitable to Moore. The most common response to this scene that I have heard, from people who despise Heston, is this: "Moore did what I would have thought impossible—he made me feel sorry for Charlton Heston." The maudlin appeal to Heston's conscience that ends the scene, in which Moore exploits the image of Kayla Rowland,[11] is almost gruesome.

■   ■   ■

While making *Bowling for Columbine*, Moore's path intersected that of his old friend Sam Riddle, not once but twice—an interesting coincidence that says a lot about American media, American politics, and those who manage both.

Riddle was the media representative for Isaiah Shoels, the only black student killed by the teenage berserkers Eric Harris and Dylan Klebold. "Our position is that hate pulled the trigger," Riddle told me. "It wouldn't have mattered if they'd had billy clubs or rocks or knives. They were bent on killing. It was a state of mind." That's clearly true enough, but Riddle's implication that Shoels was *especially* hated because of his race seems as questionable as the claim, frequently made by evangelicals in the aftermath of the massacre, that student victim Cassie Bernall was "martyred" because she refused to renounce Jesus. The possible deployment by the killers against Shoels of the most powerful word in the English language doesn't necessarily prove anything; people filled with hate will use any hook that presents itself, and Shoels's blackness might have been convenient for them rather than determinative. But we can't ask Harris and Klebold what they were thinking, so we'll never really know.

Riddle also represented the mother of the boy who shot Kayla Rowland. The section of the film that addresses her situation is the closest Moore ever comes to real policy engagement, and although it is a digression from his main themes, the fact that it is grounded in particular facts with actual solutions makes it one of the most moving and effective parts of the film.

We learn that the boy's mother was kicked off public assistance by Michigan's draconian welfare-to-work laws. Without resources to care adequately for her child, she was forced to leave him with the crack-dealing uncle and to commute for hours every day to a fast-food restaurant in a white suburban mall, where she worked for the standard low wage provided by such jobs. Before Moore, the national media usually took the blame-the-monster-mother approach.[12] It took Moore's movie to raise the question of the consequences that follow when a society that professes to be concerned with "family values" cuts loose its most vulnerable members and leaves them with only bad options.

In this part of the film, Moore truly raised some important points, and he also left himself vulnerable to even more reactionary attacks. The usually careful Dave Kopel, in his article cited earlier, makes an atypically specious argument that lets the state of Michigan off the hook. And Michael Wilson, the director of the film *Michael Moore Hates America*, says that he was inspired to go after Moore by this very sequence in the film: "My mom worked two full-time jobs when I was growing up, and she went to school full-time. And I never shot anybody, you know? We were poor. I grew up in Missouri in a house that was right between the projects and the trailer court. My mom worked really long hours, but she put her job as a mother first, you know? And to me, that's what you do as a parent: you make choices; you're accountable."[13] In saying this, Wilson—probably from pure naïveté, untainted by political malice—shows an enormous lack of understanding of the realities of class, realities that are so much at the heart of Moore's work.

■   ■   ■

Moore has never seriously attempted to objectively prove any of the social theories he advances in *Bowling for Columbine*. Speaking about the film, he flings connections around as casually as this one: "I see bowling as a very American thing, an all-American sport. The other all-American sport is violence. [The Columbine killers] went to their favorite class—bowling—in the morning. I think they just went from one to the other."[14]

As it happens, the Columbine killers skipped their bowling class that morning; Moore's journalism here is as sloppy as his reasoning. Sloppy or not, Moore never questions his conclusions, which allow him to blame American gun violence on an amorphous "culture of fear" or the war in Yugoslavia while simultaneously dismissing right-wing attempts to blame it on Marilyn Manson's shock rock[15]—an explanation no more implausible than any that Moore offers. In a speech given at the University of Denver in February 2003, Moore made it clear that he believes his generalized argument about a violent society is the *actual* key to understanding the Columbine assaults, and to understanding America: "I want everyone to be able to draw the connection between Columbine and Iraq and everything else."[16] The scale of Moore's mission, and his revolutionary pretensions, are perhaps revealed in a small but telling detail. While working on *Columbine*, he arranged for his staff to watch Gillo Pontecorvo's classic anticolonial film, *The Battle of Algiers*.

Michael Moore's inflated sense of his purposes illustrates what is so corrosive about the view of American society expressed in *Bowling for Columbine*. Moore did not set out to address the problem of gun violence in America; he set out to proclaim that America itself, American society and culture, *is* the problem. Two leftist Canadian philosophy professors, Joseph Heath and Andrew Potter, who have written about the danger inherent in the idea of the "counterculture" and its rejection of political engagement with the mass culture, get it exactly right about Moore:

> [T]he countercultural critique makes it all but impossible to distinguish between "good" repression—enforcement of the rules that enable mutually beneficial cooperation to emerge—and "bad" repression—gratuitous violence inflicted on the weak and disadvantaged. . . . If society is a giant system of repression, then every act, no matter how violent or antisocial, can be seen either as a form of protest or as "blowback" caused by excess repression in the system. . . . For Moore, the Columbine massacre was not simply a criminal act, it was an indictment of all American society and history. . . . Not only does he insist upon a revolutionary change in the culture, *he rejects anything less*.[17]

■ ■ ■

Widespread skepticism about *Bowling for Columbine* as a documentary didn't prevent it from accruing honor, fame, and riches. In addition to its Oscar, Moore took home the Cannes International Film Festival's special fifty-fifth anniversary Palme for *Columbine* in 2002—the first time in fifty years that a documentary had been in contention—which set the stage for his 2004 Palme d'Or for *Fahrenheit 9/11*. *Columbine* won awards at international film festivals from Amsterdam to São Paulo, Australia, Sweden, Norway, Vancouver, Toronto, and many other places where the film's thesis about the basic antisociability of Americans found a warm response.

The film won plaudits at home as well as abroad, scooping up awards all over the United States, including the Dallas/Fort Worth Film Critics' Association Award. Made for around $4 million, in six months it grossed over $21 million in the United States and over $35 million abroad. That's not even counting DVD and video rights, where most movies make their real money. This was absolutely astonishing for a documentary. It was unprecedented.

But, of course, what really cemented *Columbine*'s place in American culture was Moore's behavior at the Academy Awards. Everyone who has any interest at all in politics or film knows what he did. In March 2003, with the bombs falling in Iraq, Moore took to the stage in his tuxedo and didn't abide by the unwritten law of the tightly scripted, harshly time-limited Academy ceremony: thank your actors, your parents, and God, and be gone. Clutching his statue, Moore addressed the elephant in the public room. "We live in a time when we have fictitious election results that elect a fictitious president. We live in a time where we have a man sending us to war for fictitious reasons, whether it is the fiction of duct tape or the fiction of orange alerts. We are against this war, Mr. Bush. Shame on you, Mr. Bush. Shame on you. And any time that you have the Pope and the Dixie Chicks against you, your time is up."[18]

In an irony little remarked upon, the rich movie people in the audience cheered while the working-class technical people booed. On the bonus features disk that accompanies the DVD release of *Bowling for Columbine*, Moore, speaking with theatrical humility to the camera in a backyard "somewhere in Michigan," explains his unorthodox acceptance speech: "They had just honored me for my film, a film that was about guns, violence, American violence, American violence exported to other countries . . . so my comments were very much in keeping with this film. . . . If I'd made a film about birds or insects, then maybe it wouldn't have been appropriate. . . . I try to live my life in an honest and sincere way, and at the end of the day, I'm Michael Moore. What else am I going to do?" The speech was a supremely calculated grab for national attention, whether for Moore's movie, for opposition to the war in Iraq, for Moore himself—it hardly matters.

The speech and the accompanying publicity may well have improved box-office takings for both *Columbine* and Moore's forthcoming *Fahrenheit 9/11*, but it also spawned endless right-wing screeds and Internet rants—far too many to begin to attribute here— on how Moore was a traitor who worked against the troops and the president in wartime and, more diabolically and significantly, someone who *represented the left and all opposition to George W. Bush.*

There were people close to Moore who understood the danger

here. His wife, Kathleen Glynn, was reported to be unhappy with his outburst. Sam Riddle told me that a week before the incident, when Moore's film was in nomination, he'd e-mailed Moore and told him, "I know what you're thinking of doing. Don't do it." And Moore himself understood whom he was dealing with, even as he indulged in casting himself as a victim: "I forgot that the right wing and the conservatives don't really believe in free speech. They were not going to give me my forty-five seconds uninterrupted and then boo if they wanted to. Their job was to try and stop me from saying another word."[19]

Moore's speech was an easy hook on which the right hung the following non sequiturs: to question Bush's legitimacy is to hate America, to be a whiny ideological has-been, an elitist Hollywood slob (the right was certainly not above bringing Moore's appearance into the equation, and the fortuitous Hollywood location gave its well-funded attack machine yet another opportunity to go after the "liberal elite"). For many Americans, of all political persuasions, this was the moment that Moore became indelibly associated with the left and with opposition to Bush. It was a controversy that would linger and bloat in the blogosphere. Many who weren't particularly political felt that he had offended some deeply rooted American sense of propriety.

■　■　■

Bowling for Columbine's success meant that Moore was free, as an artist and as a political activist, to do whatever he wanted. Money trumps content or propriety or politics. Mel Gibson made a movie much admired on the right that also happened to be a disgraceful piece of Jew-hating sadomasochistic religious pornography, but after *The Passion of the Christ* broke box-office records for an independently distributed film, he will always be able to get money for his projects. That's how it works, and in the same way, Moore's financial success assures him that those concerned about the controversy will never be able to turn their backs and prevent him from working.

But the success of *Columbine* also had a certain slow-motion, built-in drawback. The film captured very well the fears and concerns of many Americans regarding gun culture and violence, but its flaws would be noticed, and noticed anew, when Moore took on even larger causes. The film is emotionally satisfying in many ways, but there is nothing in it that stands up to statistical analysis or even deductive logic, and several viewings can reduce it to a joke.

It's more than likely that, in the cold light of day, as the problems with *Bowling for Columbine* as a documentary began to be widely known, this fact contributed to a certain wariness toward Moore on the part of many who were in a position to make institutional judgments and, combined with similar questions about his next blockbuster, contributed to keeping *Fahrenheit 9/11* out of the running for the 2004 Academy Awards.

PART THREE

SPOKESMAN FOR THE LEFT

HOW MICHAEL MOORE FOUND HIS AUDIENCE, AND HIS AUDIENCE FOUND HIM

6

THE STOLEN ELECTION OF 2000

O n November 6, 2000, the day before the American presidential election, Michael Moore was a successful filmmaker who'd worked in television and had written a left-populist, lowbrow book of political entertainment, *Downsize This!* He'd stirred up a lot of people and gained a fan base with his first film, *Roger & Me*. He'd made a bit of money, and this gave him something of a platform. He'd created the Michael Moore brand. But could he really be said to be influencing the way Americans think, or to be a major figure on the political scene? Certainly few on what passes for the left in the United States would have identified him as a national spokesman for their causes, although perhaps he could be counted on, in general, to be in tune with the left agenda. Two things in particular, two historical events, pushed many on the left into Moore's capacious embrace.

The first of these was the Republican attempt to unseat a sitting Democratic president on specious grounds involving his personal life, led by a special prosecutor, Kenneth Starr, who seemed to confuse his personal religious views with a public policy mandate. It is a truism that often those who feel most threatened by their own sexuality do the most damage in society, and it is at least interesting that while

Republicans chanted their mantra of "It's not the sex, it's the perjury," Starr's final report to Congress on his investigations dwelled sternly, but in fetishistic, fine-grained detail, on the sex. One of the finest American essayists captured the sickness behind the Starr report very well. Adam Gopnik wrote in the *New Yorker*, "A supposedly dispassionate account of a man's sins becomes so overwrought that the reader gradually realizes that the point of the story is not that the hero is wicked but that the narrator is mad."[1]

But Starr was merely the instrument. The plan was a seizure of power by extra-constitutional means, or, failing that, an attempt to cripple a sitting president of the opposition party and damage any potential Democratic candidate to be his successor.

This cynical morality play had two effects: it made nonconservatives very aware of the lengths to which conservatives would go to seize power, and it made some of them seriously consider playing by the same rules. Indeed, while there were many who recognized the damage that mixing sex and governance was doing to the republic, there were few liberals who denied a certain satisfaction in the sex scandals that broke over the heads of Newt Gingrich and his presumed successor as Speaker of the House, Robert Livingston, in the aftermath of the Clinton impeachment. Liberals, to their shame, didn't have much to say about pornography publisher Larry Flynt "outing" Livingston's affair and threatening to expose the affairs of other Republicans, even though it was hard to find liberals who thought that Flynt had done a good or honorable thing. The refrain "Live by the sword, die by the sword" was much bandied about.

The Clinton scandals were the prelude. More than anything else, the event that primed nonconservatives for bare-knuckled political brawling was the stolen election of 2000.

■   ■   ■

In order to understand the anger against Republicans and conservatives, in order to see how Michael Moore's polemics could come as a relief, we have to understand what happened in Florida in 2000. It's a vexed and complicated issue, but it is worth going into in some detail, because it is at the root of much of the polarization in American politics today.

George W. Bush won Florida's twenty-five electoral college votes, and therefore the election, under the following circumstances:

Bush's brother Jeb was the governor of Florida, and had ultimate oversight of the election machinery.

One of Bush's eight partisan Florida campaign co-chairs, Katherine Harris, was also the officially nonpartisan Florida secretary of state, in charge of supervising and administering the election.[2]

Harris and Jeb Bush did something interesting prior to the election. They kicked a lot of legitimate voters off the rolls, and a majority of those who stayed off were Democrats. How they did this is known in rough outline, but their method is usually misunderstood and misinterpreted. It wasn't, contrary to popular belief, about disfranchising people by race.

The secretary of state spent much effort prior to the election on purging the voter lists of people convicted of a felony, who, if the conviction was in the state, do not have the right to vote in Florida. The state spent more than $4 million on hiring a private contractor, Database Technologies, to compare lists of known felons with names on the Florida voter rolls and to prepare an "exceptions list" of matching names. (After winning the contract, Database Technologies merged with ChoicePoint, Inc., in February 2000 and changed its name to DBT Online.) Those whose names ended up on the exceptions list were supposed to receive letters informing them of their status. If they wanted to regain the right to vote, they either had to prove to the State of Florida that they were not in fact felons, or apply for clemency from the governor's office.

So far, so good with the voter purge. There's nothing illegal or, arguably, anything wrong here. Florida passed a law that had not been rescinded by the legislature or overturned by the courts, and no one forced anyone to commit a felony. If, for historical and socioeconomic reasons, blacks are overrepresented in Florida's felon population, and if, for not-unrelated historical and socioeconomic reasons, blacks in the post–Civil Rights era are more likely to be Democrats than Republicans, and if therefore more Democrats than Republicans happened to be purged in this manner, the purge may have helped Republicans but it was not necessarily a political act. Even if Republican election officials knew and were happy about the differing rates of disfranchisement, they were just doing their jobs, doing what the law told them to do.

But it's more complicated than that. The purge was riddled with errors, errors that the Florida Division of Elections and the secretary of state actively and knowingly encouraged. Staff at the Florida Division of Elections, supposedly nonpartisan but overseen by Republicans, instructed Database Technologies to use the loosest criteria for the matching process: Disregard the middle initial. Disregard the subject's date of birth—a close but not exact match is acceptable. Disregard "Jr." or "Sr." Consider it a match if 90 percent of the subject's last name matches. Match real first names with nicknames. Switched first and middle names can also match: to use the example given in the testimony of DBT Online's vice president for operations, George Bruder, before the U.S. Commission on Civil Rights, "Ann Deborah" would match "Deborah Ann."[3]

Katherine Harris and the Division of Elections were repeatedly and explicitly told by precinct officers and by Database Technologies itself that this "loose" method of identifying felons would result in a lot of false positives, but consistently responded that this was all to the good. Marlene Thorogood, a product manager with Database Technologies, sent an e-mail to Emmett "Bucky" Mitchell IV, an assistant general counsel for the Division of Elections, in which she wrote, "Unfortunately, programming in this fashion may supply you with false positives." Mitchell replied, "Obviously, we want to capture more names that possibly aren't matches and let the supervisors [of elections] make a final determination rather than exclude certain matches altogether."[4] George Bruder, in his testimony, confirmed that Mitchell had been notified of the poor methodology and confirmed that Mitchell had responded that the list should be broad and encompassing. "[T]he state dictated to us that they wanted to go broader, and we did it in the fashion that they requested."[5] According to Mitchell, the loose criteria were approved by Ethel Baxter, the head of the Division of Elections, after consultation with Katherine Harris. The state's response to repeated warnings about the looseness of the match criteria was to further loosen—not tighten—those criteria.

Harris and Jeb Bush went further: in addition to felons convicted in Florida, they instructed Database Technologies to include in the database of felons people convicted of felonies in the states of Texas,

Ohio, Wisconsin, South Carolina, Kentucky, New Jersey, Virginia, Washington, Connecticut, and Illinois, states for which Database Technologies had access to conviction records. This meant that if a Florida voter's name and birth date were a *rough* match with a *felon in one of these states*, the Florida voter would be struck from the rolls. But Texas, Connecticut, South Carolina, and Wisconsin automatically restore civil rights after felons have served their full sentences or complete parole; Illinois and Ohio restore their voting rights on release from prison. The idea that felons whose civil rights had been restored in the state in which they committed their crimes could be barred from voting was a position that the Florida Supreme Court had specifically rejected as illegal in 1998.

The standard conspiracy theory that has developed in the wake of the 2000 election, the one suggested by Greg Palast and John Nichols and sometimes by the NAACP, goes something like this: by setting the exceptions list criteria so loosely, Harris and Jeb Bush and Florida's Division of Elections were deliberately drawing blacks disproportionately into the list, deliberately disfranchising them, figuring that blacks were most likely Democrats. As Michael Moore expressed it in the opening sequence of *Fahrenheit 9/11*, where he discusses the Florida voter disfranchisement, "You can usually spot them by the color of their skin." But that theory doesn't hold up.

Think about it. If you set your criteria to produce false positives, you will get a lot of incorrect matches with nonfelons—but not necessarily black or poor or otherwise likely-to-be-Democratic nonfelons. Matching Jonny Ray Jones Jr. with John A. Jones is just as likely to match an urban unemployed black Democratic felon with a rich white suburban Republican John Bircher. *Unless*, in addition to the loose name criteria, you match exactly on race; in that case you're much more likely (although still nowhere near certain) to incorrectly match the felon with a nonfelon of similar background and political affiliation. But it seems that Database Technologies did *not* match on race, and the State of Florida didn't filter the results that way. The exceptions list included more than a thousand racial mismatches.

The numbers don't support a "black exclusion" strategy. Blacks are 14.6 percent of Florida's general population and 11 percent of the over-eighteen, U.S.-citizen potential voting population,[6] but almost 49 percent of all of Florida's felons are black;[7] blacks were 44 percent of those named on the exceptions list as suspected felons. On this basis, U.S. Civil Rights commissioners Abigail Thernstrom and Russell Redenbaugh dissented from the commission's postelection finding that there was disproportionate black disfranchisement, since 44 percent is below the 49 percent of blacks in the Florida felon population.

■   ■   ■

Does all of this mean that the felon purge was innocent and nonpolitical? Not at all. It was just diabolically clever. What were Jeb Bush and Harris and Mitchell and Clayton Roberts, the director of the Division of Elections, up to? Why would they want to cast a wide net?

They were using a rebate strategy. Think of how rebates work: A company offers a product at a certain price, but a partial refund is available, which encourages sales to those who might not buy the product at the full price. Only motivated customers take advantage of the offer, though, since the rebate application process is intentionally annoying and designed to discourage a response.

The Florida purge criteria were designed to kick as many people as possible off the rolls, in two groups: genuine felons, and those who roughly matched their names. The first group could be reasonably assumed to be disproportionately black, poor, and likely Democrats, but felons were legitimately excluded, by law. The second group might be people of any race, background, or political affiliation. It was randomly selected.

Remember that if a person's name turned up on this list, the process of getting voting rights restored put the onus on the voter. He or she, first of all, had to receive the notification letter, and to receive the letter this voter needed a stable address. The voter needed to have the documents to prove nonfelon status, which would include having a valid photo ID. The voter would have to know his or her Social Security number. The voter would have to have a reasonable level of literacy, and to be confident in interactions with officials. The voter would have to not fear contact with the authorities on account of things like unpaid parking tickets or child support. Above all, the voter would have to be motivated, would have to have enough of a sense of citizenship to be willing to jump through some hoops to get the right to vote restored.

Now in general, what group would more often be able and willing to go through the "rebate" process? Not the poor, the transient, the uneducated, the marginally literate, those alienated from mainstream political culture—which, since the Republican Party serves the interests of the rich, disproportionately describes Florida's Democrats. Since race is related to class, it also happens to disproportionately describe Florida's blacks.

People in these categories, if they were citizens and residents of Florida and over eighteen and had not been convicted of a felony, had the right to vote. But if they were on the list, *they had to actively claim this right.*

The response to notification of disfranchisement in fact followed exactly the pattern that a rebate strategy would suggest. Out of 4,678 blacks on the Miami-Dade exclusions list, 239 objected when they were notified that they were ineligible to vote and had their voting rights restored. They represented 5.1 percent of the total number of blacks on the felon list for that county. Of the 1,264 whites on the list, 125 objected, 9.9 percent, and had their rights restored.[8] The higher absolute number of blacks *targeted* is most likely explained by the disproportionate number of black genuine felons. The higher rate of *reinstatement* of whites is most likely explained by lower felony rates *and* by higher literacy rates, more stable residency patterns, and greater comfort levels dealing with officials, which determined their response to the exclusion notification. We don't know anything about how those who were reinstated, black or otherwise, voted, but we do know that as a group, blacks in Florida voted for Al Gore by a factor of more than nine to one, and whites favored Bush.

That's why the Republican officials cast a wide net. Exclude as many as possible, and disproportionate numbers of Republican voters will self-select. They'll take the rebate. The strategy was about class, not race. But like so many things in the United States, class looked like race.

The beauty part, from the point of view of the Republicans, is that unless someone finds a strategy memo that Bush and Harris and Mitchell never needed to write—they would have understood each other too well—partisan intent to skew the election is entirely unprovable, and without that intent, the plan wasn't illegal. The exceptions list wasn't meant to disfranchise blacks. That idea was a red herring, and it totally confused those Democrats and black activists who tried to figure out what was happening but couldn't quite do it. Unimaginatively turning to the tired tropes of past battles, they trapped themselves into having to prove disproportionate black disfranchisement, into having to explain why there were anomalous rates of Hispanic disfranchisement and high rates of white disfranchisement, and they couldn't do it. None of that was to the point. What mattered were the *numbers* of those who were excluded, and they were in the tens of thousands. The higher the numbers, the more the rebate effect would show up.

Contrary to the U.S. Commission on Civil Rights report and the indignant claims of the Republican Party, it is quite reasonable to conclude that there was a preconceived plan designed for partisan effect. Did it work? The impact of the purge list was somewhat ameliorated by the fact that it was so widely known to be flawed that many county elections supervisors did not use it, or used it only partially. This was a decision taken at the county level. But in a very close election, its effect should not be discounted. George W. Bush won Florida by an officially certified margin of 537 of the 5,825,043 votes cast in Florida. That's less than one one-hundredth of one percent. The Republicans always knew it was going to be close. They knew it wouldn't take much.

Can we be sure that this was what Jeb Bush, Harris, Roberts, and Mitchell were thinking and planning? Of course not. But they talk to plenty of party statisticians and sociopolitical analysts. They are pros. They know how these things work. And the behavior of Harris and Bush in other election matters is instructive. Acting in their capacities as government officials—supposedly responsible to the process rather than to their party or candidate—they did everything they could to help George W. Bush win.

■   ■   ■

These are some things that Moore left out of *Fahrenheit*: Bush's narrow margin of victory triggered an automatic recount. When a Miami-Dade County hand recount of questionable ballots started to show Gore gaining, there was a threatening demonstration outside the county offices that intimidated officials into stopping the recount. Although the demonstrators claimed to be a spontaneous crowd, it later turned out that they were a group of Republican Capitol Hill staffers, more than two hundred of them. Republican Party operatives paid their airfare down to Florida, as well as all their expenses, so that they could demonstrate against the recount and generally disrupt Democratic events. There is a picture of a group of these rioting Republican staffers, each of them identified by name and position on various Republican staffs, in John Nichols and David Deschamps's *Jews for Buchanan: Did You Hear the One about the Theft of the American Presidency?* (New Press, 2001).[9] New York Republican representative John Sweeney was there, and was heard to shout, "Shut it down!"[10]—that is, shut down the recount, a legal process put in place by the institutions of democracy. John Bolton, a lawyer working for the Republicans who would later be George W. Bush's nominee as ambassador to the United Nations, arrived in Miami to announce, "I'm with the Bush-Cheney team, and I'm here to stop the count."[11]

It happened that absentee ballots for Bush had glaring irregularities: no postmark, filled out or requested by someone other than the voter, filed after the deadline, and so on. When the Republicans starting slamming the Democrats in the press by insisting that Democrats were trying to disfranchise military personnel serving overseas, Al Gore's running mate, Joe Lieberman, conceded that while some of the absentee ballots might be very questionable, it looked too bad to go after the military vote, so the Democrats dropped that line of challenge. But the joke was on them: while the Republicans had made an enormous outcry about supposed Democratic plans to block the military vote, they in fact had put in place their own plan to challenge absentee ballots, including military absentee ballots for voters registered in Democratic but not in Republican counties, insisting on using the tightest criteria in the former and the loosest in the latter. They also effectively challenged civilian absentee ballots while fighting to count military overseas ballots with exactly the same flaws. Reporters for the *New York Times* thoroughly documented the double standards of the Republicans. Referring to the Supreme Court decision that eventually decided the election, they concluded, "The court did not consider the varying treatment of military and civilian votes. It did not address the unequal treatment of the 2,490 ballots that finally determined the election's outcome. Those issues were never raised."[12]

After the election, it turned out that if ballots in which the voter had both written in the candidate's name and checked the box next to the candidate's name were counted, or else had crossed out one marked circle and marked another—the so-called "overvotes"—a statewide recount would have shown that Gore picked up 315 net votes of the first type and 682 net votes of the second type, enough to wipe out Bush's 537-vote victory margin. The optical scan ballots were supposed to work by recording the voter's choice from a darkened circle, but included a line at the bottom for a write-in candidate. Next to this line the instructions said, "Write in candidate's name here." Many voters thought they should write in the name of the candidate whose circle they had selected. The intent of the voter would not seem to be ambiguous for both kinds of "overvotes," and Florida law specifically mandates that it is the intent of the voter that must be considered. The Bush team successfully argued that these votes should not be counted.

The Florida Supreme Court ordered a statewide recount of *all* questionable ballots. However, the Bush campaign couldn't accept this. Bush brought suit at the Supreme Court, demanding that all recounting stop and that he be named the winner. In *Bush v. Gore*, in a 7–2 ruling the Court held that Florida's recount was unconstitutional because of varying ballot-counting standards in the different counties (nothing was said about the varying *voting method* standards in those counties and, indeed, nationally). Then, rather than insisting that the Florida Supreme Court develop a single standard for counting, and extending the arbitrary counting deadline, in a 5–4 ruling the Court forbade *any* recount before the arbitrary statutory deadline of December 12.[13] All five of the justices who ruled in Bush's favor had been appointed by Republican presidents.

These five judges were known, or quite reasonably presumed to be, Republican partisans personally. Justice Sandra Day O'Connor, on first hearing that Gore was apparently the winner on the close election night, was overheard to remark, "My God! That's terrible!" Two of Justice Antonin Scalia's sons were working for the Bush legal team during the recount battle, and his son Eugene had already obtained a job with the incoming Bush administration, assuming Bush won. The wife of Justice Clarence Thomas, Virginia Lamp Thomas, was working for the Heritage Foundation, vetting possible Bush administration appointments. O'Connor, Scalia, and Thomas refused to recuse themselves.

The court emphasized that its decision was not to be read as setting any kind of precedent. Quite extraordinarily, the decision was rendered per curiam; that is, it is not signed by the individual justices. These facts led many to suspect that the justices are secretly ashamed of what they have done and aware that it would lead to electoral chaos if applied as a precedent. No wonder that, after *Bush v. Gore*, many of the court's own clerks "thought that the Court was a fraud, that the place had sacrificed its legitimacy, and that there really wasn't much point in taking the whole institution seriously anymore."[14]

After the election, a consortium of news groups counted all of the disputed ballots cast in Florida and found that if there had been a statewide recount of all of these ballots using the standards in effect in each county, Gore would have won by 171 votes. Using various combinations of the various standards that were proposed at different times and in different counties for the recount, Gore wins under twelve scenarios and Bush wins under twelve scenarios. Ironically, under the standards Gore sought from the Florida Supreme Court, Bush wins. But using the tightest combination of standards—completely filled circles for optical-scan ballots and full punches for punch-card ballots, and stipulating that all observers agree on the condition of the ballots, Gore would have won by 134 votes. You have to loosen at least one of those things for a Bush win.

You can check this for yourself. The *New York Times* has posted a Web-based data tool that uses the results of the media consortium investigation in configurations that you can specify. The tool is at www.nytimes.com/images/2001/11/12/politics/recount/results/A2B1C6.html. (This link was active as of August 2005.) By the way, if anyone out there still takes Ann Coulter seriously, she's on record as saying of the 2000 election, "The media consortium study . . . [showed] that Bush had won on any count."[15] The anti-Moore film *Celsius 41.11* also claims that "the media consortium declared George W. Bush the winner no matter how the votes were counted." In support of this statement, the film flashes a written summary of the consortium's findings on the screen for a few seconds, too fast to read it. If you pause the film and read this summary, what you can see of it says this: "George W. Bush would remain as the winner of Florida's electoral vote . . . under one limited set of rules, those prescribed by the Florida Supreme Court in December of 2000. . . . . Bush's title, however, rests on narrow legalistic grounds. . . . Under a full accounting, Gore probably would be president."

■ ■ ■

Of course there is a Republican counternarrative to this description of events. A representative example is Bill Sammon's book *At Any Cost: How Al Gore Tried to Steal the Election* (Regnery Publishing, 2001). Sammon is a long-time Clinton hater and a reporter for the reactionary *Washington Times*. Since the election, he's written adoring books about Bush in office.

Sammon's work is forthrightly partisan. He clearly despises Al Gore and paints him as a ruthless, selfish schemer without any sense of national responsibility. Sammon does a good job of showing that the Florida elections were poorly organized and administered and that, in the aftermath of the vote, many decisions by judges, canvassing boards, and individual poll workers were taken on a sloppy, ad hoc basis. But he tries to paint every hardball decision that the Gore team made to try to turn the procedures to Gore's advantage as some sort of illegitimate scam, and he completely ignores the fact that the Bush team was doing the same and worse on the other side of the question. The book's focus on Gore allows Sammon to keep almost silent about the thuggery of the Bush people, and to portray Bush as an innocent bystander, a noble man above the fray. But even some of Sammon's own details condemn the Bush advocates, as when he describes how Katherine Harris, again and again and again, refused to allow recounts and, when they were forced upon her, refused to allow enough time for them to take place. Harris allowed the extension of only one deadline: that for the absentee ballots, widely expected by both Democrats and Republicans to favor Republicans because of the large number of military ballots. Sammon, a Republican partisan, shows that *every single decision that Harris took in the aftermath of the election favored Bush and hurt Gore.*

Sammon makes one legitimate point: that thousands of voters in the western Florida panhandle, which was dominated by Republicans and which was in a time zone one hour earlier than the rest of the Florida precincts, were discouraged from voting when NBC called

Florida for Gore at 7:49 P.M. Eastern time; thinking the contest was over, many potential Republican voters standing in line to vote may have gone home. Sammon believes this may have cost Bush as many as 10,000 votes. But Sammon also believes (and I agree with him on this) that the confusing Palm Beach "butterfly ballot" was no excuse for a recount in that county; if voters couldn't figure out how to vote properly, if they couldn't see which arrow led to which candidate on the form, that was their problem. According to the media consortium findings, poorly designed ballots probably led to a net loss of more than 8,500 votes for Gore. So what about those Bush voters who supposedly just stepped out of line the minute they heard the very first, unconfirmed call that their guy had lost, just eleven minutes before the polls were scheduled to close? Isn't that their problem too? Besides, Sammon undermines his own point just a few pages later, when he notes that John Ellis,[16] Bush's first cousin, who was heading up the Fox News "decision desk," called Florida for Bush just three minutes after Tom Brokaw at NBC said it had gone for Gore. Ellis made the call after speaking with his cousin, the candidate—surely this procedure is as irregular and illegitimate as any mistake made by NBC based on faulty information.

Astonishingly, Sammon makes *no mention whatsoever* of Katherine Harris's inaccurate purges of the voter rolls that just happened to favor Republicans, something that may have cost Gore tens of thousands of net votes. And when he discusses the lingering effects of the election, he drifts into complete fantasyland. "During Bush's first months in office, most Americans closed ranks behind their new president. . . . Bush demonstrated a sure-footedness that reassured Republicans and Democrats alike that an adult was now in charge. The new president deftly cultivated a bipartisan bonhomie that silenced most cries of illegitimacy."[17]

Which begs the question: What planet was Sammon living on? The new administration was the most viciously partisan in living memory. Bush seemed to relish crushing and humiliating his political opponents, making no concessions whatsoever to the fact that he had lost the popular vote and won the electoral college under extremely questionable circumstances. The newly installed vice president, Dick Cheney, actually boasted of how little respect this administration had for its clear lack of a mandate: "From the very day we walked in the building, a notion of sort of a restrained presidency because it was such a close election, that lasted maybe thirty seconds. It was not contemplated for any length of time. We had an agenda, we ran on that agenda, we won the election—full speed ahead."[18] The arrogance is mind-boggling, and sadly predictive of the wartime crimes of hubris and incompetence that Bush and Cheney were later to add to that of their election theft. But according to Sammon, this administration was cultivating *bipartisan bonhomie*? The fact that Sammon could write this without any apparent sense of shame casts serious doubt on the credibility of his entire book.

■　　■　　■

Let's try a thought experiment. Let's go to opposite-land. Suppose all of these things happened just as they did, but *the other way around*. Suppose it was Gore's brother who was the governor of Florida, and the Florida secretary of state was one of Gore's campaign chairmen. That the Florida secretary of state/Gore campaign chairman had been using a flawed database methodology to kick legitimate voters off the voting lists prior to the election, in a manner that subtly favored the reinstatement of Democrats. That she had continued to do this even after being informed of the errors, and that election officials had explicitly instructed the database contractor to use a methodology that would give "false positives." That Democratic partisans had disrupted a legitimate recount and forced it to close down. That many of the absentee ballots that went for Gore had serious irregularities. That the Supreme Court that handed the election to Gore had a majority of known Democratic partisans who had obvious conflicts of interest. That an examination of the disputed votes showed that, under the strictest standards, Bush had won. And that, after all, more Americans had voted for Bush than for Gore, a fact that may have no constitutional relevance but that is very important for a popular sense of political legitimacy.

Given this opposite-land scenario, would the Republicans have shrugged their collective shoulders and said, "Well, it was close, but Gore's the president now, he won it fair and square. We Republicans will just have to accept that and maybe we can turn it around in four years."

Of course not. The entire Republican congressional delegation, led by Republican capo Tom DeLay, would have walked out if Al Gore had tried to take up his duties, leading to a constitutional crisis. I think we all know this. The fact that the Democrats did not do this when Bush was appointed to the presidency in exactly this manner was a huge failure of responsibility, and very hard to forgive. It made many people anxious to listen to anyone who would stand up and tell the obvious truth about Bush's illegitimacy.

■　　■　　■

To be clear, then: it is more than plausible—it is very likely—that Jeb Bush and Katherine Harris and their confederates in the Florida Republican Party stole the 2000 election. Not accidentally, not due to unanticipated chaos, but according to a well-thought-out, preconceived plan, first with the purge and then using every official tool at their disposal to help their man win. Most of the people who knew this did not grasp the mechanics of the first aspect of the plan, believing that the voter purge was designed to directly disfranchise blacks. But it hardly matters. It was designed to disfranchise Democrats. They knew they'd been cheated, and they were right about that.

The outrage lingers and can't be assuaged—certainly not by the protests at Bush's 2001 inauguration, which I observed and which Michael Moore discusses in the opening sequence of *Fahrenheit 9/11*. In his film, Moore describes Bush's armored limo being hit with eggs and forced to stop, and says that Bush was not able to make the traditional walk for the last few blocks of the route. This last part is not true. Bush did get out and walk, but not very far, and only when he was in the safe, restricted zone among his ticket-holding supporters.

I remember that the fury was like a living thing. There was applause from the Republican stands when Bush and Dick Cheney took the stage, but the boos and calls of "Thief!" from the crowd were quite audible on the steps. Chief Justice William Rehnquist got the biggest applause from the Republican seats during the administration of the oath, which struck me as candid acknowledgment of what had happened.

A few Republicans along the motorcade route were deeply

offended by the protesters. One apparently middle-class, middle-aged, well-dressed man spotted two men in their thirties who were holding up a large sign reading STOLEN ELECTION, PHONY PRESIDENT and yelled that they were "a couple of sore-loser queers." A group of ten or so Republicans, in tuxedoes and party dresses for the inaugural balls, suggested that the protesters would feel more at home in Cuba. "Yes, they have phony elections there too!" a protester replied.

The police had to delay the parade because a group of protesters had burst through the police lines at Fourteenth and Pennsylvania and were blocking the route. Finally, when the motorcade rolled, there were really loud boos and taunts as the cars turned onto Pennsylvania Avenue. Bush must have heard it. I can testify that, just as Moore showed it in *Fahrenheit 9/11*, the street was very densely packed with signs reading HAIL TO THE THIEF! ILLEGITIMATE! GORE GOT MORE! and BUSH CHEATED! And my own personal favorite: SORRY BARBARA, YOUR SON'S ILLEGITIMATE. He must have seen them. It wasn't just in one place along the route; it was all along it. In some places, the protesters were the very large majority, and they were loud.

It angered me when the protesters taunted the cops and military, who after all were just doing their jobs, jobs that are worthy of respect. I had a more complicated reaction to the treatment of the high school marching bands. I certainly felt sorry for them; after all, this was supposed to be their big moment, a celebration, and they'd practiced hard and it was wet and rainy and freezing and they (especially the Texas bands) were drawing a lot of boos and thumbs-down signals as they marched along, gamely giving the "W" salute with their fingers. (This confused me at first. I thought they were giving the Satanic biker horns symbol while looking straight ahead, as if they'd collectively lost patience with the crowd and had decided as a group to give it back to us. That would have been great, in a strange way; under the circumstances, the parade should have been as much of a bummer for all concerned as possible. But no, it was the "W" salute, I eventually realized, just following the drill.) I thought it was important for them to realize that there was nothing to celebrate here; important that they go home to Amarillo or wherever and tell people that the crowd was focused and furious, that there was a depressed mood. So I felt for them and I hated to see them take flak from the crowd, but perhaps it was a lesson that had to be learned. Innocence is not always a virtue.

Those who protested the installation of a usurper who had an unwarranted sense of entitlement were in no mood for finesse. Michael Moore might be a loudmouth who occasionally makes unjustified, even scurrilous attacks on Bush, but many of those who knew that Bush stole the 2000 election thought, "Well, more power to Moore." The election showed that it was no time for fine-grained reason and delicate, balanced argument in political debate. What was wanted was a return to democracy itself. Yes, and revenge. The blunter the instrument, the better. A significant part of the broad opposition to Bush was ready to coalesce around a populist demagogue.

7

A DEBATE ABOUT REALITY

On July 28, 2004, there was a showing of Michael Moore's *Fahrenheit 9/11* in Crawford, Texas, where the fake cowboy George W. Bush had purchased his "Prairie Chapel" ranch to serve as a backdrop to his presidential campaign. The showing was arranged by the Crawford Peace House, the Waco and Dallas branches of the Friends of Peace, and John Young, a columnist at the *Waco Tribune*.

Waco is the town nearest to Crawford that is large enough to have movie theaters, but *Fahrenheit* wasn't playing there—not because the cinemas refused to play it, as some locals thought and as Young suggested in his columns, but because the Wallace Theaters chain, which owns all the screens in Waco, was having a dispute with Lion's Gate Films over how to split the take from a previous Lion's Gate release, an adaptation of Marvel Comics' *The Punisher*. Conspiracy made a better story, and there certainly were upstanding citizens of Waco who were trying to keep the film unseen and out of their town.

John Young and the Peace House thought that people should have a chance to see it, and the symbolism of showing it in Crawford was certainly not lost on them. Michael Moore himself promised to show up, inviting George W. Bush to join him. (Moore likes nothing better than to write open letters to Bush, and may well believe that Bush reads them.) Bush had no comment, and in the event neither man showed.

Lots of other people did turn up. The movie was shown on portable equipment set up by the Alamo Draft House of Austin in a nearby park and was viewed by a few thousand people, most of whom didn't like Bush. Although the $8 admission charge was supposed to be waived for card-carrying Republicans (the organizers said that they did not want to preach to the converted), most of the Republicans who wanted to see the film were asked to pay.

Galvanized by the prospect of disrespect toward their leader, Republican Party activists of McLennan County had gathered several hundred protesters. Rather than allow any of what they considered Moore's propaganda to wash their brains, most of the Republicans stood and heckled from the sidelines rather than watch the film. Near the end of the evening, perpetrators unknown dumped several tons of bagged manure on the parking lot of the local middle school—the place where TV anchors do their standups when Bush is in town—and sped off, making a pungent statement of contempt for the media. Local police officers had to clean it up. If the perpetrators are ever caught, Crawford police chief Donnie Tidmore told me, they will be charged with illegal dumping.

I guess it was the shit that got me out to Texas. A week later I was heading west out of Waco on Farm Road 185, into the heart of darkness, seeing the billboard for the McLennan County Electric Cooperative that reads PROUDLY PROVIDING ELECTRIC POWER TO THE PRESIDENT AND FIRST LADY—and, in much smaller letters, "and the Surrounding Area." For a man whose just-folks act won him a lot of Texas votes, Bush is treated around Waco with an almost royal reverence. Huge pictures of him and his wife mark the road at both ends of town; Bush wears an expression that is not too thoughtful, not too smiley: that of a simple but honest son of the soil who means what he says and says what he means.

After stopping off at the Yellow Rose of Texas gift shop, which displayed slogans suggesting that we will win the war on terror in spite of the obstructionism of the liberal elites, it was already clear that Crawford has fully bought into the "red-state" foolishness: Westerners are real Americans, straightforward folk who prize their own everyday competence, are incapable of irony, and don't need anyone else's help in this world, certainly not that of effete Eastern-establishment latte-sipping intellectuals. This is complete nonsense, of course, and every time I come across this attitude, I think of the net redistribution differential between the East and the hard-bitten, independent residents of those red states. Those central, southern, and western states take in, on average, about $1.23 from the federal government for every dollar they pay in federal taxes,[1] and this difference comes right out of the pockets of those effete, elite, parasitical blue-state loafers and academics, who, as it happens, actually produce most of the wealth of the nation.

The "heartland" could not maintain anything like its present population without massive transfers of wealth from the Northeast, and not only as a result of those net tax subsidies. There are also federal farm subsidies, ethanol subsidies, grazing subsidies, mining and water concessions, and the tourist dollars of all those Easterners who come to Montana and Wyoming, Arizona and the Dakotas, to hike, hunt, and fish. But the mistaken belief in Western independence is no doubt comforting to those who live there.

I was going to see Cathy Horton, a local Republican woman who describes herself as "an activist and an environmentalist." We met at the Coffee Station, at the only real crossroads in this small town, where Bush has been known to drop in to chat and where partisan feeling runs so deep that not only is the entire place covered in Bush–Cheney paraphernalia and anti-Clinton and anti-Kerry signs (FLUSH THE JOHNS IN '04!) but the only ketchup served is Hunt's (wouldn't want to add to the [Teresa] Heinz [Kerry] fortune).

Horton is intense. She asked me directly about my politics but was not fazed when I told her I'm a Democrat. Her sister is, too, she told me, and they get on but don't discuss politics. Her startlingly light eyes flashed as she told me what a great job President Bush was doing. She was one of the people who organized hundreds to come out and protest the Moore film, calling everyone she knew and everyone on her list of McLennan County Republican volunteers, using mass e-mail, alerting the media. She told me that she is well informed and gets her news and views from a diverse range of sources: from Hannity and Colmes to Bill O'Reilly, even though "it's really hard to find conservative sources in the media. You have to really dig for the conservative point of view. I watch Hannity and Colmes. They give both sides. They're balanced. You can flip over to CNN and see what they say, too."

When I suggested to her that the media is dominated by right-wing propaganda, she recoiled from me in astonishment. "I'm just amazed that you could think that," she said.

Our conversation drifted to a discussion of September 11 and her plans for an elaborate McLennan County monument to the victims of the terrorist attacks, to the idea of freedom, and to America's wars. She told me how, on that memorable day, she drove the rural route to her son's school and pulled him out of class, there in the rolling land-scape of central Texas. There was no way of knowing what was going to happen next.

Horton's plans for the monument feature a "liberty tree" and a granite slab commemorating the victims. There will also be slabs for each of the many fire and police departments that responded on that day. And still more slabs, one for each of America's wars since World War I. There will be a Texas flag that was flown over the state Capitol on the 2002 anniversary of the attacks, and an American flag that was flown over the national Capitol. Horton tried to get pieces of the World Trade Center itself, but these were no longer available. She did, however, get a piece of the wreckage from the Pentagon.

It turns out that she did not attend the screening: "I have no idea what happened there. It was their chance to voice their opinions. They have the right to do it. I didn't need to be there. I have my own agenda."

Of all the Republicans I asked about the film and their protests of it, only one had actually seen it. M. A. Taylor, chairman of the McLennan County Republican Party and a former member of the Texas leg-islature, told me he hadn't seen it and probably never would, but that it was important for Republicans to get out and protest. "I think what you saw here was that there were a great many people who were look-ing for an opportunity to get out there and support the president." Many people like Cathy Horton did just that. Like her concern for the symbolic content of a largely imagined polity, there is much power in a shared belief about the world.

At the Crawford Peace House, on the other side of the train tracks from the Coffee Station, the ambience is quite different. I sat on the porch there and spoke with Joshua Collier. For the last four years he'd been living in Ecuador, where he'd gone to study Spanish and women's studies, staying on to teach world history at a private school and to work as a production assistant at the International Women's Dance Festival. He's the resident assistant at the Peace House, which means that he greets visitors and the press and provides a welcoming atmosphere for this lonely outpost of opposition to Bush in Crawford. He's just the sort to play a leading role in a vicious Ann Coulter caricature, but he's smart and focused, articulate, nobody's fool.

Collier insists that the Peace House is not just antiwar but propeace, that they are in the business of providing real alternatives to war. When I pressed him on this, however, the alternative he offered was "creating a more diverse discussion" about the war rather than uncritically accepting the government line as presented in the mainstream media. He told me that the point of bringing *Fahrenheit 9/11* to Crawford was not to promote the film but to promote discussion, to get people to see each other as "people first, and then people who have politics." He walked me out to where the film was shown, in a lovely little tree-ringed field near a swimming hole and a picturesque waterfall, watching me carefully the whole time with a sharp and quizzical eye—never confrontational, never less than friendly. He hadn't quite made up his mind about me.

When I came back the next day, there was an event that might have been right out of 1969, without the anger, drugs, or violence: earnest young people in tie-dye, strumming guitars and proclaiming that "peace is possible"; poems read in honor of the life spirit of the universe; a vegan buffet. Collier gave an intelligent and insightful talk on the rush to war with Iraq, in sharp counterpoint to the surfeit of vague brotherly love. The event as a whole, however, struck me as being exactly as relevant to the real problems of international relations and of war and peace as Cathy Horton's odd mélange of patriotic signifiers.

To its credit, the Jewell 16 multiplex in Waco did eventually show *Fahrenheit 9/11*, even though the management had received hundreds of letters urging it to suppress the film. I'd seen the film in New York, where the audience (I think I'm on safe ground when I say that there were few Republicans present) loved the film, were deeply moved by it, and saw it as a decisive and irrefutable blow against

Bush, so I wanted to see it in Texas. I asked a teenage employee of the cinema who'd seen the film several times what he thought of it. After making me promise to protect his identity ("We're not supposed to say a word about this to the press"), he said, "I think Moore's a brilliant propagandist, but the film is nonsense. He gets Bush totally wrong and twists all the facts." What you take away from the film is what you bring with you.

■　■　■

Waco is an endless landscape of shopping malls and car dealerships amid desolate highways, thrown down without any apparent plan, relieved only by the elegant but very small umbra of Baylor University. It's not surprising that people there would look to their churches for fellowship; there is apparently very little other public space, few other public institutions.

Outside of Waco, the countryside is lovely, with rolls of harvested hay sitting in the fields, gently rolling hills that cradle expanses of ranch. Driving around in this bucolic landscape, looking at the cows as George W. Bush supposedly loves to do, I found it instructive to listen to the radio program of the evangelist James Dobson's Family Research Council. I heard a woman's voice speaking to me in the most dire tones: "A scientific study released recently by the Beverly LaHaye Institute [an arm of the ultraconservative Concerned Women for America] shows that John Kerry's policies are so unfriendly to families that the institution of the family may be entirely unrecognizable after four years of a Kerry administration, if it even exists at all."

I felt as if I'd entered a parallel universe where none of the rules of logic or induction that I know apply. It occurred to me that this is what arguments about *Fahrenheit 9/11* are all about—not whether Michael Moore manipulates the facts, but about the very nature of reality and the rules that we use to assess it. That's why things that didn't matter quite so much in the past—a partisan position, a movie—suddenly matter a great deal more. No less than we do when we debate whether Saddam really had weapons of mass destruction, we're arguing about what is real and what is an illusion.

■　■　■

Fahrenheit 9/11 got noticed. It won awards even before hitting the theaters. Its premiere was a cultural and sociological event. Leonardo DiCaprio was there. Salman Rushdie was there. So were Spike Lee, Tom Brokaw, Lauren Bacall, and Martha Stewart.

Citizens United, a right-wing political organization led by the commentator and Clinton investigator David Bossie, filed a complaint with the Federal Election Commission about the film, claiming that advertisements for it violated federal election laws. Another group, Move America Forward, tried to stop the film from being shown at all, writing to cinema managers and asking them not to show "Michael Moore's horrible anti-American movie." Move America Forward describes itself as a grassroots, nonpartisan organization, but it shares offices with a high-powered Republican consulting firm, Russo Marsh & Rogers. Sal Russo, who has worked with a long string of right-wing Republicans, including Ronald Reagan, George Deukmejian, Jack Kemp, and Orrin Hatch, is its chief strategist. Howard Kaloogian, a former assistant Republican leader in the California State Assembly and a leader of the movement to recall elected Democratic governor Gray Davis and of California's fiscally disastrous Proposition 13 "tax revolt," is a co-chair. Move America Forward endorsed the Swift Boat veterans' anti-Kerry accusations, and engaged in a very aggressive media campaign in support of Bush's nomination of John Bolton to be the U.S. ambassador to the UN These are, of course, decidedly not nonpartisan activities.

In a prerelease screening in May, the film won the Palme d'Or at the Cannes International Film Festival, and the screening was followed by a twenty-minute standing ovation. Moore was somewhat more gracious on this occasion than he was in accepting his Academy Award for *Bowling for Columbine*: "I've almost forgotten to thank my actors! Thank you, George Bush. Thank you, Dick Cheney. And above all, thank you, Donald Rumsfeld for the love scene!"[2] The White House, unsurprisingly, was less happy. George W. Bush's campaign staff referred to the award privately as the "Palme de Bitch Slap," a term that originated with a correspondent on Jon Stewart's *The Daily Show*.[3]

The success of the film was helped by a shrewdly manufactured controversy in the United States. *Fahrenheit's* production had been funded by the Disney Corporation through its subsidiary, Miramax, but when Disney got wind of the film's subject matter and the fact that it used footage from al-Jazeera and al-Arabiya, it refused to distribute it. Michael Moore got a good deal of free publicity from claiming in TV interviews[4] and in the press that this was a last-minute betrayal of an existing agreement, an attempt at political censorship aimed at appeasing Disney's right-wing constituency. Moore's agent Ari Emanuel told the *New York Times* that Disney feared that if it distributed the film, it would lose tax breaks for its ventures in Florida, where Jeb Bush was governor.[5] But Moore hadn't been blindsided by Disney. He'd been told a year before the film was completed that Disney would not distribute it, as he was later forced to admit.[6]

The distribution was eventually handled by Lion's Gate Films and Columbia Tristar Home Entertainment, and everyone involved ended up making a lot of money. Part of the reason there was so much buzz and so much profit, of course, was the ginned-up controversy about censorship. What was it about the film that was too hot for Disney to handle? A lot of people wanted to know.

Fahrenheit 9/11 was proving to be more than a movie; it was a perceptual test, a magnetic pole of ideological attraction or repulsion charged by the brutish certainties and edgy uncertainties of a crucial moment in American politics.

■   ■   ■

Moore is a talented filmmaker. The apparent sloppiness of his work is highly calculated, part of how he gets his audience to trust him. He seems to be taking the viewer aside and marveling at a secret, lifting the curtain on special information that is all around us but that somehow we never knew about. How did Moore get all that film of the Bushes clowning with powerful Saudis, of Bush looking like an idiot whenever he's not primed by his handlers? How did Moore discover those connections between the Bushes and the bin Ladens?

There is some good stuff in *Fahrenheit 9/11*. When Moore leaves his undisciplined commentary behind, the film can be revealing. His most damning material is more personal than factual. There's something profoundly off about Bush shooting a bird and saying, "Somebody say, 'Nice shot!'" getting the praise he asked for, and then saying, with fake modesty pitched to be charming, "Thank you." It reveals a great deal about a man of privilege who never questioned his luck, never doubted his right to the praise of sycophants and hangers-on.

There's that painful moment when Bush gets halfway through a standard adage about "Fool me once . . ." and it's clear from his face that he has no idea how it ends, so he improvises: "Well, you don't get fooled again!" Look at him playing golf, making an announcement condemning terrorism—and, contrary to Moore's detractors, it really doesn't matter whether he's actually talking about al-Qaeda or Hezbollah—and then saying, "Now watch this drive!" without missing a beat. Look at him preparing to make a speech about the nation going to war and fooling around like a six-year-old, profoundly unaware of the seriousness of the moment but no doubt aware that when he goes live, in a few moments, he will have to *appear* that he is aware it is a serious moment. And note how his staff has prepared the moment: it wasn't until I sat through the film three times that I noticed how the family pictures of Laura and the twins on Bush's desk face *outward*, toward the viewer and away from anyone sitting at the desk; even the most personal detail is made to serve the manufactured image.

In the special features section of the DVD, a clip of Bush talking to the press after his "conversation"—not testimony—with the 9/11 Commission is devastatingly revealing of Bush's pathological narcissism, his complete lack of any adult sense of accountability or responsibility.[7] It is in these scenes, when Moore—almost accidentally—peers into the soul of a little boy playing at being president, that the film has real power.

Ultimately, there is some truth here—the truth about Bush—and it is separate, or can be separated from, the means Moore uses to tell it. Other parts of the film are more problematic. There is that long sequence with Lila Lipscomb, the woman from Flint whose son was killed in Iraq. Of course Lipscomb is devastated, as any mother would be. But Moore's presentation of her pain seems highly manipulative and emotional; it's hard to discern the point here. Decent people can agree that wars should be fought only when they are truly necessary, when the consequences of not fighting are worse than the consequences of fighting. Decent people can also agree that when soldiers are killed in war, the effect on their families and loved ones is devastating. That fact belongs in a documentary about the horrors of war. But what exactly does it say about the *necessity* of war? However

tragic any death is, the tragedy of war is a different issue from its justification. It is the particular demagogic genius of *Fahrenheit 9/11* that
it blurs this distinction and suggests that if people die, if their loved
ones feel pain, then war is insupportable. This direct emotional
appeal makes national security issues disappear.

On the DVD of *Fahrenheit 9/11*, there is a feature about the film's
release. A woman interviewed at the National Education Association's
2004 convention says, "I was one of those kids who joined so that they
could get the GI bill and become a teacher. That's what a lot of these
kids did: they joined the army to go to school. And now they're fighting and dying. It's senseless."

The expectation that an army will be used only to deliver education and never to fight wars seems more than a little disingenuous. Of
course, a principled pacifist might demand that the army never fight
wars, in which case the institution might as well be abolished. There
would then be no subsidized military education, which would be
unfortunate. There'd be another unfortunate effect, too: the likes of
Hitler, Stalin, Pol Pot, Mao Tse-tung, and Saddam Hussein would
rule the world.

∎　∎　∎

Louis Menand, in his *New Yorker* piece on Moore,[8] traces the history
of the idea of objectivity in the documentary. He goes back to the film
Nanook of the North, released in 1922, and describes how the filmmaker Robert Flaherty took liberties in that piece with what we
would nowadays call the objective truth of the Inuit way of life. Flaherty had his subjects stage hunts for the camera and reenact obsolete
traditions. Although he thought he was doing ethnography instead of
entertainment—or as well as entertainment—in 1922 no one found
these practices to be a problem.

Menand then discusses Frederick Wiseman. He points out that
Wiseman's classic documentaries *Titicut Follies*, *High School*, *Hospi-
tal*, *Juvenile Court*, and *The Store* are objective in the sense that they
make no explicit commentary, but that Wiseman's editorial choices
give enormous power to a subjective point of view.

In making these historical observations, Menand seems to be suggesting that objectivity is always, and inevitably, open to question in

the documentary, and that Moore's work is a documentary in the same sense that these earlier works were documentaries. But Menand is far too gentle. The problem with Moore's films is not the same kind of problem that Menand identifies in *Nanook* or in Wiseman's work. It is not the question of the legitimacy of a staged but in some sense authentic ritual; it is not the editorial dilemma of what raw footage to run and what footage to cut, and of how these decisions build in a point-of-view bias, a bias that may still be called honest because it is unconscious.

Blatant untruths are indeed hard to find in *Fahrenheit 9/11*; Moore was careful about this. Alan Hayling, who knew him from his work on *The Awful Truth* and *Columbine*, insists that Moore was always anxious to get the facts straight, and also that he had a right to present them in ways favorable to his thesis. He does, however, stress the importance of truth and accuracy in documentary:

> I don't accept the argument that if a documentary is funny, then lesser standards apply; I don't accept that at all. A documentary is a documentary, and it has to be factually accurate. If you look at *Fahrenheit 9/11*, it's a very considerable piece of work. Whether you like it or not politically, that's a different matter, whether you think the arguments are fair or unfair, that's a different matter. In my experience of working with Michael, I have to say that he was always concerned with factual accuracy.

But there is a deeper question about whether it is legitimate, without actually saying anything untrue, to make an editorial point that is not supported by an underlying reality. Suggestion, innuendo, and unwarranted associations can all be used to distort events and motivations without telling any lies. Making judgments about this sort of thing is an area of murky subjectivity, and it is where there are disagreements about the limits of legitimate polemic.

In *Fahrenheit 9/11*, Moore uses his familiar techniques from *Roger & Me* and *Columbine*, but he's so committed to his vision of America as conspiratorial evildoer that he hardly bothers to build a case that will stand up to scrutiny; he just lets fly with the version of events that best suits his worldview. When I saw *Fahrenheit 9/11*, I was amazed at a scene of a Bush speech, in which the president, gazing out over a privileged crowd, says, "This is an impressive crowd of the haves and have mores. Some call you the elite; I call you my base." He's admitting it! He's *boasting* of representing the plutocracy! There was no context, I thought, that could make this right. This scene seems to show the sheer blundering nastiness of Bush.

A short piece in the obscure journal *Catholic New York* provides the context. The event was a fundraiser, but not a political one. It was from the annual Al Smith Dinner, which benefits Catholic medical services in New York State. The dinner is bipartisan and comes with a long tradition that speakers poke fun at themselves and their reputations. This particular dinner took place in October 2000, in the run-up to the presidential election. Al Gore spoke just before Bush, and, parodying himself and incorrect news reports that he had claimed to have "invented the Internet," he said, "The Al Smith Dinner represents a hallowed and important tradition, which I actually did invent." Referring to his oft-repeated plan to put Social Security funds in a "lockbox," he promised to put "Medicare in a walk-in closet."[9]

Although the mood was self-parodic, it is of course true that Bush and the Republicans represent the interests of the rich and not of the poor and the middle classes, and even a casual examination of their record should make this very clear. But Moore's point in showing this moment seems to be that Bush is proud of his ruthlessness, proud of his plutocratic associations and agenda. Indeed, he might be, probably is, but there's a double-wrapped irony in Bush's dinner statement, meant as a joke about how his party is perceived and not about how Bush himself perceives it. To Moore, the *essential* truth of the moment justifies the distortion of the context. Using the clip in this way is not fair, and when Moore does this, he degrades democratic debate.

This out-of-context moment reveals something about Moore's technique and about its impact not only on his audience but also on our culture's evolving ability to evaluate evidence. In fact, it points out something that Moore and Bush have in common. Both men would probably roll their eyes at a conversation that turned to the subject of academic postmodernism, with its radically leveling thesis that all interpretations are equally valid, all evidence equally corrupt. This is the territory of "intellekshools," not a group that these carefully scripted public characters, Union Joe and Tex, care for at all. But *Fahrenheit 9/11* and Bush's foreign policy are both deeply postmodernist artifacts. Both insist that there is no truth out there, only a contingent reality defined as whatever serves the preferred political narrative; both use pastiche and abuse context to present a highly massaged "truth" that has earned its scare quotes, and both end up insisting that reality is what the author says it is.

■   ■   ■

In *Fahrenheit 9/11*, Moore suggests that the war in Afghanistan was fought in order to enable the Unocal corporation to build a pipeline through Afghanistan. In fact the project was abandoned in 1998, after feminist groups made clear to Unocal and the Clinton administration that there would be a domestic price to pay for investing in gender-apartheid, Taliban-ruled Afghanistan, and after Unocal executives realized that the security situation in Afghanistan just wasn't workable.[10] The pipeline planned after the fall of the Taliban is entirely different from the one envisioned by Unocal in the 1990s.

Moore says that just five and a half months prior to September 11, Taliban representatives were "welcomed" to the United States by the State Department when in fact their request for diplomatic recognition was rebuffed, although they did meet with State Department officials. In his Web site defense of the facts in this section of the film, Moore quotes a *Los Angeles Times* article describing the Taliban visit. In Moore's own citation, the title of the article is "Overture by Taliban Hits Resistance."[11] Of the two articles quoted in Moore's *The Official Fahrenheit 9/11 Reader* in support of the film's statement, one says that the Taliban representatives "appealed" to the Bush Administration to lift sanctions on Afghanistan,[12] and one says that a Taliban representative was "scheduled to deliver a letter to the Bush administration."[13] Nothing about any administration "welcome." Moore also implies that because Taliban representatives had earlier visited Texas "when George W. Bush was governor," Bush had something to do with their visit, although state governors have no role in foreign policy.

In *The Official Fahrenheit 9/11 Reader*, Moore proves very adept at a skill that Ann Coulter has also mastered: using an abundance of irrelevant or misinterpreted "sources" to suggest to those who don't have much experience with research that his work is grounded in deep and careful scholarship, and to appeal to the paranoid with a dense agglomeration of questionable connections.

Moore presents the Clinton-appointed counterterrorism expert Richard Clarke as a heroic voice of rationality in the Bush administration, because Clarke's urgent recommendations to the Bush administration before September 11 to focus on al-Qaeda were ignored, and because Clarke played down any connection between al-Qaeda and Iraq; and Moore castigates the Bush administration for allowing members of Osama bin Laden's family to leave the United States after September 11, without giving security authorities the chance to thoroughly interview them for any knowledge they might have had about the attacks. Yet nowhere does Moore mention that the decision to allow them to leave *was made by Richard Clarke*, who gave the final authorization for the departing flights.[14]

Moore builds a conspiracy out of the fact that the Bush and bin Laden families both have business ties to the Carlyle Group, without mentioning that the billionaire sponsor of Democratic and progressive campaigns, George Soros, also has such ties. In both cases, so what? Saudis also have extensive investments in Disney, the studio that financed the production of *Fahrenheit 9/11*.[15] By his own logic of guilt by association, Michael Moore is himself a September 11 plotter. And most obviously, if Bush is really doing the bidding of his friends the Saudis, why did we go to war against the wishes of the Saudis in both Afghanistan and Iraq?

Does it make any sense, by the way, that the Iraq war is a war for cheap oil *and* that Bush is paid to please the Saudis? Would the Saudis want us to have cheap oil? And if this were a war for oil, and if the Bush people didn't really care about the tyrannical, dangerous, destabilizing nature of Saddam's regime, there was a much easier way to get the oil. Bush could have just made friends with Saddam and dropped the sanctions, and Saddam would have pumped all the oil he wanted. This is, of course, exactly the cynical strategy pursued by the French and the Russians.

Moore is equally facile throughout the rest of the film. His suggestions that Saddam wasn't that dangerous (to which he seems committed *except* when he is discussing U.S. support for Saddam in the 1980s) are bizarre. It is true that Michael Moore is not the only person on the left who has argued by innuendo[16] that, since the United States once supported Saddam Hussein as a counterweight to the power of Iran, this somehow means that the United States has no moral right to attack its former client, but the argument makes no more sense from Moore than it does from anyone else. Surely, as Christopher Hitchens has observed, a historical alliance with a brutal dictator confers an *obligation* to rectify past mistakes by action against that dictator, not a restriction on doing so.

Moore's visual suggestion that Iraq was a happy place under Saddam's rule—in several minutes during which Moore shows peaceful Iraqis sitting in cafés, flying kites, walking in parks—is deeply offensive and truly callous. Moore's portrayal of Iraq under Saddam includes no mention of rape as a weapon of terror, of the omnipresent web of surveillance, of tongues cut out and victims disemboweled on suspicion of speaking ill of Saddam, of the Thursday hangings in the stench of shit and entrails at Abu Ghraib, of one in six residents of Baghdad having at least one relative who had been killed by Saddam, of one-sixth of the entire people of Iraq having been driven into exile by the brutality of his rule. No mention of the destruction of the land of the southern Marsh Arabs, of the rooms in which Saddam's police would torture children as a means of getting information from their parents.

Moore cuts from the bucolic interlude in Baghdad to an explosion of terrifying intensity, showing the evil unleashed on the innocent Iraqis by the American "shock and awe" campaign. Many of the structures shown are Saddam's palaces and military and police installations. These were the most legitimate targets imaginable, but Moore never tells his audience what is being bombed.

■   ■   ■

Bush has mostly gotten a free pass on his constructions; Moore has not. Dave Kopel, who previously debunked *Columbine*, has done as much as anyone to destroy the flakier propositions in *Fahrenheit 9/11*. His "59 Deceits in *Fahrenheit 9/11*" is an honest and well-crafted piece of criticism, and Kopel goes into great detail about Moore's misstatements, gaps in logic, and deceptive editing techniques. Christopher Hitchens, who has spent some time in Iraq, wrote a devastating attack on both the facts in *Fahrenheit 9/11* and the good faith of its director.[17] In the ongoing argument about reality, no one did a better job of exposing Moore's shattered and inconsistent approach.

Hitchens starts with Moore's various and contradictory positions on the Saudis and moves on to his contention that Saddam Hussein never posed any threat to Americans or to the United States. He then assesses Saddam's crimes against Iraqis and his support for international terrorism. He has many words about the conduct of the war against bin Laden, and his interpretation differs markedly from that of Moore. In the wake of the release of *Fahrenheit 9/11*, there were few writers on the left who were willing to challenge Moore on his facts, and even fewer who challenged him on his intentions. Hitchens did both. His article rendered Moore's moral universe shabby and contingent, and made admiring statements such as those of John Berger—Berger would later call Moore a "people's tribune"—seem utterly bizarre.[18]

As does much of Moore's work, *Fahrenheit 9/11* gave the political right wing much ammunition with which to attack him, liberals, and the left, along with openings to advance the right's own fantastic takes on truth. For those who were so inclined, the fact that Moore could frequently be shown to be wrong was seized upon as evidence that Bush was right.

But many of the hordes of right-wing bloggers who reference Kopel's "59 Deceits" still flunk Logic 101: because something is false, it does not necessarily mean that its opposite is true. Because Moore comes up with a fantastic, simple-minded conspiracy based on connections between the Bushes, the Saudi princes, and the bin Laden family, it does not mean that the real connections between the Bushes and the Saudis are not sinister and that they do not damage U.S. national security. Because Moore plays down the real dangers of militant Islam, it does not mean that there were compelling connections between Iraq and al-Qaeda. Because Moore believes that the war was fought to enrich arms conglomerates, it does not mean that the Bush administration made the case for war honestly. Because Moore is mistaken when he insists that there were no legitimate national security reasons for war with Iraq, it does not mean that Bush is motivated solely by national security considerations, or that he is a competent military leader.

For those viewers who despised both Bush and Moore, it was absolutely maddening that just when Bush was vulnerable to a thousand legitimate attacks, Moore chose to waste the cultural moment, and six million Disney dollars, on overhyped connections and ahistorical polemics that the right could easily refute.

■ ■ ■

The Iraq war is a frustrating and challenging subject. It is enormously important, and the degree to which it lends itself to silly reductionism on both sides of the question is proportionate to this importance. It is hard to find anyone who is able or willing to make an informed and objective critique of *Fahrenheit 9/11* that keeps in mind the genuine interests of the U.S. and Iraqi people, and policies that can realistically be expected to advance those interests.

That's why I was so lucky to find Erik Gustafson. Gustafson is the executive director of the Education for Peace in Iraq Center, EPIC. The name suggests a certain vagueness of the "Kumbaya" school, but EPIC is a hard-headed organization that looks for real solutions and is uncompromising on human rights and democracy. It's quite unusual in that its founders (Gustafson is one) are military veterans as well as human rights activists. EPIC is serious about policy as well as advocacy, and has intense and extensive contacts with Iraqis both in Iraq and in exile. The organization opposed the Iraq war, but it does not advocate an immediate troop withdrawal, understanding that this would be a disaster for the Iraqis, the region, the United States, and the world.

Gustafson is a good example of the kind of skills and experience that EPIC's officers bring to the debate. He enlisted in the army right after high school and served in the 1991 Gulf War with the 864th Engineer Battalion. On his return he studied at the University of Wisconsin at Madison. He was something of a campus radical. But when he came to Washington and began actually doing the hard work of policy analysis, he saw a bigger picture.

When I asked him for his thoughts on *Fahrenheit 9/11*, he responded: "[T]he film was so clumsy and manipulative that I left the theater not wanting to ever be viewed as though I was on the same side as Michael Moore. He totally lost me with that film." Gustafson agreed to watch it again, including all the extra features on the DVD release, and to give me a point-by-point critique. He had a lot to say:

What's missing in the film is a discussion about how awful the Saddam regime was to the Iraqi people, how many people died. In the special features on the DVD where they're going through Baghdad just before the invasion, they're interviewing Iraqis and there's no indication that these interviews are being done in a police state where people aren't free to say what they want to say. That footage particularly bothered me. I can tell you, if you're with a camera crew in Baghdad under Saddam, you have a government minder with you at all times. Period. Do you think people could say what they honestly thought? Knowing that it would go right back to the Mukhabarat [the Iraqi secret police], and the consequences of that?

Those scenes of Iraqi civilians who've been killed. These are horrifying scenes. But you don't know exactly what happened. In some of the scenes, like with the soldiers talking about how they'd called in napalm and families and children had been killed, that was a clear example of a mistake where civilians were killed. In the extra features, it talks about what was known as the "leadership bombings," and how with fifty "high-value targets," not a single Iraqi official was killed, and an unknown number of civilians were killed. Those kind of criticisms are quite valid, and there's a great Human Rights Watch report that goes into it, points out that the leadership bombings were a complete failure. When U.S. forces, the Marines, and the infantry were going into Baghdad, there were a lot of incidents in which civilians were killed. But over the years, because of the kind of work that our organization does, I've seen so many cases where we can't tell whether it was mortar fire from Republican Guards—or now from the insurgency—or from the firepower of U.S. and Coalition forces. A lot of times, especially fighting against the Mahdi Army in Najaf, the Mahdi Army was raining mortar all over the place and a number of civilians were killed because of this. In the movie, it is implied that things happened in a certain way, but you never know exactly what happened. So there's some footage that I don't exactly trust.

In the special features section, I thought it was pretty powerful when Corporal Abdul Henderson talks about the convoy that was fired on, about the soldiers having to order in the air strike, which is totally understandable. But Michael Moore doesn't really explore that. He just asks the question "Did people die?" Which is *so* annoying. Hmmm, let's see, they were firing on us, and we knew what their positions were, and we called in an air strike . . . well, what do you think, Michael? Of course people died. This is a challenge for anyone who goes through combat, having to live with the fact that you killed people. But Moore just asks leading questions: "You didn't feel like you were defending your country when you called in the air strike?" He's asking that as a question. Why don't you just put the words in the corporal's mouth, Michael? The corporal answers, "Killing poor people in a Third World country," which sounds a lot like Muhammad Ali about Vietnam. And that definitely is what Moore is trying to get across, I think.

It's easy for Moore to editorialize without giving the context of the situation, and he does this continually throughout the film and the special features on the DVD. There's nothing wrong with having a point of view, but Moore's point of view was based on no particular reliable information, and this was something that people like Gustafson—and others with political views quite different from either Moore's or Gustafson's—would come to notice. For example, in Moore's interview Corporal Henderson talks about securing the oil fields, which of course was an important part of the mission. Moore asks, "You were there to protect the oil fields for American companies?" This is one way of presenting the mission, but it doesn't gain any particular validity from Moore putting the question like this or from Henderson's agreement. Oil, after all, is a resource that is essential to the health of the world's economy. And to the health of Iraq's economy, and essential to any incoming elected Iraqi government, which will need resources to rebuild. It would have been grossly irresponsible—even more irresponsible than their actual behavior in failing to prevent looting in the aftermath of the invasion, which was bad enough—had the occupying forces failed to protect this resource on behalf of the Iraqi people. What would Moore have liked to see them do? If the oil fields had been looted, he'd no doubt be criticizing the occupiers for their carelessness with the patrimony of the Iraqi people.

There are real and serious questions about the aftermath of the Iraq war, but they're mostly questions that Moore ignores. Will U.S. policy be good enough to allow for the establishment of a permanent government in Iraq, a government that's elected and accountable to the people and made up of all the parties of Iraq, that's sustainable, and not dependent on U.S. military force to keep it in power? That would be an accomplishment that would allow the United States and its allies to leave with pride and security. But if that happened, the Iraq war would have been a success, and therefore it's a scenario that doesn't interest Moore, since, as he's made clear in *Fahrenheit* and many of his writings on the subject, he believes two things: the war was unjustified, and no success can or should come from an unjustified war. But there would be consequences of a failed war in Iraq.

Erik Gustafson puts it like this:

The idea that if the U.S. pulls out, somehow Iraqis sort it out for themselves, and then there's a stable peace—that's the most preposterous thing I can think of. If the U.S. exits Iraq before Iraqis are able to provide for their own security and governance, then the country's transition to a sustainable new political order would abruptly end. That would likely lead to a full-fledged civil war. And an Iraq civil war would quickly become a regional war, drawing in Iran, Saudi Arabia, Turkey, Syria, and Jordan. The results would be catastrophic for the region, international security, and the world economy. That's the irony behind the position of those who claim that they want the U.S. to leave because that would be better for Iraqis. In fact, we would be abandoning Iraqis to a hell that we helped create.

At the end of the film, looking through the credits, I didn't see one single Iraq expert or organization that I recognized. Not one. You've got all these special credits, these

links to more information. I paused it and I was looking
through the names: not one person. 9/11 Families for Peaceful Tomorrows, Military Families Speak Out—those are
activist organizations, they're not policy organizations, they're
not authorities on Iraq. I correspond with folks in 9/11 Families, I like a number of them, very committed, amazing people. But they don't know Iraq. And they call me when they
need to understand Iraq. If there had been any consulting
done with authorities on Iraq who would have talked about
what's required now, complicated the picture at all, they
would have ended up on the cutting room floor. And clearly,
he didn't even attempt to talk to any of us.

■   ■   ■

Not all of Moore's contributions to the war debate can be easily dismissed. In 2004, he edited a book of collected letters from American
soldiers, those serving abroad and veterans of previous wars who have
doubts about our present deployments. *Will They Ever Trust Us
Again? Letters from the War Zone* is an interesting and, in many ways,
important book. It is a necessary corrective to the work of right-wing
radio hosts like Melanie Morgan, who recently organized a trip to
Iraq to find her preconceived "truth" about the war that the "Mainstream Media" (the right-wingers dismiss it as the "MSM") weren't
telling; of course, Morgan and her colleagues found, and reported,
exactly what they were looking for, which is not so much evidence of
bad faith as of the blindness of ideology.

   In giving voice to the soldiers who aren't so happy with the war or
with George W. Bush, Moore can also be said to have found what he
was looking for, but he's perfectly right to point out that the MSM was
telling a false story about gung-ho soldiers even though there was better information out there, and that it's a disgrace that bringing this
truth to light was left to the efforts of entrepreneurial individuals with
a political agenda, such as himself. Beyond making clear that the
right-wing, politically correct view of solid grassroots military support
for the war is a hoax, the soldiers' letters offer a fascinating window
into the conduct of the war and the reconstruction: the incompetence, the corruption, the lack of interest in the political, cultural, and

historical truths of Iraqi society, the Republican cronyism, the Bush administration's indifference to the safety and well-being of the troops. In bringing these things to light, the soldiers—and Moore himself—have done their country a service.

Yet the book is not quite the call to resistance that Moore seems to have hoped it would be. Reading it, one recognizes the legitimacy of what the troops are saying, and respects the political risks that they are taking in doing so, without forgetting that griping and subversion are age-old aspects of military life, integral parts of the soldier's culture in every war in history. It is fascinating—and in this context, strangely edifying—to read that the number one request for nonfiction books made by American soldiers serving in Iraq is for the books of Michael Moore, and that hundreds of bootleg copies of *Fahrenheit 9/11* have been acquired and viewed on U.S. military bases in Iraq.

But in presenting only the ideologically simpatico letters, Moore is urging the reader to draw a conclusion that is not necessarily warranted: that there is widespread disgust and dissatisfaction with the Bush administration among soldiers in Iraq and Afghanistan. Although Moore does get e-mails from troops who think this way, he undoubtedly also gets e-mails from soldiers who call him a traitor, an America-hater, a communist, a fat slob, and much worse—quite possibly many more of these letters than the ones calling him an American hero. It's understandable, and not illegitimate, that Moore chose not to publish any of these hostile letters or to give any statistics on relative proportions of fan mail versus hate mail. But these statistics would be relevant to the truth of his thesis. So would the fact that in 2004 a significant majority of the military vote went Republican. Maybe not as high a percentage as in previous elections. But still.

Michael Moore and Melanie Morgan should both take in a screening of Garrett Scott and Ian Olds's stunning documentary about soldiers of the 82nd Airborne in Iraq just prior to the April 2004 assault on Falluja, *Occupation: Dreamland*. To watch this tough, intelligent, utterly nonideological film is to understand that American soldiers are profoundly affected by their experiences in Iraq, that they have a wide diversity of views on that experience, and that ideological grandstanding on their suffering and sacrifice, from any political point of view, is both irrelevant and in terribly poor taste.

The film follows the soldiers on patrol in Falluja and in their barracks nearby. These guys are very smart, very aware of their situation, very competent and professional. They're nobody's fools, and they don't buy any ideology at face value. Some of them believe in the mission, some don't. They want to win the war, but they have no illusions at all about what it will take, and no illusions about their own military and political bosses. Some like Bush, some hate him. When one soldier starts bitching about him, his sergeant, Chris Corcione—a former metal rock bassist who joined the army to get some structure, and has clearly learned well—tells him flatly that "you don't talk like that on camera." Corcione is not expressing a political opinion; he is making a profound point about how certain First Amendment rights are, explicitly and for very good reasons, forfeited in the military workplace. And it's very true and wise, without giving a damn thing to right-wing ideological nonsense, right-wing political correctness, or the political manufacture of "heroes."

Corcione and his men *are* heroes, in their own quiet way, but it's not for any of the reasons the Bush people would like to call them that. Although they won't all express themselves publicly, they reserve the right to have unpredictable and nuanced opinions, something that most definitely does not fit into the plans of the Melanie Morgans and Michael Moores back home.

What would these soldiers think of Michael Moore and his redacted version of military life and opinions? What would they think of *National Review* editor Rich Lowry purveying the hilarious claim that the inhabitants of Falluja left out cookies for the American soldiers assaulting their homes in November 2004, and invited them to sleep in their abandoned beds, in gratitude for freeing them from the terrorists?[19] (What absurdity would it take to give Lowry, so innocent in the ways of the world, a sense of cognitive dissonance? Those allegedly cookie-leaving Fallujans recently voted down the U.S.-sponsored constitution by a margin of 80 percent.) To see *Occupation: Dreamland* and then to read Lowry's nonsense or hear Melanie Morgan on TV is to appreciate just how far from reality some on the right, as well as some on the left, have drifted over this war.

8

NEW YORK 2004:
AMONG THE REPUBLICANS

I n the wake of the success of *Fahrenheit 9/11*, Moore had a national platform as the 2004 elections approached. He was just where he wanted to be.

He was even at the Republican National Convention, courtesy of the newspaper *USA Today*, which thought it would be cute to hire him to write a daily column on the goings-on there. They also hired right-winger Jonah Goldberg of the *National Review* to cover the Democratic Convention in Boston.

Actually, *USA Today* hired Ann Coulter first, but she proved a bit too much for them. Her first column opened, "Here at the Spawn of Satan Convention in Boston," and spiraled downward from there. She didn't much care for those "corn-fed, no-make-up, natural fiber, no-bra-needing, sandal-wearing, hirsute, somewhat fragrant hippie-chick pie wagons they call 'women' at the Democratic National Convention."[1] *USA Today* was in the market for political trash talk, not nastiness for its own sake, so they took a pass. Goldberg was hired to replace Coulter and wrote boring, predictable, and empty pieces about how boring, predictable, and empty the convention was. He was mostly right about this, though, and he didn't get too personal.

Goldberg and Coulter have a bit of a history, and this history instructs about the standards of right-wing journalism, the charged atmosphere of post–September 11 political commentary, and the level of seriousness of what *USA Today* was trying to accomplish in hiring Moore and Coulter, then Goldberg.

Before September 11, Goldberg and Coulter were both featured columnists at William F. Buckley's *National Review*, where Goldberg was also an editor. Coulter's provocative, far-right rants had attracted attention since long before September 11. Her friend Barbara Olson died on American Airlines flight 77, the hijacked plane that was flown into the Pentagon. Like Coulter, Olson was a telegenic political commentator and the author of numerous hate pieces aimed at the Clintons. Two days after the attacks, Coulter wrote a piece in the *National Review* that started as a tribute to Olson ("she was really nice") and to Olson's relationship with her husband, Ted, who'd helped to make Bush president after the 2000 election by arguing the Republican side of *Bush v. Gore* before the Supreme Court and was rewarded for his legal thuggery with the office of solicitor general of the United States.

Then Coulter famously had this to say:

> This is no time to be precious about locating the exact individuals directly involved in this particular terrorist attack. Those responsible include anyone anywhere in the world who smiled in response to the annihilation of patriots like Barbara Olson. . . . We should invade their countries, kill their leaders and convert them to Christianity. We weren't punctilious about locating and punishing only Hitler and his top officers. We carpet-bombed German cities; we killed civilians. That's war. And this is war.[2]

National Review ran this, but Coulter followed up with a column that helpfully suggested, "Congress could pass a law tomorrow requiring that all aliens from Arabic countries leave. . . . We should require passports to fly domestically. Passports can be forged, but they can also be checked with the home country in case of any suspicious-looking swarthy males."[3]

This was a bit much even for the institution presided over by

William F. Buckley's callused old patrician soul, and the column was spiked. Coulter then had a temper tantrum so extreme and unprofessional that a consensus developed at the magazine that she had to go. Goldberg broke the news in a piece in which he tried to blame Coulter's departure not on institutional intolerance of psychotic right-wing raving but on bad writing. Defending Coulter against charges that she hates Muslims, he wrote, "But this was not the point. It was NEVER the point. The problem with Ann's first column was its sloppiness of expression and thought. Ann didn't fail as a person, as all her critics on the left say; she failed as a WRITER, which for us is almost as bad."

Goldberg insisted, correctly, that giving Coulter the boot was not censorship, and lest we miss the point that the *National Review* has no fear of looking like a haven for mentally unbalanced ranters, only of looking like a haven for mentally unbalanced ranters who can't write, he concluded:

In the same 20 days in which Ann says—over and over and over again—that the *National Review* has succumbed to "PC hysteria," we've run pieces celebrating every PC shibboleth and bogeyman. Paul Johnson has criticized Islam as an imperial religion. William F. Buckley himself has called, essentially, for a holy war. Rich Lowry wants to bring back the Shah, and I've written that Western Civilization has every right to wave the giant foam "We're Number 1!" finger as high as it wants.[4]

Ann waded back in and called Jonah, Rich, Bill, and the rest of the crew at the magazine girlie-boys, and that was that. Coulter's and Goldberg's paths crossed again in the summer of 2004, when Goldberg took over Coulter's forfeited Democratic Convention gig with *USA Today*. Goldberg had the virtue—for the purposes of *USA Today*—of being no more of an actual journalist than Coulter or Moore of his post-*Voice* years. He is a young reactionary who writes with a charm and casual sophistication that distracts from the fact that his work is awesomely unoriginal. If there's a right-wing *thème du jour*—the perfidy of the French, the suddenly urgent need to fight the politically correct secularization of Christmas, gay marriage as a destabilizing force in society—he can be counted upon to enter the bray. Goldberg once speculated, with a weird satisfaction, that John Allen Muhammad, the black Muslim "Washington Sniper," would turn out to be gay—something that, although Goldberg never quite says this, would have given the right-wing propagandists a chance to accuse three different disfavored groups at once: a "threefer," as he put it.[5]

Goldberg also happens to be the son of Lucianne Goldberg, the powerful literary agent who played such an important role in the Clinton impeachment. Undoubtedly this has not hurt his career in right-wing circles.

■ ■ ■

Moore was much better behaved at the Republican Convention than anyone expected him to be, at least in print. When he got away from putting the main focus on himself, his articles were remarkably restrained and politically calculated. He wrote about how what Republicans think are Republican values are actually, mostly, American values. He praised George and Laura Bush for having been good parents to their girls. He also wrote a lot of criticism of the war in Iraq and of Bush's economic priorities.

Moore had a good time with the Republicans, possibly a better time than he had at the Democratic Convention. Neither group welcomed him. The Democrats pointedly did not invite him; John Kerry wouldn't come anywhere near him. He slipped in under the rope as a guest of the Congressional Black Caucus, which honored him for pointing out in *Fahrenheit 9/11* that they were the only ones who seemed to care about democracy in the wake of the stolen election of 2000. Moore attended the Democrats' gathering with five bodyguards in tow, and he managed to delight Republicans and fuel their propaganda machine in all sorts of predictable ways when Jimmy Carter inexplicably invited him to sit in his VIP box.

He also had a brief encounter with Paul Farhi, the reporter who had been deposed in Moore's 1986 lawsuit against *Mother Jones*. Farhi noted Moore's effect on the proceedings:

> He was swamped by the press. We see this show coming, we see what he's doing; it's performance art. I introduced myself

and asked if he remembered me. I was a bit surprised that he
did. He didn't seem resentful. He asked me what's going
on; he was pretty nice about it. We followed him the rest of
the evening. It was a great show. The whole point of it was a
distraction from what was going on on the floor. The Republicans were actually pretty polite to him under the circumstances. On the other hand, he had to have a whole phalanx
of security guards and cops around him just because of all the
media. The DVD version of *Fahrenheit 9/11* was coming out
soon. It was a great publicity stunt.

At the Republican Convention, Moore didn't have to please anyone. He must have been very gratified that John McCain referred to
him in his speech, although not by name. McCain got as far as saying
"a disingenuous filmmaker" when he was interrupted by a roar of
boos directed at Moore that went on for a minute and a half and
finally broke into a robotic chorus of "Four more years." McCain,
playing to the crowd, eventually got a chance to repeat "disingenuous
filmmaker" and to add, "who would have us believe, my friends, that
Saddam's Iraq was an oasis of peace, when in fact it was a place of
indescribable cruelty, torture chambers, mass graves, and prisons that
destroyed the lives of the small children inside their walls." As
McCain spoke, Moore was up in the *USA Today* press area, in a
secure bubble.

In one of his columns in *USA Today* on the Republicans, Moore
gives us his take on what happened during this speech. He starts out
with a justified astonishment that McCain is working for Bush, considering that the Bush campaign slimed McCain in a particularly
nasty way when McCain was running against Bush for the Republican
nomination in the 2000 South Carolina primary. McCain had previously won the New Hampshire primary, and Bush desperately
needed to win an important contest to stay in the race. Just at this
point, a shadowy "polling group" began to call up voters in the South
Carolina Republican primary and ask them, "Would you be more or
less likely to vote for John McCain if you knew that he had fathered
an illegitimate child who was black?" McCain and his wife have an
adopted Bangladeshi daughter named Bridget. McCain, who had
been ahead in the polls, lost the primary to George W. Bush, and

Bush never looked back.[6] Now McCain goes around saying that Bush deserves not only our vote but also our admiration.

Moore wrote, "[McCain said] some gibberish about my movie. Everyone then sees me, I start laughing my ball cap off, the crowd goes bananas. . . . Thousands of Republicans turned to me chanting, 'Four more years.' . . . As for McCain, he had to beg the mob to be silent and listen to the rest of his speech. He must have wondered why a party that promises to protect us from terrorists booed my name more loudly than Saddam's or Osama's."[7]

Moore disingenuously avoids McCain's quite reasonable accusation, but he asks a good question. In the video of the convention moment (the cameras go back and forth between Moore and McCain), Moore looks absolutely delighted, glowing with the thrill of public recognition.

Valerie Duty, an alternate from Crawford with the Texas delegation who was in Madison Square Garden every night of the convention, has a different view of what happened between Moore and McCain. "I looked and there were all these people pointing and staring, saying, 'Michael Moore is right there,' and I saw him. There he was, no farther away than that column over there"—she pointed out a column about ten yards away from where we were talking in the lobby of the New York Hilton. "And we decided that McCain wasn't going to have to look at him. We got all these Bush/Cheney signs and held them up high, totally covering his secure little area. So McCain was talking about him but never knew he was there. We didn't want Moore to make that moment about himself."

Valerie is a small woman with dark hair and a charming, slightly shy smile. She runs a Republican-themed gift shop back home in Crawford, selling shirts and mugs and buttons supporting Bush and other Republicans. Her personal Web site features a memorial to "Spot Bush," one of Bush's dogs, recently deceased. She was one of the organizers of the *Fahrenheit 9/11* protests in Crawford, and she stayed and saw the whole thing but was not moved by Moore's arguments, having inoculated herself in advance by reading Dave Kopel's "59 Deceits in Michael Moore's *Fahrenheit 9/11*." She's clearly a kind and decent person, and she clearly believes that George W. Bush is the same, speaking of him in the language of evangelicals; she knows his "heart":

What angered me most about Moore's movie was the idea that Bush was willing to send kids off to war without a second thought, without caring about them. I've seen him in person and I can tell you, that's not how he is at all. He's a caring and thoughtful person, and he would never have just sent our soldiers into harm's way unless there was no other choice for our country. I know it hurts him. I've been with him in church. I've prayed with him. We used to have a politician in Texas who talked like a Christian but it was all for show; he didn't really live it. You can tell the difference. George W. Bush is for real.

Valerie would like to have talked to Moore, to have asked him why he does what he does, why he wanted to present his film in Crawford, and why he didn't show up. When she spotted him at the convention, she handed up her card in his direction and saw that someone gave it to him and that he did not throw it away. She had some hope that he would call her cell phone number. I told her that this was not very likely.

"But he knew it was me. I saw him looking at the card, and then the person who had handed it to him, and then over to me. And he put up his hand like this." Valerie held her right thumb horizontally up by her forehead while extending her index finger straight up.

"What's that mean?" I asked.

"L for 'loser.' Somebody told me. I didn't know."

It is appalling that Moore would insult Valerie Duty, who after all was only trying to engage him in honest debate, and who in some sense could be called working class, just as, in an even more attenuated sense, Moore himself still could be (class is determined by much more than one's bank balance). George W. Bush, however, could in no conceivable sense be called working class. The question of why he has gained the loyalty of Valerie and people like her is a fascinating, complicated, and important one. Moore has never expressed much interest in this question, and this is a great failing of his work.

Valerie and her husband are not rich. She was in New York on her own dime; the political party doesn't pay expenses for delegates. Delegates like her were not much represented among the Republican high-rollers who attended that party in a bank building, where the right-wing radio talk show host Michael Reagan hosted a broadcast surrounded by Wall Street bankers and lawyers, in the course of which Reagan and other right-wing radio talkers lambasted the "elites" for the benefit of the rubes who were back home watching TV on the prairie.[8] Nor were they represented at the party on the yacht. Or the one at Cartier's jewelry shop.

Valerie went into debt to start a business, worked hard, and made a go of it. The Bush tax cuts made a big difference to her and her family, and this is one of many Bush policies she supports. I could have made my standard counterargument: are you really better off with a few thousand dollars in your pocket than you would be with that money in the national treasury, joined by the billions of dollars that others would have paid but didn't because of Bush, with that money spent on projects that benefit us all—schools, roads, law enforcement, hospitals, the military, the environment, medical research, paying off the national debt, and so on and so on? But looking at Valerie's kind, hopeful face, seeing her so glad to be here in New York, even though most New Yorkers emphatically did not welcome her or her party to town, this seemed excessively theoretical. I felt that I was winning on points but that, even so, I would have to concede this round.

■　■　■

I must say that a few days later it became harder to sympathize with Valerie, or any Republican, although I still struggled to see her as a well-meaning, hard-working individual and not as a stand-in for her party. Over the next few days, as the convention dragged on, I had to watch turncoat Democrat Zell Miller and then Dick Cheney make speeches steeped in the most astonishing demagoguery; I had to hear Rudy Giuliani claim that, amid the chaos of September 11, he had turned to Police Commissioner Bernard Kerik and said, "Thank God George W. Bush is our president," going on to say that the United States as a nation "owes" it to the victims of September 11 to keep George W. Bush in the White House.[9] I had to hear about Republicans passing out "Purple Heart Band-Aids" mocking a man who chose to go to Vietnam while cheering for a man who supported the war but used his family connections to get a safe haven in the Texas Air National Guard.

As I watched in disbelief, I imagined myself a part of an emergent community of Americans who, perhaps for the first time, were glad that there was someone like Michael Moore preparing to respond to this. Partisanship in the face of this assault seemed normal and natural. Suddenly, the polarization of American politics began to look inevitable, and therefore not regrettable. I wondered how Valerie reacted. Her online journal of her experiences at the convention is full of glowing praise for everyone she meets, for all the speeches, for all the Republican functionaries. She expresses no doubts whatsoever.

The arrogance of Cheney, the ignorant hysteria of Miller, are the kinds of things Moore loves to attack when he goes on tour in Europe, where he will pander to his audience by describing Americans as the "stupidest people in the world," deaf, blind, and, especially, dumb: deaf to the cries of the world's oppressed; blind to the devastation wrought by the Imperium; dumb about anything outside our own very narrow field of vision. As always, the extremes teach us very little. If *Fahrenheit 9/11* is a debate about reality, Michael Moore and Zell Miller truly need each other, for how could each know that his preferred version is correct without the other—or some stand-in—at work to prove that it is not?

9

FAHRENHEIT VERSUS CELSIUS

M ichael Moore invented his own way of doing populist, tendentious, political film, and his style has become part of popular culture. But nobody owns popular culture, and the Moore attitude has been widely copied. Populist insurgency develops spontaneously and from the bottom up. The growth of amateur political commentary "blogs" (from "weblogs") is a good example of this, and a particularly unfortunate development that has contributed to poisoning the political atmosphere. In the United States, blogs have been very politically influential, particularly, for some reason, on the right. An informal survey gives the strong impression that they are maintained by people who don't know very much about the world and who stridently parrot the party line, often fed back to them in an amplifying feedback loop by the right-wing media. Optimists believe that blogs represent the power of true grass-roots democracy, but they've had a destructive effect in helping to turn politics into partisan entertainment. Blogs have no fact checking, no professional hiring requirements, and no editorial oversight process.

You don't need $10 million to make a film or a political advertise-ment nowadays. Digital and broadband have changed everything.

The sheer availability of information in our society is something quite new. In many ways, this is good; it is good that there was a built-in corrective to the abuses at Abu Ghraib prison, in the form of the cheap digital cameras and the worldwide distribution network to which everyone—including soldiers and civilians in war zones—has access nowadays.[1]

But what are the implications when anyone who can lay hands on some relatively cheap equipment, clip and image archives, and a distribution network—preferably a national theater distribution arrangement, but an Internet server will do—can get public attention for any partisan pastiche? There's no real oversight, no mandatory fact checking in a still mostly free society, and this is as it should be. But it has consequences.

Many on the right have seized on the methods Moore pioneered, and while they might not have made as much money as Moore, the propagandistic documentary slapped together with little regard for the truth has been heartily adopted by conservatives, to great effect. It is a tribute to the format's power that, in the wake of the success of *Fahrenheit 9/11*, there were almost immediately some frenzied efforts to produce a right-wing version of it, and taken together these efforts say a great deal about where American political culture is at present. As the right-wing activist David Bossie put it, "I will credit Michael Moore with [opening] up a new genre in politics. . . . Whether you agree with it or disagree with it, he did make people open their eyes to that. And delivering political messages through that medium is now going to be commonplace."[2]

Bossie was right. One great example is a film titled *Celsius 41.11: The Temperature at Which the Brain Begins to Die*, produced by Bossie's own organization, Citizens United, which exists to attack Democrats while pushing the most childish conservative causes ("Boycott France!"). Citizens United has agitated in defense of the "under God" line in the Pledge of Allegiance taken in American classrooms, for Dick Cheney's "right" to hold secret communications with for-profit energy corporations in setting energy policy, and in support of Texas legislation criminalizing gay sex. During the 2004 election, it also energetically created and disseminated material attacking John Kerry's war record, which it advertised on its Web site, along with anti-Kerry petitions.

Bossie himself is a frequent contributor to the *Washington Times*,[3] which makes no pretense of objectivity in its news stories, much less its editorial pages, and proudly employs convicted right-wing felon Oliver North[4] as a columnist.

Bossie has been a volunteer fireman for fifteen years. His work is highly cognizant of where working people are coming from politically, and although the conservatism of his Virginia firefighting brethren is for me tragically ironic, he does not agree with me that they vote against their own interests. When I visited him at Citizens United's townhouse offices in Washington, he struck me as a likable and very sincere guy who enjoys a good argument, and he kept talking with me long after many right-wingers would have kicked me out of the office. He clearly believes that Bush cares deeply and Reagan cared deeply about democracy and human freedom, that Reagan was a brilliant man, that the Strategic Defense Initiative is a reasonable idea that is technologically achievable, and that low taxes and a private, for-profit health care industry benefit working people. For me the conversation was a bit like stepping into an alternate universe where facts mean the opposite of their manifest meaning, and I'm sure the feeling was mutual.

Bossie used to work for the House committee investigating the Clintons' Whitewater affair, and he is convinced that he discovered great wrongdoing on the part of the Clintons, even though the clearly partisan Special Prosecutor Kenneth Starr, after spending millions of dollars investigating the Clintons, declined to recommend any charges against them relating to Whitewater. Bossie's experience with the investigation gave him an insider cachet that allowed him to write several books attacking Bill Clinton, Al Gore, and John Kerry, accusing them of every sin of corruption, cupidity, stupidity, irresponsibility, and dissoluteness under the sun.

Some of Bossie's stuff is just silly. He has co-authored, with Christopher M. Gray, a lengthy disquisition on why Osama bin Laden and his followers hate the United States that includes amateurish discussions of Islamic theology, the life of Muhammad, the Crusades, and the Muslim fundamentalist synthesist Sayyid Qutb but makes *no mention whatsoever* of the history of European colonialism, of American support for repressive Arab governments and for Israel, of Ronald Reagan's support for and encouragement of Islamic fundamentalists as a way to resist the Soviet Union's invasion of Afghanistan, and of historical European and American attempts to block the development of democracy in the Arab world, all of which built frustrations that fed bin Laden's grim cult.[5] Bossie has written that attempts to look for historical explanations of terrorism in reactions to U.S. policy are an attitude of "blame America first"; he has even gone so far as to write that it was primarily the Iranian people, and not the CIA, who were responsible for the overthrow of the democratically chosen prime minister Muhammad Moussadeq in 1953[6]— a bizarre attempt at freelance history that is not supported by a single reputable Iran scholar, nor, in fact, by the CIA itself.[7]

With the election looming, Bossie produced *Celsius 41.11: The Temperature at Which the Brain Begins to Die*, truly a gem of a propaganda piece. Its writer and producer, Lionel Chetwynd, had done previous work on the highly fictionalized *DC 9/11*, which portrayed Bush as a great and resolute leader in the aftermath of the attacks.

Unsurprisingly, the Republican Party made the trailer for Bossie's film available for free viewing on its Web site, and it got many mentions on Fox. Purporting to be the truth behind Moore's lies, it opens with exploitative clips from September 11 and the most idiotic and unrepresentative statements of antiwar protesters: "With a dictator, there are pros and cons. A dictator that provides universal health care—I *like* that dictator!" Bossie told me that this attitude is typical of those who oppose the war, and he seemed to sincerely believe it.

Several sections of *Celsius* feature "terrorism expert" Mansoor Ijaz speaking at length on the mistakes of Bill Clinton's antiterrorism policies—he even makes the seemingly preposterous claim that Clinton did not read his daily CIA briefings, something Ijaz would hardly be in a position to know about—but the film never mentions that Ijaz is the chairman of Crescent Investment Management, a group that had extensive contacts with the Sudanese government, or that he and Crescent donated very large amounts of money to the Democratic Party and that he may have been expecting to get some Sudanese oil money to invest when U.S. sanctions on that country were lifted. Ijaz must have been disappointed when, instead, Clinton tightened sanctions on Sudan for sponsoring international terrorism. Could it be that he was bitter about this? The film gives us no way of evaluating this possibility, since none of this is disclosed.[8] Although his analysis of the

Clinton administration seems ludicrous, Ijaz is generally quite convincing in his discussion of the goals of al-Qaeda and what is necessary in response.

The film utterly distorts the facts about the election of 2000 and completely misrepresents the scope of the Patriot Act. Speaking on Israel and the Middle East, the right-wing commentators Charles Krauthammer and Michael Medved prove once again that their actual knowledge of these subjects is inversely proportional to the strength of their prejudices. A parade of "experts" from the American Enterprise Institute and other right-wing think tanks tell us about the threat of terrorism, but seem to want to make history meaningful at times and places of their own choosing. Michael Ledeen of AEI proclaims that terrorism directed against the United States probably all started with the Ayatollah Khomeini and the Iranian revolution; in this particular manifestation of the game of he-started-it, it would be inconvenient for Ledeen to acknowledge that the United States overthrew an elected Iranian prime minister and installed Shah Muhammad Reza Pahlavi, who crushed dissent and pushed Iranian politics into the one corner of society he could not control or co-opt: radical Islam.[9] Cause and effect are not really so easy to judge.

For good measure, *Celsius* throws in the usual accusations about how John Kerry would fail to protect the United States while replaying many of George W. Bush's charged statements about the war on terror, some of them merely emotional rhetoric, many of them proven to be untrue. This is topped off with an iconic, highly manipulative sequence of Bush throwing out the first ball at a baseball game, looking just as sincere and American as can be. Say what you will about the right: its partisans understand where Americans are psychologically vulnerable.

Citizens United sent tape-recorded messages in Bossie's own voice to phones across the country saying in part, "It's the answer to *all* the lies in Michael Moore's *Fahrenheit 9/11*, as well as exposing John Kerry's *dismal* record on the war on terror. If you care about defending America, if you don't want the liberals anywhere *near* our national security, if you were as offended as I was by Michael Moore's propaganda, then you need to go see *Celsius 41.11*. Unlike *Fahrenheit 9/11*, we have the *truth* on our side." These messages even went to telephones in California, where Bossie knew, or should have known, perfectly well that Bush was not going to win; he just wanted to get up liberals' noses with his movie.

■ ■ ■

While *Celsius*, in its concern with propaganda at the expense of truth, has a great deal in common with *Fahrenheit*, the Moore-debunking vehicle *FahrenHYPE 9/11: Unraveling the Truth about 9/11 and Michael Moore* is a bit more respectable on the facts, and it is very good at calling Moore out on his grandiose conspiracy theories and on his lack of concern for any truth that doesn't serve his purposes. There are powerful sequences that take apart the war-for-oil idea, the Carlyle conspiracy, and the particular nature of the Bush–Saudi connection. The film is honest enough to point out that the ties between the United States and Saudi Arabia are very seriously not good policy, but it also quite fairly makes the point that these ties do not begin and end with the Bush family. Like *Celsius*, the film misrepresents the 2000 election results in claiming that the recounts and the media-consortium investigation both unambiguously showed that Bush won. Neither of them did that, and this statement avoids the larger issues of fraud that took place before anyone stepped into a voting booth.

FahrenHYPE also rightly castigates Moore for his insistence that terrorism is just a mirage, an irrational fear that Bush uses to consolidate power, with no real policy implications or significant human impact. But it is precisely on the question of terrorism that it crosses a very subtle line into propaganda. This is important at a time when the war on terror, and misrepresentations thereof, are shaping U.S. society. Moore gets the war on terror wrong, but so does *FahrenHYPE*.

The film spends a good deal of time taking sentimental testimony from those who witnessed September 11 or who lost loved ones on that day. In doing this, like many other post–September 11 American cultural artifacts, it elevates the event to an unfathomable evil while conferring on its victims the status of holy suffering—a uniquely American suffering. This is sadly predictable; the idea of extraordinary victimhood has been used again and again in human history as a call to unite under the caller's banner. We see Bush somberly intoning on September 11, "Freedom itself was attacked this morning by a faceless coward. And freedom will be defended."

FahrenHYPE enlists some sketchy characters to make this point. Former Clinton adviser Dick Morris, Bush speechwriter David Frum, and former Democratic mayor of New York Ed Koch weigh in to insist that anyone who questions Bush on strategy does not understand the threat, and they imply that any disagreement with Bush is tantamount to advocating appeasement. So does Steven Emerson, the author of *American Jihad*, whose questionable research has been supported by the right-wing paranoiac Richard Mellon Scaife.[10]

Morris makes the astonishing claim that even if the United States had had advance notice of the attacks of September 11, it would have been legally impossible to stop them without the Patriot Act—and that this was Bill Clinton's fault. Ann Coulter asks, rhetorically, when will she ever hear liberals mention the plight of the Kurds under Saddam? This question can be only ignorant or dishonest, since (if we stretch "liberal" to mean "those who don't agree with the conservative worldview," as Coulter habitually and promiscuously uses the term) the list is long and includes some who support and some who do not support the Iraq war: Christopher Hitchens, Michael Ignatieff, Mark Danner, Todd Gitlin, Paul Berman, and many others. But to make this point is to take Coulter more seriously than she deserves to be taken.

The film keeps returning obsessively to the terrorist threat, even in sections that have nothing to do with al-Qaeda. Zell Miller, the Democrat who spoke such nonsense at the Republican Convention, talks about how he once found a nest of poisonous copperhead snakes in his backyard: "I didn't go before the city council. . . . I didn't call Shirley, my wife. . . . I didn't call any of my neighbors. I just took a hoe and cut their heads off. Now you might call that preemptive action, or unilateral action. But those things were dangerous. They could kill my grandchildren. . . . I had to do something about their safety. And that's kind of how I see this situation right now. We're in a war with a bunch of snakes, a bunch of vipers." Here, again, is the right-wing delusion that terrorism can be fought effectively without any insight into its logic and its roots. Terrorists are not forces of nature, animals following a genetic imperative without thought or understanding. To look at them this way is a tactical and strategic mistake.

Ironically, by dwelling so righteously on the obvious danger, the film almost gives the impression of upholding Moore's thesis: that the fear of terrorism is a ruse by the right, an induced hysteria used to exert political control. *FahrenHYPE* focuses almost entirely on themes of fear and on sentimental presentations of American virtue. Fine, but so what? These things don't help us fight the war on terror.

■　■　■

There's another pro-Bush film that deserves a mention just because, for anyone who is not a hard-core evangelical, it is so very weird. The coyly titled *George W. Bush: Faith in the White House* was released at around the same time as *Fahrenheit 9/11*. It was billed as an antidote to *Fahrenheit 9/11* and was pushed hard at the 2004 Republican National Convention in New York City.

The film is a blatant hagiography of Bush. Not only is he a strong religious believer, it seems, but he's a kind man who wants only to serve and to help others, never asking anything for himself. The man who admitted to trading on his father's name during his presidency,[11] who doles out no-bid contracts to Halliburton and who engaged in insider trading at Harken Energy,[12] the man whose vice president met with many members of the energy industry in order to hear their thoughts on energy policy and environmental regulation and whose administration then fought hard and successfully to keep the meeting notes secret, is supposedly appalled at even the slightest suggestion of corruption in politics or business.

The narrators present what they believe to be inspirational messages about Bush's faith, messages that might almost have been calculated to terrify nonevangelicals. When Bush is shown answering the question "Who is your favorite political philosopher?" with "Christ, because he changed my heart," Christians whose faith suffuses every aspect of their lives might be impressed, but the rest of us are appalled at the possibility that Bush—a politician for much longer than most people think and the son of a sophisticated politician—is using religion as a political tool; or perhaps that he has not read or cannot think of anyone else; or, most frightening of all, that he is completely sincere. The film sets out to prove that Bush's faith is genuine, that faith has always been a necessary part of American political leadership, and that Bush is doing brilliantly *because* of his faith. It also takes for granted that, as Rabbi Daniel Lapin of the American Alliance of Jews and Christians tells us, "There is a struggle going on inside America, and it's a struggle between those who regard Judeo-Christian values as vital to our nation's survival and those who view those values as horrible obstructions to progress. The future of our nation depends upon the outcome of this struggle." As Lapin speaks, the film shows images of marchers with signs calling for safe and legal abortion and ominous music plays. Lest the point be lost, Bush biographer Tom Freiling follows up with "[Bush] has given strength to Christians who are in the middle of fighting a culture war, whether it be the issue of abortion or same-sex marriage."

The film dwells on the story of Bush's former drinking life and his redemption in Christ, a sentimental narrative that has been tremendously helpful to Bush in his political endeavors—and one that he and Karl Rove have exploited shamelessly, if through proxies—because it is the surest mark of sincerity in Christ that he has to offer to his followers. *Faith in the White House* blithely asserts that "a majority of churchgoing Americans believe that George W. Bush is the right man at the right time" and that only Washington, Lincoln, and George W. have had to lead the country during a time of attack on its own territory. Franklin Roosevelt, the father of the New Deal, who rallied the nation in the wake of the attack on Pearl Harbor, is strangely absent from this version of history.[13] The film is also adept at couching its most ridiculous assertions in the form of judicious rhetorical questions: "Is it possible that George W. Bush, by his faith-based example, is leading the nation in a reawakening of the principles on which it was founded?"

The film quotes the deeply religion-averse Christopher Hitchens's view that Moore's work is "an exercise in moral frivolity." Although it is scathing about the "propaganda" of Michael Moore, *Faith in the White House* unabashedly recycles some of the most offensive White House propaganda about Iraq, repeating as if it proves anything Donald Rumsfeld's assertion that "America is not interested in conquest or colonization." It also perpetuates—as many right-wingers have—the canard that Bush's forceful actions in Iraq and Afghanistan brought Muammar Qaddafi of Libya to his senses and were the reason why Qaddafi gave up his nuclear-weapons program. This idea is plausible, and the Iraq war certainly played some role, but Qaddafi's decision was also the result of a firm and longstanding U.S. policy, pursued under Clinton and the first President Bush, of isolating Libya and of Libya's desire—as shown by many actions over the preceding decade—to end its pariah status and return to the world trade system. The film makes no mention of another kind of reaction to the Iraq war: the apparent realization on the part of Iran and North Korea that if a country is named by Bush as a member of the "Axis of Evil," it had better speed up development of a nuclear weapon.

∎   ∎   ∎

Faith in the White House was clearly produced for a very specific audience, and its message was probably not intended or expected to resonate much beyond those who already believe that America is rightfully and properly a Christian nation. If everybody who does not consider Jesus to be his or her personal savior and that of the United States had seen this film before November 2004, it is hard to believe that Bush could possibly have won. This is primarily a film about religious faith, not about acts of governance or war, but there is enough comment on public affairs to hold the film to journalistic standards, and here it fails dismally. When it takes on Michael Moore's contentions, its contempt for him is palpable, but it uses his methods to further its thesis. No right-winger who accepts this abuse of the facts has any right to object to Moore's own idiosyncratic presentation of reality.

∎   ∎   ∎

There is one film about Moore, however, that is interesting on its own terms. Despite its provocative title, Michael Wilson's *Michael Moore Hates America* is less overtly tendentious than the others, and its hook is that it's about America and truth rather than about politics. Wilson doesn't want to destroy Moore; he wants to help him find the long-neglected core of decency in himself that Wilson earnestly believes is there, deep within every American, every human being. It's *Roger & Me* in reverse, as Wilson tries endlessly to track down Moore so that Moore can explain himself, and Moore's dodges look increasingly cynical, hypocritical, and unfair.

Wilson opens with his own biography, a conscious emulation of

Moore's introductions to *Roger & Me* and *Bowling for Columbine*, and just as Moore does, he uses his life story to establish his working-class credentials: his father worked in construction, was laid off when Wilson was young, moved, was laid off again but never gave up hope, never stopped believing in America. Now Wilson has a small daughter of his own: "I was the one responsible for making sure she had a shot at the future she deserved. Michael Moore had told her that she couldn't do it, that she was enslaved by corporations and greedy politicians."

The film is divided into two themes: seeking to show how Moore sets up situations dishonestly, and showing the sunny, optimistic side of Americans and American society that Moore ignores. On the debunking side, Wilson is dogged and comes up with much good stuff discussed earlier in this book, from Charlton Heston to the gun in the bank to Moore's penchant for conspiracy theories. He does a good job of showing Moore's unscrupulousness in the service of his cause. But the heart of the film is the ordinary Americans Wilson interviews, who talk about working hard and fulfilling their dreams and not giving up. Sometimes Wilson seems innocent to the hilarious bathos of what he learns from America. At one point in the film, he is talking to a sandwich-shop owner who has pulled himself up by his bootstraps, when a dissatisfied customer breaks the store's front window. The stoic owner faces it like the brave American he is. He will rebuild! "It's just a bump in the road. I guess that's what separates us from all other countries."

Wilson then goes to Washington and finds an affirmation of the indomitable American spirit in the fact that there are people playing street hockey in the section of Pennsylvania Avenue that was blocked off after the Oklahoma City bombing of 1995. Innocent or not, he knows his audience will eat this stuff up. Wilson is never nasty (although he does briefly indulge in some mild Francophobia) and he walks through the film with a sort of wide-eyed wonder that only a liberal elitist could find irritating.

Wilson quite legitimately makes much of Moore's repeated refusals to give him an interview and borrows a page from Moore's playbook in showing the runaround he gets from Moore's staff, endlessly calling the office, endlessly being told on speakerphone that Moore would certainly give him an interview if he could; it's just that it's impossible right now.[14] In a very Moorian touch, Moore is shown in a media clip explaining that he doesn't like to appear in films other than those he directs; as he speaks, Wilson scrolls a long list of films in which he has done just that.

This should be an existential question for Moore: If he refuses to talk to his critics, how can he continue to self-righteously demand interviews with public figures whom he clearly despises and claim to have shamed them when they refuse? If he won't talk to Michael Wilson and Alan Edelstein, why should Ira Rennert talk to him?

Wilson has some truly wise and good quotes from some unlikely public figures. Penn Jillette, half of the illusionist duo Penn and Teller, says, "When you start thinking that you're so right that you can twist things a little, it's a wonderful warning." The respected documentary filmmaker Albert Maysles says, "The essence of tyranny is the denial of complexity," and "I don't think that you think clearly, or film clearly, when it's hate that motivates you in the making of a film." Asked what he would say to Moore if he could ask him anything, Maysles says, "If you worked more the way I do, to set out to discover things, let the chips fall where they may . . . do you think you'd be unhappy about that?"

The moral crux of the film comes when Wilson interviews the mayor of Moore's hometown, Davison, and misrepresents what he is doing because he is afraid the mayor will clam up if he hears the name Michael Moore. Wilson says he is doing a film about small-town values and the American dream. It's less of a lie than even Wilson knows, because these things exist in the sentimental imagination, which is also whence Wilson's film springs, and they're all mixed up together. But it's still not right, and his cameraman says he will walk off the job if Wilson doesn't get straight. Wilson has a crisis of conscience: he writes to the mayor confessing all and asking to be forgiven. The mayor is disappointed but gives him permission to use the footage as long as he doesn't run down Davison.

Wilson is right: he's a better man for doing the right thing, and the film is a better film because of it. Indeed, it is this sequence that makes the film, and Wilson is sharp enough to know it.

Wilson's final narration unfolds against the background of a small-town parade. His calm, soothing voice intones, "Most of us are looking for that quick fix: 'Take the red pill! Take the blue pill!'—anything to make our problems go away—but that just doesn't exist. If it were that easy, I don't think anyone would appreciate the satisfaction of working hard for what we have and realizing that we solved our problems on our own." Wilson's understanding of the American idiom is masterful and far beyond anything Moore can do. Moore's style may provoke, may win him fans and riches and acclaim and enemies, but Wilson's style is what wins American elections. Neglected among all the optimism and decency is the possibility that Moore's exploitative corporations, greedy bosses, and evil politicians might share the American reality with Wilson's plucky strivers.

■   ■   ■

Wilson's movie has the potential to be a real breakout hit, and with the new fashion for right-wing film festivals he'll have plenty of places to show it. One such event, the Dallas-based Renaissance Film Festival, was set up by Jim and Ellen Hubbard, who seem to have a fairly narrow idea of what appeals or should appeal to the American moviegoing public:

> We were in law school and we took a study break and visited our favorite art-house theater and noticed that *Frida* [a widely respected biography of the radical Mexican artist Frida Kahlo] was playing, and *Bowling for Columbine* . . . was also playing. And we just looked at each other and said, "Where are the films for the rest of us, for real Americans?" So that's how the idea got started, from that time when we realized that we needed to do something about the lack of films that existed for people like us.[15]

The populist appeal is assumed. The identification of anti-Moore beliefs and anti-international cultural tastes with "real Americans" is treated as an obvious fact.

■   ■   ■

Although all of Michael Moore's films and all of the right-wing responses to them contain some kernel of truth, none of them are really concerned with truth; they are about restating and reaffirming a political identity that transcends any mere truth, in the service of

which all is permitted.[16] This is why the right-wing Internet provocateur Matt Drudge can admit to professional respect for *Fahrenheit
9/11*. His acknowledged jealousy over the manipulative power of
Moore's technique is telling:

> I give [Moore's work] major props as a piece of art. I was
> filled with steamy jealousy throughout. . . . It's all about the
> close-up. . . . One reason *American Idol* does so well is the
> close-up; they announce who lost and zoom in to the eyes.
> When I saw [*Fahrenheit 9/11*]—even the opening three min-
> utes of the movie, [when] you see his love of close-up—I
> said, "Aw, he's got it." You put that with a Harvey Weinstein
> campaign ad and you're good to go; Palme d'Or, baby. . . .
> Nixon said history belongs to those who write it. That's what
> it is. You see things through your own prism. I feel what I do
> on the Internet is just one guy's outlook on the world.

The medium is the message, in a way that Marshall McLuhan
only partially comprehended.

This has consequences. Commenting on the phenomenon, R. J.
Cutler, the producer of a 1993 documentary on Bill Clinton's campaign, *The War Room*, remarked:

> What complicates it now is that at this point, if you look at
> Condoleezza Rice on the *Today* show and you take her at her
> word when she says something, it's almost like you're naïve.
> It's your own fault if you're not a sophisticated-enough
> viewer. To that extent, the blurring . . . the distance between
> the word and its meaning has grown very far apart, and that's
> something that television has accelerated dramatically. And,
> of course, that's been exploited by those who are controlling
> the message out of government administrations.[17]

∎ ∎ ∎

This kind of thinking may not disturb commentators at the level of
Rush Limbaugh, whose only mission is to provoke. Rush doesn't
care that he's spawned an entire cottage industry dedicated to

debunking him.[18] But for sincere liberals and progressives (and, it must be said, for sincere conservatives too), it can be a trap. Political work that emphasizes emotional appeal over factual content is dangerous, often most dangerous to those who try to harness it for their own purposes. It did not do liberals any credit, or advance their political standing, when many famous Democrats (including Richard Ben-Veniste, a member of the commission investigating the September 11 attacks; former Clinton adviser Paul Begala; former Clinton aide Representative Rahm Emanuel of Illinois; Terry McAuliffe, the Democratic national chairman at the time; Senator Tom Daschle of South Dakota, the Senate minority leader at the time; and many other Democratic members of Congress) attended the Washington premiere of *Fahrenheit 9/11* and treated the event as an important anti-Bush moment. Perhaps some of their enthusiasm can be explained by their contempt for a president who stole an election and who governs like a schoolyard bully, but this is not really an excuse for accepting a piece of demagoguery as a legitimate political statement. As time went on and the serious flaws in Moore's work began to be widely exposed, the lack of initial criticism on the part of prominent Democrats who saw the film became a common complaint on the right, and a legitimate one.

10

MOORE ABROAD

M ichael Moore is the same phenomenon in Europe that he is in the United States, but different. In the United States there are several kinds of lines drawn, and they're more complicated than pro or con: there is the line between those who see patriotism as defined by support for the president and those—both left and right—who see patriotism in principled dissent; and then there is the line between those who are eager to believe Moore's view of the world and those who oppose Bush but question Moore's evidence and his logic. Call them "right patriots," "dissenting patriots," "conspiros," and "left skeptics" respectively. These categories break down in different ways, and there are overlaps. Some left skeptics are also dissenting patriots who have contempt for both Moore and Bush but who understand the seriousness of the war on terror. The conspiros are Moore's base, the right patriots Bush's.

In Europe it's a bit simpler, and it comes down to the question of whether the United States is a force for good or evil in the world—a way of putting it that already reduces the scope of argument considerably. And Michael Moore is extremely popular in Europe, where the left is less marginalized and where his work has been greeted with less skepticism and analysis than it has in the United States.

Moore's star quality was imported early and caught on in a big way, at least in the United Kingdom. Alan Fountain, professor of television studies and program leader in television production at Middlesex University, knows the medium inside and out: he's worked in all aspects of the film and television industry since the 1970s as director, writer, and producer. In the 1980s he was a commissioning editor with Channel 4, where he specialized in independent film and video. On a trip to the United States, he was invited to see a rough cut of Moore's *Roger & Me*, was impressed, and put up some money for its completion, in effect prebuying it for the channel. Warner Bros.' eventual buyout brought it to U.K. cinemas first. A major release for a leftish documentary in the United Kingdom was extraordinary; *Roger & Me* did very well, and Moore's reputation was solidly launched in Europe. Beyond that, the film opened the door for a resurgence of interest in documentary film, and Moore established a particular style. Fountain told me:

> The success of [Moore's] films has—not single-handedly, but near-single-handedly—turned around the prospects for new mainstream releases of documentaries in Britain and perhaps Europe. It's not unusual now for there to be five or six documentaries going around in the art houses and in mainstream release, and most of them are somewhat politically left. . . . I teach a "history of the documentary" course to young people who are about twenty-one. Moore is one of the few documentary makers they've ever heard of when they start. Many students really like his films. One of the things I ask them to do as part of their assessment is to choose a documentary and write a case study about it, and probably a third of the class has chosen one of his films. Most of these kids haven't heard of indigenous filmmakers like Nick Broomfield; Michael Moore is the name that they all recognize.

Moore has been lambasted by the American right for criticizing the United States abroad in a time of war, but it's not as if the Brits need Moore to educate them about the war in Iraq; the situation itself is highly instructive, and the BBC, unlike the American media, has done a good job of presenting the facts, so there is a political environment in which Moore's presentation will resonate. "The whole situation with the war is another dimension," said Fountain. "There's a very intricate tie-in with American culture, media culture, television culture. The vast majority of the people who live here are very uncritical of the American mass media. There's a minority that are more critical. As the war continues, most of the people are now opposed and see Blair as doing what Bush tells him to do. Moore is seen as someone who is offering a different analysis, a different viewpoint from the official American view."

■   ■   ■

On the Continent, it is different again. The British share a language with Americans, and in the satellite age U.S. media are readily available in the United Kingdom. Consequently, the British have many direct sources for ideas and impressions about American politics and culture. Beyond that, the basically Anglo-Saxon American cultural tradition—modified by a myriad other influences, just as Britain's own culture has been—is familiar and transparent in the United Kingdom. Certainly many Europeans speak at least some English and can read it quite competently, but American broadcasts and American news and culture are not ambient in non-English-speaking societies in the same way that they are in Britain. Consequently, while Michael Moore is perhaps a popular representative of one part of the American political reality in Britain, on the Continent he is more likely to be seen as the single antidote to the Bush administration, a kind of orthodox counterorthodoxy.

There are other elements. Europeans are angry at the international role of the United States and at Bush's apparent preference for unilateral action, and this has given Moore a strong platform. The anger has some complicated roots. The European demographic profile is aging alarmingly, meaning that a shrinking tax base, a growing nonworking population, and extensive social welfare commitments leave little left over from social needs to invest in European militaries (or, as now seems increasingly possible, a European military). Unwilling and increasingly unable to invest in their own military capacities, and weighed down by the baggage of an explicitly colonial past in ways that Americans are not, Europeans have become humiliatingly dependent on and subordinate to U.S. policies in the world arena, and this of course feeds resentment.

With American military subsidies through NATO having largely paid for their welfare states, Europeans are unaccustomed to taking responsibility for security threats (the Yugoslav wars are a good example of this European abdication of responsibility) and many in Europe therefore see the war in Iraq—and even that in Afghanistan—as simply imperial aggression.

It is also true that long-standing ties to much of the developing world dating from the colonial era mean that Europeans often have a better sense than Americans do of what's happening sociologically in their former colonies. It's unlikely that the French, say, would have been so blindsided by the genuine sociological power of Saddam Hussein's hold on Iraq's people; they would have realized that it was based on tribal and ethnic clientelism seen as legitimate by many if not most Iraqis, and would not have just barged in, expecting to be welcomed as liberators.[1] This more subtle knowledge of how the world works can lead to contempt, at best, for the American approach, especially in its most incurious Texan manifestation. It can also lead to deeper suspicions and downright silliness. Thierry Meyssan's *L'Effroyable Imposture* (The Shocking Deception) has been a huge best seller in Europe. Meyssan suggests that the Pentagon was actually hit by a missile transmitting a friendly identifying code, not an airliner, and that elements in the U.S. government plotted other parts of September 11. Three years after its release, this book is still in the top five thousand sellers of the millions of items sold on Amazon France.

Some of Moore's appeal may be less historical or political. I suspect that Europeans are secretly pleased by Moore's personal slovenliness, which allows them to patronize him and, in a certain way, all Americans: "Look, he's an honest American, but a reassuringly ugly American too." It's like the French solemnly anointing Jerry Lewis as the greatest American comedian. It confirms something about the order of the universe. As Christopher Hitchens puts it: "They think Americans are fat, vulgar, greedy, stupid, ambitious and ignorant and so on. And they've taken as their own, as their representative American, someone who actually embodies all of those qualities."[2]

All of this means that many Europeans are primed to respond to an American who apologizes for being such. Moore is the anti-Bush, and he plays up the image of America as a rapacious Imperium inhabited by ignorant, holy-rolling fools whenever he speaks in Europe. An invariable part of his routine before any audience, at home or abroad, is to talk about how little Americans know, how dangerously isolated they are. Eighty-five percent of Americans can't find Iraq on a map. Eleven percent can't find the United States. He likes to face off non-Americans against Americans in his audiences and have them compete in pop quizzes on their respective countries' geography, history, and politics, and he usually finds that the non-American knows more about America than the other way around. Strictly speaking, this is not surprising, since non-Americans have many more practical reasons to study America than Americans have to study other countries, and, due to the dominance of American pop culture, many more opportunities to do so. But the routine does what it is designed to do.

∎   ∎   ∎

Fahrenheit 9/11 opened different political fissures abroad than those it created domestically, and sometimes surprising ones. It brought the debate over American political reality to the whole world.

There was the predictable, uncritical reaction in certain quarters. The novelist John Berger, who wrote that Moore is "a people's tribune," speculated as to whether the film could "change the course of civilization," and, most astonishingly, claimed that it "appeals to people to think for themselves and make connections."[3] But there were less-than-glowing responses, too, even from the left—even from the French, despite that twenty-minute standing ovation at Cannes. The French showed some real objectivity and Gallic intellectual engagement in criticizing the film, and often came to the conclusion that it was less than straightforward. Jean-Luc Douin, writing in *Le Monde*, called it

> effective but simplistic and sometimes demagogic. . . . By its avowed objectives, by its tone, *Fahrenheit 9/11* reveals itself to be a militant film, even a propagandistic film, and this is not necessarily a bad thing, as the films of [Soviet Stalin-era propagandists] Dziga Vertov, Mikhail Kalazatov or Joris Ivens

have shown . . . to affirm [as Cannes jury president Quentin Tarantino did], that *Fahrenheit 9/11* won the Palme for its cinematic qualities is either a sign of incompetence, a pure lie, or a cynical joke. . . . *Fahrenheit 9/11* was crowned for political reasons. It has more in common with *Mad* magazine, the tone of Karl Zero or other investigative films destined for television than what [filmmaking] expects from a documentary creation.

Intelligent criticism grounded in a knowledge of the political history of film was probably more than mainstream American audiences were capable of, and certainly more than they would expect from the stereotypically perfidious French. "*Fahrenheit 9/11* is a new symptom of the way in which the American cinema uses spectacle as an art for the denunciation of axes of evil,"[4] Douin continued. Does the American right object to French snobbery when it is directed evenhandedly against the American left and right in the same sentence?

The French cultural critic Pascal Bruckner had an interesting view on why some French people embrace Moore while many resent him. As Bruckner sees it, Moore allows the French to remember two of their proudest traditions: their early discovery of American talent— Faulkner, Miller, Hemingway, Stein, and many of the jazz greats who couldn't be served a cup of coffee at lunch counters in the America of their times—and their solidarity with the political visionaries of the world. "Moore became our very own dissident, somewhere between Vaclav Havel and Andrei Sakharov, freed from the clutches of a totalitarian administration, protected by the good people of the French hexagon and honored by the Palmes in Cannes," Bruckner wrote. "Through Moore, the French could grab a piece of the good America and use it to exorcise the bad—the predators of Wall Street and Washington, the rich, the super-rich and their lackeys."[5]

Moore's status was a symptom of that most banal and overly remarked-upon French paradox: that of simultaneously loving and hating America. But the French are smarter than that, and while they might have little sense of Moore's place in the American debate, they know how to apply intellectual rigor. Bruckner continued:

The audience felt cheated by the director—under the guise of making them laugh, he had treated them as idiots. It wasn't simply that Moore uses blatant caricatures, dramatically oversimplifies and makes a cheap play for tears; rather, it is because, to draw voters away from Bush, he uses precisely the same weapons as those used by the Republican propaganda machine: disinformation, shortcuts, omissions. . . . This mimicking of conservative propaganda reduces *Fahrenheit 9/11* to a simplistic militant manifesto . . . but people, including French people, do not like to be manipulated like this. The hatred that Bush engenders on this side of the Atlantic alone is not enough to make Moore lovable. The French feel that Moore doesn't teach them anything new and that his arguments are aimed at their gullibility rather than their intelligence. In other words, the French people don't like being treated as though they are American voters.[6]

Fahrenheit 9/11 had pushed a much more worthy anti-Bush film—William Karel's *Le Monde Selon Bush* (The World According to Bush)—out of contention at Cannes. The organizers thought that it would be bad form and would smack of anti-Americanism to have two anti-Bush films up for awards. Karel's film covers much of the same ground as Moore's but without the childish stunts and cheap, paranoid manipulations. Karel put it like this:

Michael Moore has the phenomenal gall to take a position. He's an American, engaged in the campaign on the side of the Democrats. My conception of the documentary is that commentary should not be partisan, but should deal with facts and figures. I would have loved to be able to say that Rumsfeld and Bush are crazy and dangerous, that their unconditional support of [Israeli prime minister Ariel] Sharon is the worst service that one could render to Israel, but I never did that, not in any film of mine. . . . [In my film] there are no devastating revelations but, taken all together, everything adds a bit of force to the argument.[7]

It's very unlikely that Karel's film would ever have made more than $200 million in the United States. It covers much of the same ground as *Fahrenheit 9/11*, yet, lacking Moore's loose associations and hysterical accusations, it is a much more effective indictment of Bush and the people around him. The film is especially terrifying in its documentation of the religious fanaticism of the people at the top. Clearly, Bush believes himself the chosen of God. Without presenting an editorial position, the film successfully suggests that it is ironic, and highly disturbing, that the vital struggle against Islamic fanaticism is presently led by a religious zealot.

■   ■   ■

Back in the United States, the Republicans made much of the fact that the film was popular in the Arab world. Rumor had it that when it played in Beirut, it was the first film since the invention of cell phones for which the Beirutis actually turned theirs off. But even in Lebanon, Moore's methods were suspect. The *Lebanese Daily Star* ran a long piece by Ibish Hussein,[8] head of the Arab American Anti-discrimination Committee, on something that I noticed about the film the first time I saw it: how the exoticized Saudis are portrayed as inherently evil, money-loving, and war-profiteering, an entire nationality tainted by the sins of its plutocratic princes. As a member of a related Semitic people too often similarly rendered in propaganda as dark-eyed, hook-nosed exotics obsessed with money and addicted to conspiracy, this made me uncomfortable. No matter how much the Lebanese dislike Bush and the war in Iraq, they aren't blind to some of the nastier aspects of Moore's American populism and the larger implications that this has for his credibility.

■   ■   ■

Fahrenheit 9/11 had an ambivalent reception in the new European democracies formerly dominated by the Soviet Union, many of them, in one of the most astonishing changes of my lifetime, now NATO members; some of them—Poland, for example—contributors of not-insignificant contingents to the Iraq war. Here, reaction to Moore is, in a different way than in the West, a profound matter of political identity.

Western-style capitalist democracy has been revived quickly in these mostly Catholic countries, far more easily than in the historically Christian Orthodox and Muslim parts of the Soviet empire, because it has cultural and economic roots that predate the Soviet period. During the Cold War, a sentimental sense of the unlimited virtues of the West reigned in this part of the world, but the nations liberated in 1989 have had plenty of opportunities to get over that one-dimensional belief over the past sixteen years, during which time they have seen their job security evaporate, learned to fight for health care and social security, and come to understand the agonizing decisions involved in having to direct their own foreign policies in a world in which they must respond to pressure from both East and West. Many Poles, Czechs, Slovaks, and Hungarians feel the tension in the philosophical differences between, say, an ideological capitalist politician like Czech president Vaclav Klaus—who never had time for social democracy—and his predecessor, Vaclav Havel, the playwright and moral philosopher who led Czechoslovakia's "Velvet Revolution" and who is essentially a democratic progressive shaped by the Western counterculture. Havel was a friend of Frank Zappa and Bill Clinton; Klaus most definitely is not.

The last sixteen years have also seen another kind of political development entirely, led by Central and Eastern European politicians who merely transformed the Soviet style into a new nationalist populism: Slobodan Milošević in Serbia, Vladimir Meciar in Slovakia, Leonid Kuchma in Ukraine, Ion Iliescu in Romania, and Belarus's Aleksandr Lukashenko, a dictator in full Soviet mode. So, in the former Soviet satellite states—some of them in NATO, some of them also in the European Community, and some of them preparing to join these institutions—reaction to Moore and *Fahrenheit 9/11* takes on a different burden. In these countries, it is an argument about the interpretation of the political past, the economic present, and the multilateral future, all at once.

Poland is a particularly interesting case, since it was consistently one of the more restive Soviet satrapies. The Catholic Church was tolerated and influential, and most of Poland's farm-based economy remained in private hands, so it was always a bit of an anomaly in the Soviet Bloc. Its Catholicism meant that it always maintained close cultural ties with the West, and it had a long history of revolt against foreign rulers, going back beyond the Solidarity movement that arose in the 1980s to the Committee for the Defense of Workers (Komitet Obrony Robotników, or KOR) in the 1970s, to the Polska Armia Krajowa, the Polish Home Army that resisted both the Nazis and the Soviets in the 1940s, and even to the nineteenth-century uprisings against Imperial Russian occupation. It was so culturally disposed to be pro-Western that union-busters Margaret Thatcher and Ronald Reagan could afford to ignore the contradictions of an alliance with the union leader Lech Wałęsa, and vice versa.

Of all the former Soviet Bloc countries, Poland is most closely aligned with the policies of George W. Bush, and he has significant Polish popular support. There is the inevitable reaction to this support, too. These feelings unfold with some urgency, because Poland is not neutral in Iraq, and this has consequences that are very clear after Madrid, after London. It is not surprising that Poles take a particular interest in *Fahrenheit 9/11*.

In Warsaw, screenings of the film had an almost festive feeling, as members of the diverse antiwar counterculture took their seats and excitedly encountered each other as family, nodding and chatting in agreement at each new subtitled revelation of an American conspiracy. Web sites for Polish film fans had a more mixed reaction, expressing the national ambivalence about close military ties with the United States. Some comments called it manipulative propaganda, "a shitty product . . . and only a product." Others expressed a more sophisticated postcommunist point of view, a very Western one:

> To use the word "propaganda" in a completely negative sense is just a mistake, a confused way of thinking. Yes, this is a propagandistic film, because the filmmaker is trying to bring the viewer to certain conclusions that he has already reached. But how beautiful, how suggestive, how powerful and passionate this propaganda is! Propaganda films aren't necessarily bad; they are only bad for people of the "old times" who still think in terms of categories from more than 15 years ago. I feel embarrassed when I hear someone say that a film is "hideously propagandistic"; this Polish way of understanding film is just stupid.[9]

The movie did seem to strike a chord. In July 2004, *Fahrenheit 9/11* took in over $110,000 in its opening weekend on twenty-eight screens in Poland, which put it in fourth place nationally.

■　■　■

There is no place in Europe—and therefore no place in the world—where Moore is more popular than Germany. It's easy to speculate about this. Germany was a frontline state of the Cold War and, as such, has had an enormous American military presence for many years, something that never wins the affection of the locals. Germans were appalled at the Vietnam War and felt abused and manipulated when, in the 1980s, Ronald Reagan—with the consent of European leaders—distributed Pershing missiles throughout Western Europe, most of which, due to the logic of the Cold War confrontation, ended up in Germany. Germans are also highly skeptical of American adventurism; in 2002, Gerhard Schroeder's Social Democratic Party won reelection in a very tight race by promising not to send troops to Iraq under any circumstances whatsoever, *even if such action were authorized by the United Nations*.

Germans have their own homegrown version of Thierry Meyssan's theory in Andreas von Bülow's *The CIA and the Eleventh of September*. Unlike Meyssan, however, von Bülow once held a position in his country's government (he is a former minister of technology). There is the complex psychology of a country that was twice conquered and once occupied in large part by American soldiers, but that, due to the nature of these conflicts, cannot allow itself to resent its defeats in the way that most other defeated nations can. Perhaps all of this contributes to the cult of Moore in Germany.

And a cult it is. Over a million copies of *Stupid White Men* were sold in Germany—almost a third of the book's total global sales and far more than the 630,000 copies sold in the United States—and in 2003 it resided simultaneously at both number one and number six on the German best-seller lists, for the German and English editions. Moore's other books also sell enormously well in Germany. Half a million Germans saw *Bowling for Columbine*; a million saw *Fahrenheit 9/11*. His status in Germany has been favorably compared to that of

Jerry Lewis in France,[10] an interesting observation that inadvertently suggests the clownish nature of his popularity.

Moore is even less subtle in German translation, and this seems to reflect some craving on the part of the German market. The English-language title of one of his best-selling books is *Stupid White Men . . . and Other Sorry Excuses for the State of the Union*. It's understand-able that the "State of the Union" part of the title, with its phraseolog-ical formality, might not translate literally into German, but this doesn't quite explain the actual title of the German translation: *Stupid White Men: Settling the Score with America under Bush*.

Moore, speaking in Germany and releasing articles in German translation, never fails to deliver the message that America is a crazy and dangerous place and to urge Germans to reject American social and foreign policy. The following is typical: "[The Bush administra-tion] would not hesitate to destroy anything that got in its way, espe-cially if they are on the way to make more money. And they will punish even old allies if you don't kneel by the side of the road and bow your head as they march by on their way to the next regime change (preferably in a country which has some promising oil fields)." Moore goes on to say that 85 percent of Americans can't find Iraq on a map—as if this is relevant to the debate about the necessity for the Iraq war—and cautions Germans not to give in to right-wing argu-ments against their welfare state: "Don't go the American way when it comes to economics, jobs and services for the poor and immigrants. It is the wrong way."[11]

Dr. Peter Filzmaier is a professor of political science and the head of the department of political communications at the University of Krems, Austria. He has extensively studied U.S. elections and media culture, and has recently co-authored a book on the subject, *American Politics: Elections and Campaigning in the United States* (Manzsche Verlags, 2005). He told me that Moore's reception by German political elites was quite different from that by Germans in general, and that the German and Austrian publics were more inter-ested in his attacks on the U.S. government than in learning about the nuts and bolts of American politics:

Germans and Austrians hold certain shallow stereotypes about the United States, and Moore has appealed to these stereotypes: Americans are deeply conservative, they have appointed themselves as the world's policemen, American politics is corrupt, etc. Moore brought up all of these issues in a very simple and direct way, and this is one reason that his books and movies are so popular in Germany.

In Germany as in the United States, there are those who agree with Moore's conclusions but question his methods. He is a master of "infotainment," combining facts that are sometimes out of context with emotions, with a comedic style of reporting these facts, and this is of course how modern media democracy works. In my opinion there were two winners of September 11: One was George Bush, and the other was Michael Moore.

Filzmaier also pointed out a particular aspect of *Fahrenheit 9/11* that affected German perceptions of the United States, one that Michael Moore probably did not expect or intend:

While there are a lot of good things that Moore has done for U.S.-European relations, the good effects of his work are often undermined by his approach. Of course there are some very interesting aspects of *Fahrenheit 9/11*: the connection between the Bush family and the Texas economy, the Saudi Arabian government, and so on. On the other hand, when he does things like mocking the "Coalition of the Willing"— making fun of the Netherlands, Fiji, many other countries that were in this coalition—it's a kind of racism. In doing so, he destroys his good arguments, the points where he is laying the groundwork for more detailed research into what really happened.

Moore does show that Bush's policies are not the same as the desires of the people of the United States, and that was important for American-European relations; but overall he has a bad influence, because he appeals to emotional views of the "bad Americans." It is a little like what Donald Rumsfeld did with his idea of the "Old" and "New" Europe. He is explaining things in a too-easy way. Things are not that easy.

■   ■   ■

The combination of flattery of Europeans with anger at America does seem to have won Moore many friends in Germany and in much of the rest of the world, and this is an interesting phenomenon in its own right, but when this kind of attitude was picked up at home—and in the age of the Internet and with the help of enthusiastic bloggers, it was, and to a very great extent—it tended to marginalize Moore's domestic appeal. Most Americans, even those who don't like their government, don't like to be called fools by outsiders. The condescension in Moore's own simplistic presentation of the issues is at least as bad as that issuing from the Republican platform, and expressing anger at one's own countrymen is an unorthodox approach on the part of someone who presumably still needs and wants their support. Moore's antics in Europe have handed his domestic opponents a stick to beat him with, a rather irresponsible move for a man who says that he wants to rally the American left as a powerful force.

PART FOUR

THE ROAD AHEAD

11

POPULISM

A chastened Hollywood, perhaps remembering how *Bowling* and *Fahrenheit* had unraveled on inspection, offered Michael Moore no Oscars for the 2004 film year, not even any nominations, although he lobbied hard for the award, went to all the parties, took out full-page ads, and even wore a suit.[1] Hollywood wasn't having it; many of the Academy's voters didn't trust him, and they blamed him for helping George W. Bush win with his *Fahrenheit* foolishness.

But in 2004 *Fahrenheit* won the People's Choice Award for Favorite Film, an award that is determined in an egalitarian, popular fashion: by public voting on the Web page www.pcavote.com. Moore hasn't lost his base.

When I heard him speak near the end of 2004 at a private reception for people in the film industry, an event designed to tout *Fahrenheit 9/11* among potential Academy voters for the Best Picture slot, Moore was in his element, and he perhaps unconsciously revealed his confusion of politics and showbiz. In front of an adoring crowd, a crowd still deeply wounded and angered by Bush's November victory, he climbed some steps at the back of the room and gave a brief summation of where we found ourselves at that point in political time:

Well, we got out of bed on November third. . . .

Here's what happened. Four years ago, Karl Rove said that there were four million evangelicals who didn't vote and that he wanted to turn them out next time—and he did. Here's the good news: seventy million people—poor people, women, African Americans, Hispanics—didn't vote this time. And they don't have seventy million evangelicals.

They won because they had a storyline. It didn't matter that it was fiction. Here's their story: Bush stands at Ground Zero, megaphone in hand, and says, "I hear you. We're going to get the people who did this and no one will ever attack you again." And the people weren't attacked again. What was Kerry's story? Can anyone tell me? His story was, "I'm not Bush." And we still got forty-nine million people out to vote.

Bush has been working on his story line for four years. Crawford? That was Karl Rove's idea; he got him the ranch, the hat, the wardrobe. Americans love the movies; they love movie characters. Republicans understand Hollywood and the Democrats don't. Republicans don't run policy wonks like Gore, Rumsfeld, or Condi; they run movie stars. Americans like to vote for movie stars—Reagan, Arnold, Sonny Bono. We win when we run rock stars—Bill Clinton. Kerry was trying to tell his story in seventeen paragraphs. Doesn't work. You have to tell your story in seventeen seconds. Karl Rove is a master at that.

What's happened in America? What's changed? When I was a kid, we went to the weekly union meeting and we talked to each other about our lives and the issues, and we had a sense of solidarity in that. Nowadays, what do working people have? Where do we get that sense? The mall? What do the Republicans have? Church on Sunday. That's where they get that sense of community and fellowship.

Americans are liberals. They support liberal positions. The latest CNN/Gallup poll shows that 59 percent of Americans are outraged at the possibility of the overturn of *Roe v. Wade*. A majority of Americans want gun control. A majority think the war in Iraq is a bad idea. In fact, the only major areas in which Americans are not liberal are the death penalty and gay people marrying each other.

That's what the Democrats have to understand. The Democrats can win, but not with the watered-down republicanism of the Democratic Leadership Council. Given the choice between real Republicans and fake Republicans, leather or pleather—does anyone remember pleather?—of course people will take the real Republican! Who would choose pleather when they could have real leather? But I note that *Fahrenheit* was nominated for Best Picture in the People's Choice Awards. That's not the Academy; that's not *USA Today* or Fox News. That's where the American people are at.

We need better candidates! Who's our rock star? Well, who wouldn't vote for Tom Hanks? Who wouldn't vote for Paul Newman or Robert Redford? Who wouldn't vote for Melissa Gilbert, the president of the Screen Actors' Guild? Hey, you can't vote against *Little House on the Prairie*!

What about [Senator Barack] Obama? I'm back in Michigan now, full-time, and a guy back at home who probably never used the phrase "African American" in his whole life told me, "I like Obama." Why? "I like his story." His story! It's that kind of narrative that appeals to people.

What we need is a front man who surrounds himself with the right people. When we run a wonk, we lose.

At the question-and-answer session that followed the screening, Moore followed up on the idea that show business trumps policy in a sort of self-referential circle. He did it so well that the crowd hardly noticed when he crossed the line into silliness. Shuffling out on stage, head down, in his trademark jeans and baseball cap, a black sweater draped over his enormous belly, he appeared modest and ill at ease as he took questions, but he soon warmed to his subject and said quite sensible things about why the Democrats lost: "I know James Carville. I called him up before the debates and told him, 'When Bush goes after Kerry for being a flip-flopper, here's what he has to say: "Mr. President, I only had one position on the war, ever. I believed you.

And you betrayed my trust and the trust of the American people.'"
And Kerry just could not do it. He could not go for the kill." Moore's
proposed solution? He again called for the Democrats to nominate
Tom Hanks—but only if his first choice, Oprah Winfrey, was unavailable. He insisted that he was serious.

Moore's analysis of the problems of the Democrats is trenchant,
his solution less so. There is something simultaneously naïve and cynical about his view of American politics as a scene of competing
entertainments, with the implication that Americans will vote for
whoever is most convincing in the role. This cynicism is only slightly
ameliorated by the cold, hard fact that American voters—at least,
those since Reagan and very likely long before—tend to bear out
Moore's estimate of them. It's this gap between governance and
entertainment that gets Americans into so much trouble, and in a dis-
tinctly American way. Reagan enjoyed being a cowboy; he enjoyed
being George Gipp and that guy who lost both his legs to a crazed
surgeon in King's Row. And he undoubtedly enjoyed playing the role
of president of the United States. Bush the elder was a one-termer
because he was a "policy wonk" (a frightful expression) trying to look
like a cowboy, and because, as a policy wonk, he understood that he
had to do the right thing and raise taxes. Clinton was equal parts playboy and wonk, but he caught the collective imagination of the voters
as a playboy, a smart playboy. No one has been better at the cowboy
role than Bush the younger. Did any of these roles really deliver good
governance?

Perhaps the American people should think about that, and think
hard, before putting too much faith in developing their character
actor. Would they really want Tom Hanks as president? Would Tom
Hanks want Tom Hanks as president? He'd have to take a pay cut.
Would he surround himself with the right people? How would the
American people know that they were the right ones? How would
Hanks know? It's a clever tag line—it plays well in seventeen
seconds—but Moore can't quite separate the real business of governance from what politicians have to do to get there, the business of
entertainment. This same confusion, in a slightly different context,
offers Moore a great device for avoiding responsibility. As he once put
it on the CNN show Lou Dobbs Moneyline, "How can there be inac-
curacy in comedy?"[2]

Moore starts out by making a populist argument: Americans are good, decent, hard-working people who want to do the right thing but are kept powerless by the machinations of Republican mandarins like Rove and the Bush family, who find actors to front for them. A populist agitator of a previous age might have cast his lot with a smart, talented, theatrical candidate who understood the broad needs of ordinary people and who wanted to serve them: William Jennings Bryan, say, or in a different way (and very differently from each other) both of the Roosevelts. But Moore wants a front man who can *entertain* the people. He can't see the problem because he inhabits the world of popular culture so completely. Ironically, he *is* a rock star, as anyone who has seen him in front of a sympathetic audience can attest. In person he has a surprising charisma. When he asks the crowd for names of those who might win one for the left, his charisma calls forth the inevitable response: "You!" No, he hangs his head modestly: I'm just a filmmaker. Why would he give up that freedom?

∎   ∎   ∎

Where does Moore's rhetorical style come from? What are the origins of his appeal to the wisdom of the common people?

The language of populist opposition has been a staple of American discourse since at least the days of the American Revolution. It has always depended on the articulation, as Michael Kazin puts it in his book *The Populist Persuasion*, of "four clusters of beliefs: about Americanism, the people, elites and the need for mass movements."[3] In different political ages, the polarity of populism has shifted from the political right to the left and back again, and has often borrowed from the bedrock beliefs of both. In a contradiction that captures much about American political character, populist rhetoric has often insisted on self-reliance and a right to personal success that is limited only by one's individual merits, while condemning excess and the concentration of wealth within a social and economic elite.

In recent times, Republicans have captured populism and used it to advance the interests of the most privileged. It was no accident that the Connecticut senator's son George H. W. Bush ate a lot of pork rinds in public (although he never really seemed to like them, and people noticed). Republicans have made a point of conspicuously enjoying NASCAR stock car racing.[4] The right-wing syndicated columnist George F. Will ostentatiously enjoys the amusements—baseball, jazz—that were devised by a class he has shown every sign of despising to ease the burdens imposed on it by the class for which he advocates.

Republicans, many of whom know better, will even sink so low in their pursuit of populist appeal as to go along with the most regressive currents in American intellectual life.[5] The Republican Party in Kansas and Georgia is at the forefront of efforts to discredit the teaching of evolution in public schools, thereby crippling the professional and intellectual prospects of any students who wish to study science; and George W. Bush himself has said that "the jury is still out"[6] on evolution, which no doubt helps him win the votes of evangelical mass-media entrepreneur James Dobson's millions of followers. As Thomas Frank has described so well in his brilliant book *What's the Matter with Kansas? How Conservatives Won the Heart of America* (Metropolitan Books, 2004), these small tokens of fake solidarity have enabled the privileged people who run and benefit from the Republican Party to convince working-class people to vote Republican and to militantly *demand* that the party cut taxes for their bosses and bust their unions.

Republicans have somehow pushed these measures as *revolts against elitism*, while their leaders have been the most elite individuals and families in the nation: William F. Buckley, the heir to an oil fortune, who in his views, his tastes, and his presentation is the epitome of the privileged blueblood; the aristocratic Bush family, which has been at the intersection of high finance, industry, and politics in the United States for a hundred years; Richard Mellon Scaife, the paranoid billionaire financier of the modern right; Malcolm Forbes Jr., folksily known as Steve—these are the people who benefit from low taxes and reduced government services, and from taxing consumption rather than income, investments, and capital gains, as the Republican Party is now bent on doing. But many Americans, seduced by the manipulation of the romantic ideal of rugged individualism, seem to buy this agenda. It is not surprising that Forbes, a billionaire, might sincerely believe that his proposal for a 17 percent flat tax serves the national interest, and not merely his personal interest, but it is downright amazing that any normal person could agree.

Republicans have worked hard to redefine the extreme right as encompassing "normal" American values. Newt Gingrich, who was soon to be Speaker of the House of Representatives, said in a speech to supporters before the congressional elections of 1994 that his congressional campaign strategy was to portray Democrats as "the enemies of normal Americans";[7] the right-wing MSNBC commentator and former Reagan and George H. W. Bush speechwriter Peggy Noonan described George W. Bush as "normal."

Noonan's description is worth quoting in full for the light it sheds on the bizarre and sentimental world of Republican populist fantasy:

> Bush is the triumph of the seemingly average American man. He's normal. He thinks in a sort of common sense way. He speaks the language of business and sports and politics. You know him. He's not exotic. But if there's a fire on the block he'll run out and help. He'll direct the rig to the right house and count the kids coming out and say, "Where's Sally?" He's responsible. He's not an intellectual. Intellectuals start all the trouble in the world. And then when the fire comes they say, "I warned Joe about that furnace." And, "does Joe have children?" And "I saw a fire once. It spreads like syrup. No, it spreads like explosive syrup. No, it's formidable and yet fleeting." When the fire comes they talk. Bush ain't that guy. Republicans love the guy who ain't that guy.[8]

Political commentary is one thing, but Noonan throughout her career has been the foremost American purveyor of sloppy, sentimental fantasy, and the right-wingers eat it up. As for how "normal" George W. Bush really is, the following conversation (which took place in real life, not in Noonan's head) is perhaps more revealing of his status and outlook. Running for Congress in 1978, Bush remarked to California Republican congressman David Dreier, "I've got the greatest idea of how to raise money for the campaign. Have your mother send a letter to your family's Christmas card list. I just did and I got $350,000!"[9]

Whether or not Republican leaders are anything like "normal" Americans, the erstwhile conservative activist Kevin Phillips understood well, and early, that the battle would be won on "cultural" issues. Back in late 1972, when Nixon had just won a second term in a landslide election, Phillips bemoaned the fact that right-wing victories in 1968, 1970, and 1972 merely repudiated a left seen as violent and un-American but did not signify a national embrace of the right-wing agenda. How to get the people to give a real mandate to the right? "The fulcrum of ideological gain is not adherence to classic conservatism, but rather hostility toward the emerging liberal elite of amorality activists and social-change merchants."[10]

Phillips went on to say that practical matters that hinged on real differences of economic philosophy, such as wage and price controls, were the wrong approach. He recognized, long before Newt Gingrich and Karl Rove, that the appeal to moral righteousness was the way to achieve the right's objectives in the class war.

No matter whose interests the rhetoric actually served, American populism has always emphasized distrust of the high and mighty and faith in the humble striver, a prejudice that perhaps can be traced to the Calvinist influence on the American ideology. As Michael Kazin has noted, the trick consists in being exclusive enough to motivate with a sense of mission while being inclusive enough to have a shot at power. The Populists of the 1890s thought they'd got it right with their appeal to a broad coalition of "producers"—farm workers and laborers—that also included movement radicals such as the various types of Christian socialists and adherents to the temperance and women's suffrage movements. The realities of power seeking in America have usually meant that the rough edges of direct appeal to class or race or industrial sector are eventually filed down, but populist legitimacy still springs from a sacramental reverence for an idealized laborer—the rough, honest producer of the necessities of life—and, by association with this character, from true patriotism, unspoiled by privilege or station.

The politics that flow from this are by no means as predictable as one might think. The self-righteous polemics of Michael Moore and Bill O'Reilly are, in slightly different ways, both descended from those of the self-consciously working-class newspapers of the 1830s, in which Jacksonian editors drew glowing moral lines between hard-working "producers" and sinister elites. The split between modern left and right populism can be traced back, through many twists and turns, to the abandonment of the progressive economic agenda by religious reformers after the success of the broad social coalition that worked for the passage of Prohibition in the late nineteenth and early twentieth centuries; and, before that, to the split between the religious and economic constituencies of the Populists of the 1890s in the wake of that movement's political defeat.

The newfound—for Americans, anyway—reality of terrorism has made it easier for the right to appropriate the language of populism, which thrives on the political use of an external enemy to divert attention from matters closer to home. The patterns are drearily predictable. Michael Kazin, in *The Populist Persuasion*, directs us to Richard Hofstadter. Speaking of the very first fully American populist age, that of Andrew Jackson, Hofstadter wrote: "Class struggles did not flourish in states like Tennessee until the frontier stage was about over. The task of fighting the Indians gave all classes a common bond and produced popular heroes among the upper ranks."[11]

To get a fuller sense of what Moore is up against from the right, take a look at Kazin's description of the contemporary cult of Andrew Jackson, which resonates eerily today:

> Jackson's reputation as an uncompromising foe of the Indians, a man of action who scoffed at negotiations and legal formalities, was of immeasurable aid to his political career, especially in the South and West, where "removal" of the "savages" found overwhelming support. Jackson's journalistic backers . . . praised him as an "untutored genius" who cut to the heart of the Indian problem and solved it swiftly. They contrasted Jackson's candid, blunt approach with the outraged opposition to Cherokee removal voiced by John Quincy Adams and Chief Justice John Marshall, whose university learning and sense of racial guilt allegedly paralyzed their manly faculties.[12]

Populism's dark side comes out in other ways, too. There is a negative, brooding strain of American populism that has never been politically successful in the long run. Given the industrial and labor history of Flint, it is probably no accident that one of the most influential radio personalities of the 1930s, Father Charles Coughlin, found a comfortable broadcast home in Royal Oak, Michigan, half an hour's drive from Michael Moore's hometown. The story of Father Coughlin offers

some very interesting parallels with that of Moore, although these parallels are much more analogous than exact.

For much of his career, Coughlin preached politics in a classic
populist style, condemning the machinations of the world's bankers
and the "money power" that conspired to steal the hard-earned living
of the working man and keep him humiliated and subordinate.
Coughlin's ideas grew out of the Catholic Church's social doctrines
and its responses to the Industrial Age, but were seldom restrained by
them. He shared his Church's hatred of communism and socialism so
that, while he inveighed against the bankers and plutocrats who kept
the working man down by controlling his access to capital, he could
not advocate active redistributionism, and so was forced to a certain
vagueness as to how this situation was to be remedied.

As he made political miscalculations and found himself increasingly marginalized, Coughlin's paranoia grew, and he began to take his
ideas about social justice to sinister conclusions. Starting in the mid-
1930s, his attacks on an international banking elite gradually gave way
to attacks on communists, and then on Jews. Karl Marx was not
merely an ideological foe but a "German Hebrew," and even Alexander Hamilton was a Jew who had founded the federal banking system.
By 1938, Coughlin's newspaper *Social Justice* was excerpting the
famous anti-Semitic hoax "The Protocols of the Elders of Zion."

Coughlin eventually retreated to a form of romantic, reactionary
populism that seems to thrive from time to time in the Catholic
Church: a corporatist social doctrine claiming the lead role for the
Church and its traditions and an insistence that respect for these
things among both workers and employers would usher in a golden
era of justice and godliness and respect for properly constituted
authority, such as that which supposedly reigned under the Church in
the Middle Ages. The abuses of the capitalist class would be punished
and the working man would be taken care of, as long as he honored
the proper relationships between the Church and the larger society.

Think of Mel Gibson's Catholic chauvinism and love for authority
merged with Pat Buchanan's social agenda and populist economics. If
the imagined polity that results seems vaguely familiar, there's a reason for that. It's no surprise that Coughlin expended considerable
political capital in defense of Spanish dictator Francisco Franco's
authoritarian, romantic view of the traditional Spanish social order.

In articulating the potential damage of the right-wing agenda, Michael Moore sometimes draws on the sunny "producerist" populist style and sometimes on the negative, paranoid populism that shares roots with Coughlin. His tendency to romanticize the lives of working-class people—as when he talks about the social solidarity of the union meeting—is an example of the first type and usually works better for him than the second type, which includes his tendency to sketch sinister conspiracies and to talk about how stupid Americans are. When he goes negative, he is a man only his die-hard fans can love; when he is positive, he seems to be straining for a type of banal communication that someone like Michael Wilson, director of the film *Michael Moore Hates America*, has completely mastered.

■ ■ ■

If there is one consistent theme in Moore's work, it is his attempt to reclaim the language of working-class identity and working-class values for the *actual* working class and its interests. That's the reason for the trademark look; that's why Flint and his uncle, who was a founding member of the UAW and took part in the great sit-down strike of 1937, are never far from Moore's political discourse. As his old friend and associate Sam Riddle told me, "It's not like he's some naïve, aw-shucks, working-class bumpkin who's trying to get into politics. This guy was on the debate team in high school; he prepped himself to do everything he's doing now." Unlike George W. Bush's carefully cultivated image as an ordinary guy, this is not entirely disingenuous because, unlike Bush—who has always lived in a bubble of extreme privilege, although he never seems to notice—Moore comes by it honestly.

Todd Gitlin, a former president of Students for a Democratic Society and nowadays a professor of journalism and sociology at Columbia University and a prolific writer on politics and culture, shared some thoughts with me on the populist style and its tendency to veer into demagoguery, and on how this relates to Michael Moore. He put it like this: "Populism is nothing other than a prejudice on behalf of the ostensible common sense of the ordinary person, and the potential for demagoguery is always built into it, since the demagogue is always, almost by definition, the person who mobilizes sentiment that other people can recognize as theirs. . . . The point is to generate a Pavlovian response rather than a reasoned one."

Moore's timing is good. Gitlin puts the Moore phenomenon in perspective:

Today there's a sense of predicament that lends itself to the demagogic pseudo-solution: "They" have it in for "us," whether "they" means the terrorists or the ruling class. . . . Intellectually, there's nothing new about that. What's new is the weird hybrid fact-and-entertainment combo that Moore has worked out for it. Whenever he's in intellectual trouble, he dances away by saying that he's just an entertainer—something Bush can't do, by the way. This way of avoiding taking full responsibility for political engagement no doubt happens somewhere near the threshold of consciousness, although he's clearly intellectually unscrupulous.

Moore branded himself. In our culture, being the outsider can be a brand, a calling card, a badge of recognition. It opens up the tube of cement that can lock the outsider into an entourage. Early new-left iconography featured the gang, an affinity that linked *West Side Story* with the Cuban Revolution with the civil rights movement. At some deep level—although obviously the moralities are very different—it was the idea of a tightly knit band of brothers who were going to explode the world and change everything. . . . The '60s, by elevating youth culture to a standard of value, took Nietzsche away from the intellectuals and elevated the long-haired, grunting, drug-crazed rebel—Jim Morrison, say. The culture turned the "born to be wild" mystique into an affirmation. Then, in the mid-seventies, Moore is in the backwash when this thing reaches the blue-collar Midwest. Deindustrialization, revival of blue-collar militancy, wildcat strikes, farm foreclosures—that was real. It was part of this wild insurgency, the Midwest against the banks. Obviously, it is full of fertile metaphors.

There's a truth here about Moore the cultural outlaw, but it is very far from General Motors, the union meeting, the Boy Scouts, and baseball. Moore's a paradoxical outsider in that a big part of his whole presentation is that he's an ordinary guy who has figured out some things and is loyal to his roots.

To help explain Moore's romantic outsider status, Gitlin directed me to a little-known cultural critic of the 1940s and 1950s, Robert Warshow, who died in 1955 at the age of thirty-seven, and specifically to his essay "The Gangster as Tragic Hero." Warshow, unlike many intellectuals of his time, was deeply interested in popular culture, although at times his interest was rather condescending. Only a half century later, his outlook already seems a bit antique, and his words often serve as a measure of how much American politics have changed. When we hear, "The avowed function of the modern state . . . is not only to regulate social relations but also to determine the quality and the possibilities of human life in general,"[13] we realize that the voice of Warshow—who was an anti-communist, and who was making an observation, not a statement of principles—is coming from very far away indeed.

Likewise, when he writes of the gangster as the individual who must assert his identity and his need, the antisocial hero who seeks total freedom and is doomed to failure by the logic of both film and society, we understand the romantic attraction but not the weight of the observation. In Warshow's time, the trope of the gangster had been absorbed into cinematic convention; in ours, the trope of analysis of the trope of the gangster has been absorbed into intellectual convention. But in Warshow's collection of essays in which "The Gangster" appears, there is one piece that I thought quite relevant to a discussion of Michael Moore: the essay on Julius and Ethel Rosenberg, who came to represent—for Warshow and others—a generation of American communists. In their complete commitment to a worldview that wasn't necessarily supported by the facts (and, especially, to the cultural loyalties that this worldview demanded), they anticipated much of Moore's public style and political orientation.

The Rosenbergs were arrested in 1950 for spying. They were charged with having persuaded Ethel's brother, David Greenglass, who worked in the atomic weapons lab at Los Alamos, to give them classified information on atomic tests and of passing this information to the Soviet Union. The Rosenbergs were sentenced to death and, like Nicola Sacco and Bartolomeo Vanzetti a generation before them, became public martyrs for the American left, many of whose members, as a matter of deep belief about the nature of the world, insisted that they were framed.

But the Rosenbergs actually were guilty. The archive of intercepted and decrypted Soviet spy communications known as the Venona Project, released by the National Security Agency in 1995, refers to their spying. In his memoirs, published posthumously after the fall of the Soviet Union, Nikita Khrushchev seems sure about the Rosenbergs: "I heard from both Stalin and Molotov that the Rosenbergs provided very significant help in accelerating the production of our atomic bomb."[14]

Warshow looks at the Rosenbergs' letters and journals, published as a propagandistic effort to win sympathy for their cause while their death-penalty appeals were under way. He notes how the Rosenbergs claim all sorts of popular and politically acceptable elements of American culture. Yet none of this do they own or understand, and, as Warshow quotes from their journals, their pretentious righteousness becomes pathetic and almost unbearable. Warshow points out what is so false and wrong about their self-conscious affiliation with various American traditions:

> We need not doubt that Julius was strengthened by singing "Kevin Barry" or "United Nations" or that Ethel was cheered by hearing "Ballad for Americans" or, making allowances for her language, that she was "enraptured" by the NBC *Summer Symphony*. It is even possible to imagine that Ethel was actually excited at the "trouncing" administered by the Dodgers to the Giants . . . and that her excitement was related to the Dodgers' "outstanding contribution to the eradication of racial prejudice." We know how easily these responses could have been changed: if "Old Man Tosc" had slighted Paul Robeson, if the Dodgers had fired one of their Negro players, if *Gentleman's Agreement* had been unfavorably reviewed in the *National Guardian*. But the initial responses and their contradictories would have been equally real, and equally unreal.[15]

The Rosenbergs are pathetic because they have committed to a course in which they cannot be themselves. Their whole world is false, dictated by whatever is expedient from the point of view of a determining set of precepts, and they cannot escape this falseness or even know that they are lost. As Warshow notes, they cannot conceive that they are guilty because it is impossible that serving their cause could be a crime; if the world thinks so, the world fails to understand the meaning of crime. The grotesquerie lurking behind this delusion is that what the Rosenbergs were guilty of was helping a foreign power to acquire the means to kill millions of Americans. There is both a tremendous negation of the self involved in their service to the Soviet Union and a pathological egotism.

In their dogged adherence to a particular ideological identity, in their proud appropriation of populist symbols to which they didn't really have a right, the Rosenbergs reminded me, just a little, of Michael Moore. No, I don't think Moore would pass weapons secrets—he's a pacifist, after all, and his attitude toward politics is different and of his time—but he is committed to seeing good and evil in the world in the same one-dimensional way that the Rosenbergs did. He has expressed sympathy and understanding for a group, the "insurgents" in Iraq, that clearly wishes harm to his country and his countrymen. And he doesn't hesitate to use whatever sentimental and cultural hooks are handy to make his points. To understand the game he is playing, you need only think of how Moore castigates Bush for attacking Afghanistan—and then castigates him some more for not being worried enough about the murderous Osama bin Laden. But in fact it's not a game; if you think so, you miss something important about Moore. He believes in his role and his cause, just as the Rosenbergs did, and he completely believes every point he makes at the time he makes it. His arguments lack discipline, but his outlook does not. Orwell would have understood Moore very well.

■   ■   ■

The damage that this sort of split vision can do was described to me by Peter Ross Range, a veteran journalist, former Vietnam correspondent for *Time* magazine, and White House correspondent for *U.S. News & World Report*. He is now the editor of *Blueprint*, the online magazine of the center-right Democratic Leadership Council.[16] On Moore's approach to filmmaking, he said,

That kind of sloppy and tendentious and hilarious attack on
political enemies was not necessarily good for the Democratic Party and not good for the country, even though it was
highly entertaining. The man is a master of certain things—
the comic moment, the tendentious allegation very cleverly
presented. I think *Columbine* is a better movie than *Fahrenheit*, especially if one doesn't have the tools or information to
deconstruct it, and most people don't. Seeing it a second
time, I began to see the games that he was playing, like having the Flint sheriff comment on the welfare-to-work system
as though he knew something about sociology. There are
plenty of experts that one could interview on that subject, but
instead he interviews the sheriff, because the sheriff thinks
it's a bad thing. It's especially powerful and problematic when
this stuff is shown to our friends in Europe, where they really
don't know the details of what's going on here. It has a very
big impact on people who have no way of judging the veracity or proportionality or appropriateness of what he's doing.

Range brings up a problem that he's written about in articles on
Moore,[17] something that might be called paranoid lowbrow political
postmodernism: "What's not fine about *Fahrenheit* is what I would
call the Oliver Stone effect: to distort history and put it out there
among people who are not in a position to judge it, like the young, the
uninformed and the foreign."

The comparison with Stone is an apt one. The director of *JFK*
apparently believes that the CIA, the Mafia, anti-communist Cubans,
and the Military Industrial Complex successfully conspired to kill
Kennedy—and that the CIA, the FBI, the Secret Service, the military, the Dallas Police Department, and President Lyndon Johnson
then covered up the crime. Everyone involved kept their secrets for
forty years. Moore apparently believes that Bush is a hireling of the
Saudis who invaded Iraq for its oil, for the profits of U.S. corporations, and as a distraction from the Saudi relationship. In both cases,
an undisciplined, highly partisan take on history finds its way into the
cultural bloodstream and is embraced by many as fact, with that extra
frisson of a *secret* fact known and accepted only by the truly hip and

aware. In Stone's *JFK*, Joe Pesci, playing alleged conspirator David Ferrie, lets the mask slip in a moment of panic. The good guys and the bad guys are the same guys! It's very disorienting:

> Everybody's flipping sides all the time, it's fun and games, man, fun and games . . . the CIA and the Mafia, working together, trying to whack out the beard, mutual interest, they've been doing it for years, there's more to this than you could dream. Check out something called Mongoose, Operation Mongoose, government, Pentagon stuff. They're in charge, but who the fuck pulls whose chain? Who the fuck knows? Oh what a deadly web we weave when we practice the disease. . . . Who killed Kennedy? It's a mystery wrapped in a riddle inside an enigma! The fucking shooters don't even know, don't you get it?

Moore is far from the first person to become a hero to many by drawing the curtain from a secret world, but credit him with this: he greatly stimulated the production of political fantasy on all sides.

12

TERRORISM

On May 17, 2005, George Galloway testified before the U.S. Senate. Galloway is a British Member of Parliament. He used to be a member of the Labour Party until he was kicked out for vocal support for Saddam Hussein's Iraqi forces, for urging other Arabs to come to Iraq's defense—"Iraq is fighting for all the Arabs. Where are the Arab armies?"[1]—and for appealing to British soldiers in Iraq to disobey orders;[2] he is now, and was at the time of his Senate testimony, an MP with the "Respect" coalition, having won the votes of the heavily Muslim Bethnal Green district in the elections in May 2005.

Galloway was in the United States to refute allegations that he had received special dispensations from Saddam Hussein to profit from Iraqi oil under the corruptly administered oil-for-food program. After vigorously denying the charges, Galloway told the Senate committee—he'd earlier described it as a "lickspittle Republican committee"—that sanctions on Iraq had killed a million people, most of them children; and that the whole Iraqi invasion was a brutal and hopeless endeavor, with no connection whatsoever to the war on terror. His contempt for the senators and the government they represented was more than clear. It dripped from every syllable and was sent across the country and around the world on the radio and in print.

For some in Galloway's left and liberal audience, hearing and reading his words over the next few days was like water in the parched desert of American politics. Finally, someone was treating the reactionary Republican senators with the contempt they deserved; finally someone was calling them to account for their lies, their imperialism, their arrogance and ignorance. Galloway's testimony was carried triumphantly on antiwar Web sites, trumpeted with approval on marginal left-wing radio programs, sent in cascading e-mail chain letters around the world. Naturally, a multitude of news stories about Galloway's heroic stand against the U.S. Senate were posted on Michael Moore's Web site.

Never mind that Galloway's statement on the brutality of the war, like most of those of Noam Chomsky, Naomi Klein, Arundhati Roy, Robert Fisk, John Pilger, and too many others, completely ignores the brutality of Saddam; and the fact that the war, unlike toleration of the status quo under Saddam, offers Iraqis the possibility of an escape from that brutality. Never mind that Galloway's statement about the deaths inflicted by the sanctions has more to do with propagandistic speculation than with humanitarian concern.[3] Even without that, Galloway is a horrible man for any liberal or leftist to embrace as a hero.

Galloway has said, "Falluja is a Guernica, Falluja is a Stalingrad, and Iraq is in flames as a result of the actions of these criminals [the American and British forces]." He has described these forces as "Crusader soldiers."[4] He has said that Fidel Castro is "a hero . . . I don't believe that [Castro] is a dictator. . . . He's the most magnificent human being I've ever met." His office walls are adorned with photos of Tariq Aziz, the former Iraqi prime minister, Che Guevara, Castro, and Yasser Arafat. He has said that "If it comes to the invasion of North Korea, I'll be with North Korea."[5] He has said that "the disappearance of the Soviet Union is the biggest catastrophe of my life."[6] At a debate with Christopher Hitchens in New York on September 14, 2005, I myself heard Galloway make the appalling and ahistorical claim that the Iraqi "insurgents" are the moral equivalent of the Algerian nationalists who fought for their freedom against the French.

And whether or not Galloway accepted Saddam Hussein's illicit oil futures, he has had a peculiarly friendly relationship with Saddam.

Galloway protested Saddam's crimes in the 1980s, when the United Kingdom and the United States were supporting the Iraqi dictator, and has used his early opposition as a defense against charges of supporting Saddam; but ever since the 1991 Gulf War, when Saddam was recast as the enemy of his enemy, Galloway has greatly tempered his criticism. In 1994 Galloway stood before Saddam and said:

> Your Excellency, Mr. President: I greet you, in the name of the many thousands of people in Britain who stood against the tide and opposed the war and aggression against Iraq. . . . I greet you, too, in the name of the Palestinian people. . . . I can honestly tell you that there was not a single person to whom I told I was coming to Iraq and hoping to meet with yourself who did not wish me to convey their heartfelt, fraternal greetings and support. . . . I thought the president would appreciate knowing that even today, three years after the war, I still met families who were calling their newborn sons Saddam. . . . Sir: I salute your courage, your strength, your indefatigability. And I want you to know that we are with you, *hatta al-nasr, hatta al-nasr, hatta al-Quds* [until victory, until victory, until Jerusalem].[7]

I would like to think that all of those people around the world, all of those Americans who excitedly forwarded those e-mail transcripts of Galloway's words, didn't know much about the man and his history. No matter how satisfying it may be for people who don't like George Bush and don't like the modern Republican party to hear them lambasted, Galloway is far more troubling than anyone on the American right. The Galloway phenomenon has something to teach us about Michael Moore. It is instructive. It is a warning.

∎   ∎   ∎

Galloway is an extreme case. Michael Moore has never done anything quite so wicked as to salute Saddam Hussein's courage, strength, and indefatigability. But, as we shall see, Moore is many ways the American Galloway. He has expressed sympathy for the terrorist Iraqi "insurgents." Against the challenge of terrorism, Moore has hedged his commitments with lists of imperialist crimes, just as Galloway does. Galloway and the reaction to his testimony are indicative of a blindness in certain leftist quarters, and it's a blindness that extends to Moore's sins of omission and commission in the public debates on the war on terror.

There is a serious problem—the *most* serious problem—with Moore as spokesman for a vital, popular, and forward-looking left, and this is his failure to grasp the meaning of the war on terror. As a defining issue of the times, this failure deserves some special consideration.

Most liberals and democratic leftists (a category that, by definition, excludes the Fidelistas and those who think that Kim Il Sung was a great visionary leader), like most Americans, understand the absolute necessity of the Afghan war. Within this group, there is a smaller subset of thoughtful democratic leftists who believe, like others who are critical of Bush, that the reasons the American people were given for war in Iraq were bogus, the goals blatant lies, and the means chosen incapable of achieving those goals, even if they had been the real goals. They are appalled at a policy that rejects the Geneva Conventions and endorses torture and "extreme rendition" as tools of interrogation. They are astonished at the deep incompetence of an administration that expected its troops to be greeted as liberators and that was completely uninterested in the culture of Iraq and its sociology of power. They are incredulous that Secretary of Defense Donald Rumsfeld thought he could do an invasion quickly and easily to make a point about modern high-tech warfare, and they are furious that Bush indulged him.

But, having recognized all these things, this group of people on the left also believe that the world is a better place without Saddam. That whether or not he actually had them, Saddam was bent on acquiring weapons of mass destruction as soon as the U.N. sanctions were lifted. That he was an inspiration to terrorists around the world (yes, even Islamic ones—Saddam could play the jihad card when it served his purposes) and that, with Saddam gone, there are now real possibilities for the growth of democracy in the Middle East, as well as very serious risks of an expanding sphere of influence for terrorism and theocracy.

The conceptual problem at the heart of present U.S. foreign policy is that Bush, like a small boy, has used the most shallow, uneducated, self-interested, narcissistic, messianic reasoning to stumble upon the correct answer to certain questions. Perhaps this is the basic reason that many on the left find him so infuriating. It may also be why Bush is both necessary and dangerous. We may yet learn, to our enormous regret, that it is not only the answer to a question that matters. It matters how you get there, and there are thinkers who have arrived at a similar position by a different route.

Many who are not of the American right—Christopher Hitchens, Paul Berman, Michael Tomasky, Michael Ignatieff, Peter Beinart, Jonathan Chait, Kenneth Pollack[8]—many genuine Iraqi democrats such as Barham Salih, Jalal Talabani, and Kanan Makiya, and international leaders like British prime minister Tony Blair have all made serious and legitimate arguments for the war with Iraq. Berman, Ignatieff, and Tomasky in particular have argued the case not only for a liberalism willing and able to defend itself, but to take action against tyranny and in defense of genuine liberal principles abroad; at the same time, they have coherently addressed the differences between truly standing for freedom and human rights and, as Bush does, using those concepts to opportunistically further an ideology of American hegemony.

Although some conservatives say otherwise (Bush adviser Karl Rove said recently, and slanderously, that liberals wanted to "offer therapy and understanding for our attackers,"[9] and Shelby Steele has suggested that "American Taliban" John Walker Lindh was a product of liberalism),[10] most liberals and most Democrats supported the war in Afghanistan. Even on Iraq, there are some leftists and some liberals who see the central dilemma as being not the bromide of how to support the troops without supporting the war, but rather as how to support the war without supporting the president. There are liberals who fully understand the existential threat that terrorism poses to our civilization, and the urgency of killing terrorists, as well as the urgency (and here liberals do differ from many conservatives) of understanding the roots of terror and taking long-term policy measures aimed at destroying these roots. There are liberals who have a serious position on terrorism.

Michael Moore does not seem to be one of these liberals. Most notably in his book *Dude, Where's My Country?* and in *Fahrenheit 9/11*, but also in public speeches and articles and on his Web site,

Moore has been very unserious on terrorism. He has rhetorically compared the terrorism of Oklahoma City bomber Timothy McVeigh with the "terrorism" of companies that lay off workers.[11] He has said that September 11 was an outrage because the victims had not voted for Bush (and, the implication goes, would have been legitimate targets if they had).[12] He has said—scandalously, callously, and ahistorically—"The Iraqis who have risen up against the occupation are not 'insurgents' or 'terrorists' or 'The Enemy.' They are the REVOLUTION, the Minutemen, and their numbers will grow—and they will win." The observation that the chaos and violence of the "insurgency" is the tragic fruit of Saddam's thirty years of brutality, of his destruction of Iraqi civil society, seems to be far beyond Moore's powers.

In the same post, he wrote:

> There is a lot of talk amongst Bush's opponents that we should turn this war over to the United Nations. Why should the other countries of this world, countries who tried to talk us out of this folly, now have to clean up our mess? I oppose the UN or anyone else risking the lives of their citizens to extract us from our debacle. I'm sorry, but the majority of Americans supported this war once it began and, sadly, that majority must now sacrifice their children until enough blood has been let that maybe—just maybe—God and the Iraqi people will forgive us in the end.[13]

So we must ask the Iraqi people to forgive us for toppling Saddam. And if American soldiers die to pay for that sin, that is rough justice. I wonder if Moore ever proposed this idea to Lila Lipscomb, the grieving mother in *Fahrenheit 9/11*, or to Cindy Sheehan, another mother of a slain American soldier whose anti-Bush campaign Moore supports. Sheehan is herself a rather creepy character: she believes that Bush is "the biggest terrorist in the world," that the Iraq war had nothing to do with the war on terrorism, that the United States is in fact itself waging a terror war, and that the American system is "morally repugnant." She has implied that the Bush administration welcomed the attacks of September 11 because they were useful in furthering the neoconservative agenda.[14] She has spoken in support of Lynne

Stewart, a radical attorney who was convicted of helping her client, Sheikh Omar Abdel Rahman, communicate with his terror network. Moore has tried to make a heroine of Sheehan, and has expressed his sympathy for her loss. So is it only those bereaved parents who think the war is justified who should suffer, who deserve to suffer?

There is just no way to make Moore's statement about the deaths of soldiers in Iraq come out less than appalling. Moore may have written it in a moment of passion, which is bad enough. But it has remained on his Web site for more than a year. It's particularly offensive considering that this same Web site, in an ostentatious display of sympathy, has a page titled "How can I help the soldiers?" Apparently Moore doesn't want the soldiers to receive UN help that could save their lives. He does offer advice on how to register as a conscientious objector, however.

Moore was convinced only days after September 11 that there could be no justification for war. He had intended to fly from Los Angeles to New York on that day; blocked by the nationwide no-flight order, he and his wife, Kathleen Glynn, set out to drive across the country. His journal of the trip was posted on his Web site, and even in the aftermath of the attacks, he couldn't find much to like about American politics and culture. Already by September 14 he was blaming blowback and demanding that Bush not respond with war: "How dare you talk about more killing now! Shame! Shame! Shame! Explain your actions in support of the Taliban! Tell us why your father and his partner Mr. Reagan trained Mr. bin Laden in how to be a terrorist!"[15] In the midst of maudlin concern for the victims of the attacks, Moore has no doubt about where the real danger lies: "Coming into Albuquerque, Kathleen is leafing through the Frommer's travel guide for a place to spend the night. She finds what seems like a nice spot near the White Sands national park, but then reads this passage: 'Occasionally the road to the hotel is closed for nearby missile tests.' Yes, welcome to New Mexico, the 'Land of Enchantment,' just one big testing ground brought to you by the originators of every single weapon of mass destruction known to man."[16]

Moore has scorned the idea that the fight against terrorism was any part of the decision to go to war with Iraq: "The motivation for war is simple. The U.S. government started the war with Iraq in order to make it easy for U.S. corporations to do business in other countries.

They intend to use cheap labor in those countries, which will make Americans rich."[17] He has said that the most salient fact about terrorism is that conservatives can use it as a tool to manipulate the American people: "They know that *real* Americans are not into dominating anyone, so they have to sell it to us in fancy packaging—and that package is FEAR. In order to properly scare us, they need a big, bad enemy."[18]

And it certainly did not do Moore's moral standing much good when members of Hezbollah called up the Middle Eastern distributor of *Fahrenheit 9/11* and asked if there was anything they could do to support the film.[19] Nor when, a few weeks before the elections of 2004, a tape of Osama bin Laden surfaced in which the terrorist leader delivered taunts against Bush that seemed to have been lifted right out of *Fahrenheit 9/11*. Osama had Bush in that Florida classroom; he had him listening to "My Pet Goat."[20]

■　■　■

In December 2004, Peter Beinart wrote a long piece in the *New Republic* that will be remembered as one of the seminal articles to come out of the period of the war on terror. Beinart compares the liberal anti-communists of the 1950s with the stalwarts in the war on terror today and points out that the anti-communists were the saviors of liberalism. Those who were willing to see and to speak and to act on the evils of Stalinism gave the liberal agenda power and credibility, and those who were willing to work alongside the Stalinists in American life—if not actually condoning or agreeing with them—were doing the opposite: discrediting and neutralizing liberalism.

Beinart says that the anti-war-on-terror factions today—most notably Moore and MoveOn—are the "softs" of this generation's most important battle, and that they threaten the prospects and credibility of liberalism as a movement:

> Today, most liberals naïvely consider Moore a useful ally, a bomb-thrower against a right wing that deserves to be torched. What they do not understand is that his real casualties are on the decent left. When Moore opposes the war against the Taliban, he casts doubt upon the sincerity of liberals who say they opposed the Iraq war because they wanted

to win in Afghanistan first. When Moore says terrorism should be no greater a national concern than car accidents or pneumonia, he makes it harder for liberals to claim that their belief in civil liberties does not imply a diminished vigilance against al-Qaeda.

Moore is a non-totalitarian, but, like [Henry] Wallace, he is not an anti-totalitarian. And when Democratic National Committee Chairman Terry McAuliffe and Tom Daschle flocked to the Washington premiere of *Fahrenheit 9/11*, and when Moore sat in Jimmy Carter's box at the Democratic Convention, many Americans wondered whether the Democratic Party was anti-totalitarian either.[21]

Beinart's argument has some flaws. The doctrine of anti-communism did not prevent American anti-communist liberals from criticizing the disastrous, crusading excesses of the Cold War when those excesses were not in line with America's best interests or traditions. Clearly, leaving aside the question of the necessity of war, at least much of Bush's *conduct* of the war on terror is not in line with those interests or traditions, and there is nothing wrong with MoveOn pointing this out. And in characterizing the enemy as "totalitarian Islam" and ascribing primarily religious rather than primarily political goals to this enemy, Beinart comes close to endorsing Bush's unhelpful tautology: "They attacked us because they are evil." These points and others have been very ably addressed in responses to Beinart, especially those by John Judis[22] and Eric Alterman.[23]

But Beinart's central point is very real and true, and it should be taken to heart by liberals who want to succeed in American politics and by those who, much more importantly, are not "soft" on fundamentalist terror and who truly believe in a free, open, liberal, socially inflected political and cultural environment. Beinart raises questions that Moore, with his hodgepodge of ill-disciplined, contradictory, and ideological antiwar positions, cannot begin to resolve. The fact that Moore is so profoundly unsatisfying when it comes to taking on these vital issues in the real world—as opposed to the play world of entertainment and the emotionally satisfying world of incitement—is a measure of his ultimate failure to offer a stable and effective pole of attraction in American politics.

Moore gets too many things half-right, and often the effect of this is the same as getting them entirely wrong. It is indeed infuriating to hear Bush speak of how U.S. actions are intended to bring freedom and democracy to a part of the world in which they have long been suppressed, for what does Bush know about freedom? He, after all, by virtue of having been born into a world of extreme privilege, has always been perfectly free: free to go to the best schools and waste his time, free to drink and drive, free to make money while the businesses he ran tanked and his father's associates picked up the bill, free to use cocaine and not go to jail,[24] free to get away with insider stock trading; free, ultimately, to steal an election. And he does all of these things as if by right, denying his privileged origins with his affected redneck manner. He is truly our Paris Hilton president: lacking in any talent or ability, yet believing that he has earned his public acclaim.

Liberals cannot be expected to believe such a man's rationalization of an imperial agenda in the Middle East. But making the war in Iraq about loathing for Bush is tragic bathos. Bush is far from being in control of the situation, and unfolding history tends to take on a logic of its own. It is possible—along with other far less positive scenarios—that the events that Bush has set in motion will lead in the long term to more open, democratic, stable, and peaceful states in the region. If liberals cannot acknowledge at least this possibility, if all contemporary liberalism can do is to condemn Bush's strategy and his actions, liberals may eventually find themselves in a situation in which they are on record as being opposed to freedom and democracy. That is a bad place for liberalism to be in, and Michael Moore is leading the charge.

Ultimately, Moore's position on the Iraq war is as serious as the solutions to intractable world conflicts that he offers in *Stupid White Men*: a page or so apiece on how to handle Northern Ireland, Israel/Palestine, the former Yugoslavia, and North Korea (Moore recommends that the North Korean dictator Kim Jong Il should "watch better movies" and that Hollywood should sponsor his film proposals).[25]

Moore wants to have it both ways: to get laughs for his humor and to be respected for his world vision. As Larissa MacFarquhar astutely noted in her *New Yorker* profile of Moore,[26] he finesses his credentials as a thinker by casting issues in such a way that the conspiracists can experience the shock of recognizing a truth and the nonconspiracists can comfort themselves with the idea that "Hey, it's just satire"—and Moore picks up the support of both groups. There's an emptiness here, and in the long run it counts. People will always pay to see his movies—as Moore says, they're entertaining—but, as the 2004 election showed, millions of tickets sold do not translate into millions of votes against the radical right.

Beinart's article, no matter how flawed in its details, was a call for seriousness in the debate about the war in Iraq. If Moore is to address Islamic terrorism in a way that will not isolate him from political influence, he will have to pay attention. There may be a serious position against the Afghan war, although I cannot imagine what it might be. There certainly are serious positions against the Iraq war. Moore hasn't found one. If he continues to be against the wars in Afghanistan and Iraq, and if he wants to be effective, his opposition must be in the context of winning—not denying—the war on terrorism. Otherwise he will become slowly irrelevant, and take much of the left with him. It will be fatal for liberalism if liberals indulge themselves in hating Bush more than they hate terrorism.

∎ ∎ ∎

That's not quite the final word, though. No matter how dangerous Moore's positions would be if he had any influence on policy, he does not have any influence on policy. Moore and his ideological cohort have been effectively marginalized on the American scene. The same cannot be said of dangerous positions on the right.

The Cato Institute, one of the most extreme of the right-wing "think tanks," is staffed by political advocates who are committed to the idea of market forces as an absolute good, even when there is evidence that they damage the interests of the people they supposedly serve. Since this sort of absolutism is more in the realm of faith than of evidence, the staff at Cato can be said to approach economics as a religion rather than as a manifestation of culture. They are much farther on the economic right than, say, Ronald Reagan, although, unlike Reagan, they are libertarian on social as well as economic issues. Soon after September 11, David Boaz, the executive vice president, wrote an article denouncing people like Moore and the Italian playwright Dario Fo. Fo had suggested in a widely circulated e-mail that Western crimes of colonialism and continuing economic domination were the parents of the terrorist attacks.[27]

Boaz makes a rather striking accusation, and in doing so he demonstrates that the narratives of the right can be as confused as those of the knee-jerk pacifist left:

> [Moore's and Fo's writing] sums up the criticism of America that unites the Islamic terrorists, the anti-globalization street protesters, the resentful right and the literary left: They hate the culture of markets and liberalism. They hate the Enlightenment and modernity. They hate reason, science, technology, individualism, pluralism, tolerance, progress and freedom. And to be more specific, they hate Wall Street, Hollywood, McDonald's, Starbucks, Microsoft, Ralph Lauren ads and the casual joy of American freedom.

Boaz concludes with this bit of fluff: "One consequence of the evil acts of September 11 . . . was to give a few people an opening to reveal to us what they really think about America—they don't like our freedom, our openness, our tolerance, our prosperity, our exuberance."[28]

When I spoke with Boaz, he took some pains to point out that he was not intending to lump anyone who believes in regulated markets or anyone on some vague "literary left" (a phrase he justified by its alliteration) into the category of those who hate America and make common cause with Islamic terrorists. He was kind enough to exempt specifically mainstream, market-orientated center-leftists, mentioning Michael Kinsley, Nadine Strossen, and the editors of the *New Republic*. But he did say this: "Does Michael Moore hate reason? Absolutely. He used the emotional medium of film to distort, manipulate and mislead. . . . Does he hate individualism? Well, since he seems to be pushing socialism, I'd say so. . . . Capitalism is part of modernity, and if you're resentful of capitalism and 'conspicuous consumption' and things like that, then I think you don't like modernity."

There's a lot to work with here. Note Boaz's conflation in his article of things that many liberals and democratic leftists would consider quite reasonable objects of criticism if not of hatred—Wall Street, McDonald's, and Hollywood (criticized on the right as well)—with things that no one on the democratic, liberal left dreams of criticizing:

reason, science, technology, pluralism, and so on. Here, Boaz has himself made a classic lapse of reason. Note, too, that there is a difference between criticizing what people do with science or technology (a type of criticism that is sometimes made by liberals) and criticizing science itself (a type of criticism that is never made by liberals, although it is often heard on the evolution-denying, religious-fundamentalist right). And Boaz clearly has no understanding of at least the small-*d* democratic variant of socialism if he thinks that respect for the individual is in opposition to it.

Boaz also seems to know little about the meaning of the Enlightenment thinking that he professes to support. The Enlightenment was a movement and an era that explored what we know about the world, how we can know it, and how we can use this approach to improve the human condition. The work of Karl Marx, even though it came later, is every bit as much a part of the Enlightenment intellectual heritage as that of Adam Smith.

But most importantly, Boaz's comment implies something about the ideology of the war on terror, and shows a chasm of unreason on the right that is as deep and as harmful as Michael Moore's sinister pacifism. In preferring the moralistic language of good and evil to that of thoughtful analysis, no matter how appropriate it may be on an emotional level, Boaz denies the legitimate part of the point that Fo—very clumsily—was trying to make: that there actually were historical causes of September 11. Boaz's outrage over Fo's article doesn't really take terrorism seriously as a phenomenon with historical roots and may indirectly encourage an unhelpful delusion of the right: the conviction that the events of September 11 were simply the work of evil people carrying out the agenda of an inferior civilization that has always been at war with the West, out of some unknowable urge to fanaticism and bloodlust.

Boaz and those who argue that Islamic fanatics are motivated by hatred of our freedoms would like to draw a line under the entire history of the interaction between Western and non-Western civilizations. This history carries a complex and, it must be said, not entirely negative legacy. It is much more complicated than the proclamations by shallow agitators like Tariq Ali of an equivalence of fundamentalisms, but it is also more complicated than the Western triumphalists' insistence that the only thing that matters is the West's gift—not universally appreciated—to its former colonies of the social values and the material prosperity of capitalism.

This is, of course, blind reductionism. History and human beings don't work like that. To say so is in no way to justify or to defend terrorism. There is no doubt and very little argument that the West has an urgent need and an existential obligation to root out and kill terrorists, that no negotiation is possible with the forces of militant Islamic darkness. But we cannot win this war if we allow ourselves to be incurious about why much of the rest of the world is angry at Western civilization, and it's not because of our freedom and our exuberance.

There is a wrong kind of focus on "root causes" of terrorism. This is the kind that seeks to minimize or excuse terrorism through a relativistic comparison with the crimes of empire. There is also a right kind of focus on root causes, one that recognizes that terrorism must be defeated and that this involves war on terrorists, knowledge of what creates them, and a desire to right historical wrongs—a desire that springs not from fear or guilt or appeasement but from an understanding that this is in everyone's interest. No one has shown this second kind of focus better than the Iraqi dissident Kanan Makiya. His short essay "Arab Demons, Arab Dreams 1967–2003" should be read by everyone who is serious about winning the war on terror.

Over at the *National Review*, the far-right partisan Jay Nordlinger and the pompous faux-stoic Victor Davis Hanson, an intellectual hero of the post–September 11 political right, are apparently unable to make the distinction. They regularly write of their contempt for those who are interested in the root causes of September 11. Their colleague John Derbyshire has put it this way: "Try as I might (and I confess I haven't tried *very* hard) I can't summon up an ounce of interest in what the Arabs think about us. Nor the Bushmen of the Kalahari, neither. Though I think the Arabs should be considerably worried as to what we think about them."[29]

One problem with this attitude is that it is at least a small part of what has gotten us into the mess in which we find ourselves at present. Another is that if we continue to indulge ourselves in this way, we will lose the war on terror.

Michael Moore has not put forth a point of view that is helpful in securing a lasting victory of civilized values in this war, and that is a shame. But neither have Nordlinger and Derbyshire, Hanson and Boaz.

13

PROSPECTS

As of this writing in the fall of 2005, in the wake of Hurricane Katrina and the Bush administration's botched and cynical response to it, rumor has it that Michael Moore's next project will be about the causes of and response to the disaster in New Orleans.

New Orleans really did expose some fundamental truths about American society, about race and class and the ways in which privilege finds concern and response from a government of the privileged; about how even a disaster like Katrina can be used by conscienceless ideologues to further an agenda of class warfare, as when some on the right took the opportunity to call for the New Orleans public school system to be reconstituted with more "school choice," a cynical euphemism for "divide and conquer."

But it would be astonishing if Michael Moore proves capable of addressing these things in a reasonable, sophisticated, and objective manner designed to find and develop practical solutions to social problems. Given what we know about Moore and his work, we can reasonably make some predictions about how he would approach this subject. He will probably focus on race, ignoring or glossing over the subtle interactions between race and class in America, to make the claim that the Bush administration doesn't value the lives and interests of black people. He will probably assert that large corporations, led by Halliburton, are looting the remains of the Big Easy to make enormous profits, without regard for the needs of the people who live or lived there. He will likely try to tie federal tax cuts to the state of the levees, even though overall spending on the levees was increased under the Bush administration. He might portray the rich people of New Orleans as callously unconcerned for and out of touch with their neighbors; he may even lend credence to rumors that the rich intentionally blew the levees in such a way that the waters would flood the poor Ninth Ward and leave their own neighborhoods intact.

He will undoubtedly dwell on the time when a desperately needed National Guard contingent was not sent to New Orleans, while conveniently overlooking the fact that the request for troops was not forthcoming for several days from the Democratic governor of Louisiana, Kathleen Blanco, for reasons best known to herself. He may say that troops were unavailable for New Orleans because they were off on a fool's errand in Iraq. For good measure, he may throw in some comparison of the suffering caused by Katrina with the suffering of the people of Iraq.

It is more than likely that Moore's ultimate message will be a simple one: New Orleans suffered because of the greed and incompetence of a privileged few, of Republicans. Indeed, he's already stated his position on what went wrong, in which the central fact of a massive natural disaster is strangely absent: "[T]he manmade annihilation of New Orleans [was] caused NOT by a hurricane but by the very specific decisions made by the Bush administration in the past four and a half years."[1]

If Moore does this, will it really help us understand what happened in New Orleans, a city cursed with a long legacy of local corruption, administrative incompetence, terrible race relations, irresponsible populist leadership, and bad economic development strategies? Government at all levels was unprepared for the disaster, and individuals too often did not react well. Many looted, and not only for food and water. Some raped and killed. There is plenty of blame to go around. But it is extremely unlikely that Moore will put any of it on C. Ray Nagin, the Democratic mayor of New Orleans, or Kathleen Blanco, or any poor or black or Democratic residents. They were victims of the Republican right, and that's the central meaning of the story. Moore has his limitations.

Which brings us to the only important question about Michael Moore. How much do his radically reductionist views actually influence American politics?

■　　■　　■

Because Moore is one of the very few voices of the left who gets national exposure, it's easy to take him too seriously. But there's an important message in his popularity, if not in his broadsides. Just think of all those kids who have taken up the Che Guevara T-shirt as a fashion statement. Are they really signaling their admiration for this icon of international socialism, who was, in real life, a totalitarian psychopath who took personal pleasure in torture and murder? More likely that the great majority of people walking around with Che on their chests know almost nothing about who he actually was and how he lived his life. But his image is an inchoate protest. At least one point of promoting it is to engage and enrage the grubby zealots who admire Ronald Reagan. Why shouldn't Che be marketed as counterpoint, as balance? Why shouldn't Moore's work be sold as protest? Protest that, in going against the reactionary tide, has value in its own right?

It's a debased value, though. In making politics about identity rather than about content, it becomes hard to keep the irony of Moore as a consumer phenom separate from his chosen role of political activist. As the Che T-shirt shows, and as Joseph Heath and Andrew Potter point out in their book *Nation of Rebels: Why Counterculture Became Consumer Culture*, rebellion and dissent can be branded and sold like anything else. Heath and Potter give the example of the "culture-jamming" magazine *Adbusters*, which in 2003 produced and marketed a no-logo sneaker as a supposed act of rebellion against all things corporate. The sneaker was black, of course, the cool noncolor of punk and anarchist nonconformists, and the lack of a logo was a fashion statement.

The problem for Americans who are interested in politics, and who are not conservative, is that Moore has so thoroughly captured the market for *symbolic* rebellion. This kind of rebellion is more about the confirmation of identities taken on through assumed, highly reductionist common "truths" ("No blood for oil!") than it is about actually understanding what is happening and changing it for the better. Because of Moore, and because of the brilliant use that the right has made of his provocations, there is less room for serious, thoughtful, and balanced discussion of the issues.

Millions of people saw *Fahrenheit 9/11*. No one really knows how many votes were changed, and it is possible that—as the quotes in the beginning of this book suggest—Moore managed to fire up the right to become more active in the election, while having his strongest appeal only to the people on the Democratic side who were already solid Kerry voters. One of the most disastrous things about *Fahrenheit 9/11* was that, for nonaligned viewers capable of thoughtfully critiquing the film, it made taking Moore's side so embarrassing. And Moore's side happened to be the anti-Bush side.

Moore's faith in broad political theater has done him in again and again. He endorsed Ralph Nader in 2000—we know how that turned out—and General Wesley Clark in 2004. Clark got nowhere in the primaries, and many observers believe that at least part of the reason for his failure was Moore's "help": Taking the stand at a Clark primary rally, Moore called George W. Bush a "deserter." This may be overstating the case, although not by much. There's no question that Bush shirked his duty as a member of the Texas Air National Guard, and was allowed to do so because of his privileged family connections. But the aggressive exaggeration, especially coming from Moore, was obnoxious to many primary voters and certainly didn't advance Clark's chances. After Clark failed to advance to the nomination, Moore endorsed John Kerry. Kerry's campaign also had a lot of help from Moore, and *Fahrenheit 9/11* was a directed effort to damage Kerry's opponent. Although Kerry, wisely, avoided any public association with Moore, Kerry also failed to get elected.

■　■　■

One thread that runs through all of Moore's work is his absolute refusal to take responsibility for anything that he has done, and some of the things he has done have had serious consequences that are not the ones he intended. Ralph Nader cost Al Gore the election by splitting the anti-Bush vote. When confronted about this, Moore never fails to brush it aside with the observation that he didn't lose the election, Gore lost the election by refusing to take any principled liberal positions. The self-justification is total and obsessive. In *Stupid White Men*, Moore even goes so far as to write of how, just before the vote, he came up with an idea for how Nader could win his 5 percent of the popular vote (thus becoming eligible for federal funding in future elections) while not damaging Gore's chances: offer the Gore people a deal in which Nader would campaign hard in states that were already safe for Gore or for Bush, while not contesting states where the race was in doubt. In return for helping Gore win, Nader could demand that, once president, Gore would follow through on any one of many important liberal initiatives. How statesmanlike! The selfish Nader people turned down Moore's brilliant compromise, as he tells it.[2]

But of course this exact compromise was widely discussed at the time, from Molly Ivins's syndicated column in July 2000 to the *New York Times* in October 2000. Moore certainly wasn't the first to suggest it. Harry Levine, a writer and academic who worked on Nader's 2000 campaign, remembers Moore taking precisely the opposite position. When Levine suggested that the Nader campaign post polling data on its Web site so as to direct voters to vote for Nader in states where the election was not going to be close, Moore "poked his finger into my face, and yelled: 'You can't say that! You can't say that! You can't say that!'"[3]

It was important to Moore to insist that he couldn't be held responsible for George W. Perhaps it was his own subliminal lack of conviction in this idea—some nagging doubt—that led him to endorse Clark in the 2004 Democratic primaries, a man who is the opposite of Moore's political ideal, a military man, the architect of the Kosovo war (which Moore vociferously opposed), far less progressive than Gore, let alone Nader, in almost every way. Yet who seemed, for one brief, shining moment, capable of defeating Bush in 2004—and paying off Moore's debt to society.

■ ■ ■

Michael Moore's work will continue to unfold in the context of his political times. There isn't much left of the American liberal movement, if one defines modern liberalism as guarding and expanding the social ideals and public commitments of the New Deal. Republicans have used savvy political organization to completely marginalize Democrats in government, in ways both traditional and quite novel. Republicans control both Houses of Congress, the presidency, and much of the judiciary, where, guided by the radical right-wingers of the Federalist Society, they have installed their own right-wing activist judges and proclaimed them constitutional "originalists." Their congressional majority gives the Republicans control of the House and Senate Rules committees, which they have used in unprecedentedly partisan ways.

Republicans control a majority of the statehouses, which, in the states they hold, allows them to determine congressional redistricting. In Texas, the Republicans, under the tutelage of then–House Majority Leader Tom DeLay, used strong-arm parliamentary tactics to reconfigure the apportionment that followed the census of 2000, in order to lock in a Republican majority in the federal House of Representatives. DeLay himself, who has recently had to resign his House leadership position when he was charged with political money laundering, has informed firms that lobby the government that they should employ only Republicans. This is a tactic that has allowed DeLay and the Republicans to seize a vital, though informal and extra-constitutional, channel of power.

This domination of power both springs from and encourages a dangerous arrogance, one that is not warranted by popular support. It is important to remember that while in 2004 George W. Bush won the largest number of votes of any presidential candidate in history, John Kerry won the second-largest number of votes of any presidential candidate in history. Although Republicans currently hold fifty-five of the one hundred seats in the Senate, because of the way Senate seats are allotted (every state gets two, regardless of size, and the Republicans hold their majority by dominating in many small states), those fifty-five seats represent just over 48 percent of the population, while the forty-four Democrats and one Independent who votes with the Democrats represent more than 51 percent of the population. This argument may not be constitutionally meaningful: the Senate is not designed for proportional representation. But it goes to the heart of the Republicans' claim to be the party of an outraged, "normal" majority of Americans, and that they therefore have a mandate to drag the country to the extreme right.

Republicans are very happy to be able to present Moore as the voice of the Democrats, and they have capitalized on the perception of Moore as someone who hates America. This idea has been tremendously helpful to them. When *Fahrenheit 9/11* was released, the Web site Conservative Petitions opened a petition urging the Justice Department to "brand" (the petition doesn't go so far as to say "prosecute") Michael Moore as a "treacherous traitor" (*sic*). There are any number of specifically anti-Moore Web sites, with names like moorewatch.com, moore-exposed.com, and moorelies.com. This year, Bernard Goldberg, the author of a bizarre previous book about supposed liberal domination of the media, came out with a new book called *100 People Who Are Screwing Up America (And Al Franken Is #37)*. Predictably, Michael Moore was #1. Also predictably, the Fox network fell all over itself to help Goldberg promote the book. Within the first three weeks of its release, Goldberg appeared on various Fox shows no less than eight times.[4]

For the 2004 Academy Awards ceremony at the Kodak Theater in Hollywood (which took place after the elections), David Bossie rented the two largest billboards near the theater, on which he expressed his thanks to Moore and other Hollywood Bush opponents for contributing to the 2004 Republican victory.

The association of Michael Moore with a lunatic America-hating left has, more ominously for Moore's followers, made inroads into popular culture. The social anarchists Trey Parker and Matt Stone, in their brilliant 2004 puppet parody, *Team America: World Police*, cast Moore's puppet as a suicide bomber, and an intelligent computer refers to him as a "giant socialist weasel." On the comedy show *Saturday Night Live*, the actor Seth Myers portrayed Osama bin Laden in a pre-election address to the American people. "Osama" gave Moore a friendly mention, but even he was skeptical: "I've tried hard to follow the campaign, and to study both the candidates, and the issues. This has often been frustrating, as I am constantly moving from cave to cave here in the mountains of Northwest Pakistan, and thus have very little contact with the outside world. The only person I see regularly is Michael Moore. And frankly, I am not sure I can believe half of what he tells me."[5]

■   ■   ■

The Republican monopoly on power and its dominance of the major media is something that will be sure to feed the frustrations of liberals and the liberal left, and lead people to the uncompromising and sometimes childish polemics of a figure like Moore. It is unfortunately part of the reason that there is an emotional attraction to Moore, and part of the reason why many who should know better show up at his movie premieres.

There is also a counterreaction among liberals to this dangerous emotional attraction, a reaction that poses its own problems for a truly thoughtful, progressive, liberal agenda. In the wake of its losses in 2004, the Democratic Leadership Council, a group of centrist Democrats that has been trying to steer the party toward a more conservative Democratic consensus since the early 1990s, and many prominent Democrats (Harry Reid, Max Baucus, Evan Bayh, Joe Lieberman) have been calling for the party to abandon more of its liberal principles, even, in a particularly disastrous suggestion, to "get religion" (why the Democratic Leadership Council believes that this would be seen as anything other than the cynical, condescending ploy that it in fact would be is an interesting question).

Moore frequently inveighs against the shift to the right when he talks about the Democratic Party, but the louder he gets, and the more public attention he gets, and the more he provokes mainstream America by insulting Americans while abroad and minimizing the threat of Islamic fundamentalism, the more he encourages this shift and the more the Democratic Party shrinks from the principles he enunciates. It's a terrible dynamic for which both Moore and the Democrats share responsibility. Saying this is not to blame Moore when he tells the truth; it is to blame him for not cleaning up his act and being more careful with the facts.

Moore is committed to some good things. He wants to expand the wealth and power of the working class, since he is highly skeptical of the return to capital that its controllers arrogate to themselves, and he insists that much of this is rightly owed to labor. He advocates for women's rights, gay rights, and national health care. He believes in fairly distributing the burden of taxation. He believes in public ownership of vital public services.

Many on the left try to take the good with the bad, and there is some good that is worth acknowledging. Todd Gitlin wrote as much in a piece on Moore and his political role, "Michael Moore, Alas" (echoing André Gide on Victor Hugo). After slamming Moore's irresponsible and inconsistent approach to politics, Gitlin said:

> Benighted democracy needs the contention that Moore provokes because the newspapers don't provoke it, television doesn't, the Democrats didn't, Congress didn't, judicious folks didn't. No one who didn't get worked up about the administration's distortions re WMD, al-Qaeda and mushroom clouds has the right to pure rage against Michael Moore. He's not running for President, after all. (More good news . . .) Moore is the master demagogue an age of demagoguery made. . . . Still, Moore could be a better version of Moore and still be Moore. He could show us that war kills and Bush is appalling, and yet be more scrupulous. But Moore is the only Moore we have—alas. Moore is the anti-Bush, and damn if we didn't need one.[6]

Deirdre English, the former editor of *Mother Jones*, told me something similar, something that captures much of the ambivalence that thoughtful people on the left feel about Moore as a public advocate:

> He's done some good things in bringing things into the media that weren't there. I think one of the most important things he did in *Fahrenheit* was to bring attention to the victims of the war, to show people what it's like to be a believer, a patriot, and to have your child die for a cause that was so wrongly constructed in the first place. There are things that can only be shown effectively from the perspective of working-class Americans. As I go through my ordinary day here in San Francisco . . . well, I'm a professor at UC; I don't meet people whose children are in Iraq. But the woman who runs the little cafe I had dinner in last night, her son is there and she knows one person who lost an eye and another who lost a leg there. The carpenter who plugged a leak in my ceiling knows a lot of people who are there. But these people aren't getting into the media because the media is out of touch with them. But Moore is in touch with them; he can

get their stories out. The media do a bad job of reaching out to those people, do a bad job of understanding them, of representing their interests, writing about them, and Moore does a good job of that. To the extent that he's representing them, that's a good thing; to the extent that he becomes a paranoid, demagogic voice himself, or begins to push his own opinions down people's throats, I think that's a bad thing.

Speaking of *Fahrenheit 9/11*, Erik Gustafson of the Education for Peace in Iraq Center told me:

> I guess it was all for entertainment. Yet at the same time, with these extra DVD features, he's got one section that's all about the opening of the film, you've got Steve Earle playing "The Revolution Starts Now," and it's very exciting. And that is everything that's wrong with the Democratic Party. It's seductive. You've got all kinds of folks in the party saying, "Yeah, that's what I want to hear, that makes me feel good." But you know what? More than half of America watches that and says, "What the fuck? That's not me, that's not what I stand for." And it's that disconnect that has done the political discourse in this country no good at all. *Fahrenheit 9/11* is not going to help the Democrats find a way to be taken seriously on national security.
>
> The progressive community, and the progressive community within the Democratic party and even the antiwar left, can make a tremendous contribution; but when you have leadership like Michael Moore, they actually become more of a liability than an asset. That's what I first thought when I saw the movie, and think to this day. With the work that EPIC does, we're often battling what I call the "Michael Moore factor." I see this in the flak EPIC gets from some otherwise well-intentioned folks on the left for not saying "Bring the troops home now." What's that? That's not a policy. It's this Michael Moore factor.

Liberals and the democratic left have some hard questions to face when it comes to Moore as a spokesman for liberalism, especially in a time of war and terrorism. Does the left really want to be associated with someone who does not seem to think that the United States can ever legitimately go to war? Who opposed the war in Afghanistan? Who referred to the Iraqi insurgents as "minutemen," and who went out of his way to express a lack of sympathy for American families who lost loved ones in the Iraq war? Liberals and the left should think very hard about embracing Moore, and other such dubious voices as George Galloway; Cindy Sheehan; International A.N.S.W.E.R (Act Now to Stop War and End Racism—an affiliate of the Stalinist Workers' World Party, which supported the Soviet Union's invasion of Czechoslovakia and the repression of the Polish Solidarity movement, and which admires Kim Il Sung and North Korea); Noam Chomsky, the sinister ideologue and favorite intellectual of those who still believe that the Soviet Union wasn't really so bad, who wrote that the proper way to respond to September 11 was to bring Osama bin Laden before an international tribunal but not to make war on the Taliban; and the radical Canadian journalist Naomi Klein, who, at the height of the U.S. military's battle with militia forces in Najaf, urged war protesters to "bring Najaf to New York."[7] Do such associations really help the liberal agenda? Are they morally decent?

■ ■ ■

Moore has other kind of associations that are questionable. He has signally failed to practice what he preaches, in ways that very much compromise his public image and his credibility as a leftist. Contrary to radio host Dave Barber's belief that Moore never fundamentally changed, ever since Moore started to make serious money he has, in his own personal financial dealings, had a mutually profitable relationship with corporate America. It may technically be true, as he says, that "I don't own a single share of stock."[8] But some of his movie and book project profits were put into a foundation that is controlled by him and his wife, the gains from which they can dispose of as they see fit; the foundation has no other trustees. At various times, Moore has held stock in Big Pharma companies such as Pfizer, Merck, and Eli Lilly. Several different oil companies, including Sunoco. McDonald's. Major defense contractors General Electric, Honeywell, Boeing, and Loral.

Moore also once held stock in Dick Cheney's old company, Halliburton.

Moore sometimes talks about his foundation in interviews, describing it as one of the ways he does good in the world, funding artists and activist groups. But through 2002, of the almost half a million dollars that Moore declared for his foundation, he had given away $36,000, much of it to film festivals and other organizations in which he had at least an indirect interest. This was near the minimum of what he needed to do to keep his foundation in nonprofit status.[9]

Moore may indeed have struggled to finance *Roger & Me*, but when he started to have money, he looked after it shrewdly, and in doing so he made full use of the mechanics of capitalism. Moore's former manager, the film industry veteran Douglas Urbanski, found Moore so personally appalling that he dropped him as a client. Urbanski said of Moore that he "is more money obsessed than any I have known, and that's saying a lot."[10]

■ ■ ■

This question of Moore's political effectiveness is connected to the question of Moore as a person: someone who has, in the past, had no qualms about fudging the facts for his greater purposes or betraying people who trusted him, someone who claims the right to intrude on and interrogate others and yet does not allow himself to be intruded on and interrogated in the same way. Someone who has repeatedly threatened legal action—against at least Glen Lenhoff, Adam Hochschild and the Foundation for National Progress, Alan Edelstein, and the online magazine *Salon*—and then withdrawn his claim. Someone who has been known to treat his staff badly, who offers grand theories that incite without really explaining. As Laura Fraser, the freelance journalist whom Moore once accused of supplying drugs to the editors of *Mother Jones*, put it, "I support the politics of [*Roger & Me*], but politics are . . . personal and a social conscience has to be based on personal credibility."[11] A former Moore associate put it like this, tying up the connection between Moore's approach to his staff and the effect of his disputed factual claims: "Because he rules by intimidation, no one around him is going to point out the danger that his sloppy technique does to his cause."

Mark Dowie told me that Moore has used his anger to appeal to a lowest-common-denominator comedic tribal rage that satisfies the human need for symbolic bloodshed and a good laugh, just as the rants of Ann Coulter do. Sophisticated people may shun this sport— the *New York Times*'s public editor, Daniel Okrent, in charge of editorial oversight, wrote in his introductory column, "I'd rather spend my weekends exterminating rats in the tunnels below Penn Station than read a book by either Bill O'Reilly or Michael Moore"[12]—but this might mean only that sophisticated people will continue to be increasingly marginalized in politics, and this cannot fail to help the right. Dowie rightly laments the harm that the success of Moore and Coulter (and Rush Limbaugh, Don Imus, Howard Stern, and Jerry Springer before them) has inflicted, but he sees more of it on the way,[13] and sadly it is hard to argue with this prediction. In culture, as in markets, good coinage is driven out by bad.

Dowie went on to say:

> I don't consider Moore a major voice of the left, because his voice is so fucked up. I think one of the reasons that there isn't an effective, vocal left is because of people like Moore, who've spoiled it by taking the Ann Coulter approach to politics, just slamming and bamming and tossing around unsubstantiated points in an irresponsible way. I think he's a leftish-leaning voice of the culture, but I don't think he's a voice of the left . . . and I wish he was! Because he's got what it takes; he's got the background and the credentials to do it. And maybe he will grow up now that he's got [millions] in the bank and do something of real value that doesn't set itself up for the kind of trashing his previous work has received from the right and the center.

■　■　■

If the left gives Moore a pass, however reluctantly and with however many qualifications and notes on the extenuating circumstances, is it not collectively confirming James K. Glassman's view, expressed in the wake of the election, that Moore is all the left has got?

There is a natural temptation on the part of Democrats to find their own Karl Rove; this explains a lot of the tolerance for Moore. But this temptation should be resisted. The idea that Democrats can win with Rove's methods is a trap. Leaving aside the ethical issues, Democrats will never have anyone as good at political manipulation as Rove. Moore doesn't come close.

This is actually a very good thing for the country and for Democrats, because it means that they must reject Rove, not become him. If Democrats want to regain power, they will have to be serious about truth. They will have to start aggressively calling out the grievous distortions of the right-wing propagandists who have gotten away with a duplicitous game for far too long, but also calling out the distortions of those in their own camp who justify means by ends. When Democrats win, it is in spite of Michael Moore, not because of him.

Moore could still be effective if he decided to play it straight and buckle down to work. If he does not release a film on New Orleans first, his next movie is going to be about the broken American health care system, a serious subject for which, one can hope, he will eschew the narcissistic grandstanding involved in trying to single-handedly take down an illegitimate president. This is a good sign.

There's a real longing on the left for someone who can articulate its issues in an honest and powerful way and who can harness the traditional tools of populism in their service. Moore would have to grow up a lot and think a lot more deeply if he wanted to be that person. He'd have to accept Albert Maysles's challenge to approach his material without fear of what he'd discover and to present what he finds, rather than what he wants to find. Can he do it?

The bar will be set high for him because he has set it so low for himself in the past. That's a shame, and it's the fault of nobody but Michael Moore.

POSTSCRIPT
A CHALLENGE FOR CONSERVATIVES

The April 25, 2005, edition of *Time* magazine featured a cover story on Ann Coulter by John Cloud. The story was largely a whitewash of her radical views and her sloppy polemics, but in an age of media intimidation by the right, this was no surprise. The cover blurb was interesting, however: "Fair and balanced she isn't. This conservative flamethrower enrages the left and delights the right. Is she serious or just having fun?"[1]

Beyond any doubt, Coulter delights many of the modern breed of conservative, those who are so steeped in ideology that actual history and facts, let alone common decency, mean nothing to them. But I cannot accept that Coulter delights "the right" in general. I know many decent and sincere traditional conservatives, people who have arrived at their views through thoughtful analysis and concern for the common good rather than through a tribal identification with ideology. Conservatives of this school believe in fair play and honest debate. I don't think they are any more impressed with Coulter than their counterparts on the left are with Michael Moore.

If this type of thoughtful conservative has made it this far in this book, he or she will undoubtedly disagree with a great deal of what I've said about the right and about the left. But I would hope that he or she would think that I have approached the subject of Michael Moore's role in American politics in good faith, and that I have not flinched in taking on the American left when I found its tactics or beliefs to be dishonest or harmful.

Let me pose a challenge, then, to such a conservative. Who on the right is going to take on his own team's excesses?

Even in its more genteel manifestations, the right has done more to poison the wells of political discourse than the liberal left—and, after all, the right has the media access and the money. Political hypocrisy knows no party.

When will thoughtful people on the right take on the influential conservative columnist Charles Krauthammer? Krauthammer has disgraced himself and both of his professions—journalism and medicine—with his support for the use of torture in counterterrorism under certain circumstances.[2] He has written that the U.S. treatment of prisoners at Guantanamo Bay is "remarkably humane and tolerant."[3] Surely such statements are as repulsive as anything Michael Moore has said about the war in Iraq.

Where is the conservative who will argue with the right's problem child, Ann Coulter? Coulter uses sloppy research and the energy of her own hate-filled obsessions to smear the history, motives, and actions of American liberalism. She is sure that Joseph McCarthy, who destroyed the lives of thousands of innocent people, was a great man. She's recently written, "I think the government should be spying on all Arabs, engaging in torture as a televised spectator sport, dropping daisy cutters wantonly throughout the Middle East and sending liberals to Guantanamo."[4] Is this "tongue-in-cheek" satire, as her supporters claim? Does it matter? Coulter herself never gives any indication of being other than completely serious.

What about Rush Limbaugh? Limbaugh's inventions of fact to suit his purposes may not matter to the ideologues, who are so convinced of his meta-rightness that they are not bothered that much of what he says is provably untrue. But isn't this the kind of excuse that the most dishonest partisans of the left offer in defense of Michael Moore? And shouldn't Limbaugh's truly awesome hypocrisy—he has railed against drug addicts yet maintained an addiction to illegally procured OxyContin, a drug more powerful than heroin—embarrass the right just a little bit?

Speaking of hypocrisy, what conservative will dare to question the deeply ridiculous, pompous opportunist William Bennett? Bennett is the radio talk-show host and former secretary of education in the Reagan administration, the self-appointed guardian of public morals who lost $8 million at the gambling table—and who, far more ominously, seems to think that he is entitled to define what constitutes good American citizenship and good American values.

There's Fox TV host Bill O'Reilly, who threatens guests who disagree with him with bodily harm and misrepresents what they say on his show. When will conscientious right-wingers object to the unscrupulous attacks of Sean Hannity, who thought perjury was a terrible thing when Bill Clinton was accused of it and a minor matter when the same accusation was made against Dick Cheney's chief of staff, I. Lewis "Scooter" Libby?

At the very bottom of the barrel of conservative discourse are clowns like the nasty ranter Michael Savage, who believes that liberalism is "a mental disorder"[5] and who once told a gay caller to his television show, "You should only get AIDS and die, you pig!"[6]

And there are so many others like Krauthammer, Limbaugh, Hannity, and Savage, who have much more access to the public debate, and a much greater impact on it, than Michael Moore. While the political right complains bitterly about Moore, it completely ignores its own destructive darlings.

Debate couched in terms of blind ideology damages the nation. Sincere people on both the left and the right should be able to agree that what damages our country is bad for all of us. What are you, dear conservative colleague, going to do about it?

NOTES

Introduction

1. CBS News transcription, November 3, 2004.

2. James K. Glassman, "Will Michael Moore's Fahrenheit 9/11 Defeat a President?" *Capitalism*, June 25, 2004 (www.capmag.com/article.asp?ID=3760; active as of August 2005).

3. David Bossie, *Washington Times*, November 8, 2004.

4. See Larissa MacFarquhar, "The Populist," *New Yorker*, February 16 and 23, 2004. "Yippie" is an acronym for Youth International Party, but the Yippies were a political party only in the broadest possible sense.

5. From Phil Ochs's testimony, compiled as part of Professor Douglas O. Linder's Famous Trials Project at the University of Missouri, Kansas City.

1 Roots

1. Michael Moore and Kathleen Glynn, *Adventures in a TV Nation* (New York: HarperPerennial, 1998), p. 8.

2. Michael Moore, *Stupid White Men . . . and Other Sorry Excuses for the State of the Nation* (New York: Regan Books, 2002), p. 100.

3. *Flint Voice*, June–July 1980.

4. Michael Moore, "Who Is 'Brian'?" *Flint Voice*, December 1977.

5. See Peter Schweizer, *Do as I Say (Not as I Do): Profiles in Liberal Hypocrisy* (New York: Doubleday, 2005), pp. 46–50.

6. Ben Hamper, *Rivethead: Tales from the Assembly Line* (New York: Warner Books, 1992), p. 103.

7. Ibid., p. 2.

8. Laurence Jarvik, "Will the Real Michael Moore Please Stand Up?" *Montage*, February 1990.

2 New Vistas, New Conflicts

1. Michael Moore, "Ronnie's Kids," *Mother Jones*, September 1986.

2. Michael Moore, "A Room with a View," *Mother Jones*, October 1986.

3. Hamper doesn't agree; he says the magazine was always supportive of him, and after Moore's departure he got a letter from the communications director Richard Reynolds saying that bringing him to *Mother Jones* was one of Moore's best decisions, and inviting him to continue to write for the magazine. Hamper declined,

out of loyalty to his former editor. It's hard to believe that the cover had anything to do with Moore being fired, since Hamper's picture had appeared on the first issue that Moore edited and he had gone on to edit two more issues—both of which included Hamper's column—without any management complaints about that.

4. *Mother Jones* was and is far from uncritical of Israel and ran articles on the Palestinian issue both before and after Moore's tenure as editor.

5. *San Francisco Chronicle*, September 7, 1986.

6. Adam Hochschild, "A Family Fight Hits the Headlines," *Mother Jones*, December 1986.

7. Deposition of Paul Farhi in the case of *Michael Moore and Kathleen Glynn v. Foundation for National Progress and Adam Hochschild*, Oakland, California, February 25, 1987.

8. Jeane Kirkpatrick, "Dictatorships and Double Standards," *Commentary* 68 (November 1979). One of the most powerful refutations of Kirkpatrick's strategic dichotomy, by the way, comes from someone who truly has the moral authority to make it: the Hungarian Cold War dissident György Konrád. Konrád, who struggled mightily against Soviet intellectual, political, and military hegemony and who opposed it in all its forms, was not overly impressed by the American commitment to democracy and human rights, and unmoved by Kirkpatrick-style sophistry. His words from Budapest in 1984 are insightful, prophetic, and inspiring today:

> [W]here Americans have found undemocratic regimes of various kinds—monarchies, fascistoid military dictatorships, and the like—they were content with military and economic co-operation, and regarded the poverty and oppression of the people as an internal affair of their clients. . . . [I]n those countries where democratic popular movements or political elites mobilized autonomous forces—where the nationalism of poor nations struggled to win independence from both superpowers—the American strove for no less than the suppression of those aspirations for autonomy. . . . I would think twice about exchanging the position of a Hungarian dissident for that of a Turkish or Southeast Asian or Latin American dissenter. It is possible that, in their shoes, I might long ago have been turned over for torture or even killed. No doubt American liberals are aware of this and they deplore it as well. . . . Meanwhile the ideologues declare that human rights violations are less serious if they happen in friendly countries rather than communist ones.
>
> As I write these lines, American politicians are being moved to profound moral indignation by the violation of human rights in Poland, while Soviet politicians are being moved to profound indignation by the violation of human rights in El Salvador. This all-too-evident selectivity can only move the observer to profound cynicism about the moral rhetoric of the superpowers. It also suggests that we cannot expect our freedom from either one of them, for neither one is particularly interested in our freedom. We can expect freedom only from ourselves, from our own patient, stubborn efforts to win it.

György Konrád, *Antipolitics: An Essay* (San Diego: Harcourt Brace Jovanovich), pp. 22–24.

9. Under severe international and military pressure, the Sandinistas did allow a presidential election in 1984, but they set up impossible and unfair conditions for their opponents. The widely respected candidate of the unified unarmed political

opposition, Arturo Cruz, eventually withdrew from the campaign rather than lend legitimacy to a sham.

10. The story of the Chibchas and their role in the Nicaraguan resistance is told in Timothy C. Brown, *The Real Contra War: Highlander Peasant Resistance in Nicaragua* (Norman: University of Oklahoma Press, 2001).

11. Reagan was not alone in his apparent belief that the leftist South African opposition was worse than the apartheid government. Dick Cheney was one of the very few members of Congress who voted against a resolution to urge the South African government to release Nelson Mandela.

12. Paul Berman, "Nicaragua 1986," *Mother Jones*, December 1986.

13. Alexander Cockburn's introduction to *Snowball's Chance*, an anti-Orwell "sequel" to *Animal Farm* by the serendipitously named John Reed (New York: Roof Books, 2002).

14. Cockburn agreed to take some questions by e-mail but did not write back when I asked him about the events at *Mother Jones* and about how he would respond to criticism that he is soft on leftist totalitarians.

15. Alexander Cockburn, *Nation*, September 20, 1986.

16. Moore's note, quoted in Paul Berman's analysis of the incident in "Me and Mother Jones," *Village Voice*, September 16, 1986.

17. See, for example, writer and former vice president Sergio Ramirez's memoir, *Adios Muchachos* (Miami, FL: Santillana USA Publishing, 2000).

18. Alexander Cockburn, *Nation*, September 13, 1986.

19. Not least in his very powerful books *King Leopold's Ghost* (Boston: Houghton Mifflin, 1998), which is an exploration of the historical and continuing damage done to the Congo by King Leopold of Belgium's brutal personal rule, and *Bury the Chains* (Boston: Houghton Mifflin, 2005), a stunning and inspiring history of the British abolitionist movement.

20. Guy T. Saperstein, *Civil Warrior: Memoirs of a Civil Rights Attorney* (Berkeley, CA: Berkeley Hills Books, 2003), pp. 204–5.

3 A National Stage

1. Michael Moore, *Downsize This!* (New York: HarperPerennial, 1997), p. 142.

2. Bureau of Labor Statistics (www.bls.gov; active as of August 2005).

3. In fact, Moore originally thought of calling his film *Pets or Meat* presumably on that very analogy, but he saved the title for his follow-up project.

4. William L. O'Neill, *American High: The Years of Confidence, 1945–1960* (New York: Free Press, 1989), p. 30.

5. For an interesting analysis of GM's struggle in this period, see Maryann Keller's *Rude Awakening: The Rise, Fall, and Struggle for Recovery of General Motors* (New York: HarperCollins, 1990).

6. Ben Hamper, *Rivethead: Tales from the Assembly Line* (New York: Warner Books, 1992), p. 47.

7. John Pierson, *Spike, Mike, Slackers and Dykes: A Guided Tour across a Decade of American Independent Cinema* (New York: Hyperion Miramax Books, 1997), p. 152.

8. Harlan Jacobson, "Michael and Me," *Film Comment* 25, no. 6, November–December 1989.

9. The major layoffs had occurred in 1974, in response to the first OPEC oil embargo, and were old news by 1989. Furthermore, many of the laid-off workers had been relocated or retired with benefits rather than just let go.

10. Jacobson, "Michael and Me,"

11. Michael Moore, "Roger and I: Off to Hollywood and Home to Flint," *New York Times*, July 15, 1990.

12. Doron P. Levin, *New York Times*, January 19, 1990.

13. Rob Medich, "Look Who Talked," *Premiere*, May 1990.

14. Roger Ebert, "Attacks on *Roger & Me* Completely Miss Point of Film," *Chicago Sun-Times*, February 11, 1990.

15. Pauline Kael's review of *Roger & Me*, *New Yorker*, January 8, 1990.

16. Andrea C. Basora, "Michael & Me," *Newsweek*, April 20, 1998.

17. Moore, "Roger and I."

18. David Armstrong, *San Francisco Examiner*, January 12, 1990.

19. Ben Hamper, "Brucie Can You Hear Me?" *Mother Jones*, October 1986.

20. For Moore's take on the encounter with Marsh and this new description of his departure from *Mother Jones*, see his introduction to Ben Hamper's *Rivethead*, pp. xiii–xiv.

4 Fun with a Purpose

1. Andrea C. Basora, "Michael & Me," *Newsweek*, April 20, 1998.

2. Michael Moore and Kathleen Glynn, *Adventures in a TV Nation* (New York: HarperPerennial, 1998), pp. 4–5.

3. Ibid., p. 12.

4. Larissa MacFarquhar, "The Populist," *New Yorker*, February 16 and 23, 2004.

5. For the exchange between Moore, Talbot, and Radosh, see "Michael Moore Fires Back at Salon," *Salon*, July 4, 1997 (http://dir.salon.com/ july97/moore970703 .html). Radosh's original piece on Moore, "Moore Is Less," appears in *Salon*, June 6, 1997 (www.salon.com/june97/media/media970606.html; active as of August 2005).

6. See David C. Korten, *When Corporations Rule the World* (San Francisco: Berrett-Koehler Publishers, 2001 Kumarian Press), p. 114.

7. For the record, Humana claims that Moore's antics had nothing to do with its decision to fund the procedure, and that it had already decided to do so before Moore's visits. See Colleen Dougher, "Life, Death and the Bottom Line," *Citylink*, August 28, 2002 (www.citylinkmagazine.com/cover/coverstory082802.html; active as of September 2005).

8. Moore has said that he "wanted to pursue the case" and implied that he had been blocked in his pursuit of justice, but the court transcript shows that the case was dismissed at the plaintiff's request. See John Tierney, "The Big City: When Tables Turn, Knives Come Out," *New York Times*, June 17, 2000. When I tried to verify the court transcript myself, I was told that the records of the case had been sealed, something that is very unusual.

5 Take the Gunheads Bowling

1. See Osha Gray Davidson, *Under Fire: The NRA and the Battle for Gun Control* (Iowa City: University of Iowa Press, 1998), p. 44.

2. In a long string of judgments the Supreme Court has agreed. See *Presser v. Illinois*, 1886; *United States v. Miller*, 1939; and *Lewis v. United States*, 1980. The Supreme Court has upheld without comment lower federal court rulings that interpret the Second Amendment as a collective rather than individual right: see *United States v. Tot*, 1942, in which the Third Circuit Court of Appeals ruled that "weapon bearing was never treated as anything like an absolute right by the common law";

Farmer v. Higgens, 1991; *United States v. Warin,* 1976; *Quilici v. Morton Grove,* 1982, in which the Seventh Circuit Court of Appeals ruled that "the possession of handguns by individuals is not part of the right to keep and bear arms"; and *Hickman v. Block,* 1996, in which the Ninth Circuit Court of Appeals ruled, "Because the Second Amendment guarantees the right of the states to maintain armed militia, the states alone stand in the position to show legal injury when this right is infringed."

3. Pierce, a former physicist, wrote under the pseudonym Andrew MacDonald. For some reason, many American white supremacists consider the Scots to be the finest flower of pure Aryan development.

4. Postulating the existence of such a thing is, of course, a gross generalization, but not an unrealistic one.

5. What Moore did is recounted by the bank employees themselves, in interviews in Michael Wilson's film *Michael Moore Hates America.*

6. In an odd connection, Michael Moore had donated the school's computer equipment.

7. Current statistics show that Americans have more guns than Canadians, and both have more guns than the Swiss. Thirty-nine percent of U.S. households possess firearms, compared to 29 percent in Canada and 27.2 percent in Switzerland (including Army and Reserve households), according to "International Violent Death Rates" at www.guncite.com, a pro-Second Amendment site (www.guncite.com/gun_control_gcgvintl.html; active as of August 2005).

8. It is a fact, however, that there are military assault rifles in many Swiss households and that the Swiss homicide rate is far lower than that of the United States or Canada. (According to the *International Journal of Epidemiology,* U.K., 1998, Switzerland has 1.32 deaths per 100,000, compared with Canada's 2.16 and 5.70 in the United States.) Here, I believe that we do have to look for cultural explanations; does any person seriously believe that, were there to be a military assault rifle in every U.S. household, the homicide rate in the United States would be as low as that of Switzerland? But whether Moore's particular cultural explanation is or is not correct is an entirely different question.

9. Dave Kopel, "Bowling Truths," *National Review Online,* April 4, 2003 (www.nationalreview.com/kopel/kopel040403.asp; active as of August 2005).

10. A white supremacist who shot and killed the civil rights leader Medgar Evers in 1963, acquitted by all-white juries several times, but finally convicted—thirty-one years after the fact—in a federal court of violating Evers's civil rights.

11. Although the scene appears to show Michael Moore displaying the girl's picture while he pleads with the departing Heston to look at the little girl who was shot, David Hardy and Jason Clarke, in their book *Michael Moore Is a Big Fat Stupid White Man* (New York: Regan Books, 2004, pp. 78–79), spend some time on an examination of the camera angles, and speculate that Heston had already left the scene at this point, and that the shots of Moore holding the picture and the voiceover were later spliced into the scene of Heston walking away.

12. See, for example, Kay S. Hymowitz, "This Family Shouldn't Have Been Saved," *Wall Street Journal,* March 3, 2000.

13. Rob Nelson, interview with Michael Wilson, "The Last Patriot Standing," *City Pages,* September 15, 2004 (http://citypages.com/databank/25/1241/article12459.asp; active as of August 2005).

14. *Boston Globe,* October 27, 2002.

15. Tom DeLay, at that time the House Majority Whip, went so far as to approvingly quote a letter that blamed the Columbine events on the teaching of

evolution in the public schools. *U.S. Congressional Record*, June 16, 1999, pp. H4364–H4414.

16. The speech is included on the bonus disc for the DVD release of *Bowling for Columbine*.

17. Joseph Heath and Andrew Potter, *Nation of Rebels: Why Counterculture Became Consumer Culture* (New York: HarperBusiness, 2005), pp. 140–42, emphasis in original.

18. Joel Bleifuss, "Michael Moore Stars at Academy Awards," *In These Times*, March 24, 2003.

19. Michael Moore, interview on *The Charlie Rose Show*, January 14, 2004.

6 The Stolen Election of 2000

1. Adam Gopnik, "American Studies," *New Yorker*, September 28, 1998.

2. The office of state secretary of state is quite different from that of the federal office of the same name. This officer does not work on foreign relations, which are constitutionally reserved for the federal government. The state secretary of state is in charge of civic matters, such as overseeing fair and transparent elections.

3. George Bruder testimony, Miami verified transcript, February 16, 2001, p. 220.

4. In materials quoted by the U.S. Commission on Civil Rights investigation, Emmett Mitchell IV, assistant general counsel, Division of Elections, "Your letter," March 23, 1999.

5. Bruder testimony, p. 219. Part of Bruder's testimony can be seen on the DVD *Unprecedented: The 2000 Presidential Election*.

6. U.S. Census Bureau.

7. Florida Department of Law Enforcement, and the dissenting statement of U.S. Civil Rights commissioners Abigail Thernstrom and Russell Redenbaugh on the commission's report on Florida voting. (The relevant passage does not appear in all versions of the statement; it is present in the version posted on *National Review Online*, www.nationalreview.com/document/documentprint062701.html; active as of August 2005.)

8. U.S. Commission on Civil Rights, "Voting Irregularities in Florida during the 2000 Presidential Election."

9. No reason not to repeat here the names of some of the people who had such contempt for the democratic process: Tom Pyle, policy analyst, office of (then) House Majority Whip Tom DeLay; Garry Malphrus, majority chief counsel and staff director, House Judiciary Subcommittee on Criminal Justice; Rory Cooper, political division staffer at the National Republican Congressional Committee; Kevin Smith, former House Republican Conference analyst; Steven Brophy, former aide to Republican senator Fred Thompson; Matt Schlapp, former chief of staff for far-right Republican Todd Tiahrt, at the time of the "riot" working for the Bush campaign; Roger Morse, an aide to Republican representative Van Hilleary; Duane Gibson, an aide to Republican representative Don Young; Chuck Royal, legislative assistant to Republican representative Jim DeMint; and Layna McConkey, former legislative assistant to former Republican representative Jim Ross Lightfoot.

10. Jeffrey Toobin, *Too Close to Call: The 36-Day Battle to Decide the 2000 Election* (New York: Random House, 2002), p. 156.

11. Scott Shane, "Never Shy, Bolton Brings a Zeal to the Table," *New York Times*, May 1, 2005.

12. David Barstow and Dale van Natta Jr., "Examining the Vote: How Bush Took Florida: Mining the Overseas Absentee Vote," *New York Times*, July 15, 2001.

13. For a very interesting discussion of the U.S. Supreme Court Justices' reasoning and their states of mind, see David A. Strauss, "Bush v. Gore: What Were They Thinking?" in Cass R. Sunstein and Richard A. Epstein, eds., *The Vote: Bush, Gore and the Supreme Court* (Chicago: University of Chicago Press, 2001).

14. See Jeffrey Toobin, "Breyer's Big Idea," *New Yorker*, October 31, 2005.

15. Ann Coulter, *Slander: Liberal Lies about the American Right* (New York: Crown, 2002), p. 149.

16. "John Ellis" is something of a Bush family name. The "Jeb" in Jeb Bush is actually an acronym for John Ellis Bush.

17. Bill Sammon, *At Any Cost: How Al Gore Tried to Steal the Election* (Washington, DC: Regnery Publishing, 2001), p. 274.

18. Bob Woodward, *Plan of Attack* (New York: Simon and Schuster, 2004), p. 28.

7 A Debate about Reality

1. This average is based on data from the Tax Foundation, "Federal Spending in Each State per Dollar of Federal Taxes, FY 2003" (www.taxfoundation.org/publications/show/266.html; active as of August 2005). The central, southern, and western states I have averaged are Alabama, Alaska, Arizona, Arkansas, California, Colorado, Florida, Georgia, Idaho, Illinois, Indiana, Iowa, Kansas, Kentucky, Louisiana, Minnesota, Mississippi, Missouri, Montana, Nebraska, Nevada, New Mexico, North Carolina, North Dakota, Oklahoma, Oregon, South Carolina, South Dakota, Tennessee, Texas, Utah, Virginia, Washington, West Virginia, Wisconsin, and Wyoming. All but thirteen of these thirty-six states took in more federal dollars than they paid out in federal taxes in 2003. The exceptions were California (received 78 cents on each dollar paid), Colorado (received 80 cents), Florida (broke even at $1 received for each $1 paid), Georgia (95 cents), Illinois (73 cents), Indiana (96 cents), Nevada (70 cents), Oregon (broke even), Texas (98 cents), Washington (90 cents), West Virginia (90 cents), Wisconsin (84 cents), and Minnesota (70 cents). These thirteen states, along with the liberal northeastern states of Massachusetts (receives 78 cents for each dollar paid in federal taxes), New Jersey (receives 57 cents for each dollar paid in federal taxes), and New York (receives 80 cents for each dollar paid in federal taxes), are subsidizing the other parasitical "ruggedly independent" central, southern, and western states.

Of the thirteen central, southern, and western states that took in less money in federal taxes than they paid out in 2003, six of them went Democratic in 2004: California, Illinois, Minnesota, Oregon, Washington, and Wisconsin. Seven went Republican: Colorado, Florida, Georgia, Indiana, Nevada, Texas, and West Virginia. Twenty states both took in more money than they paid out in federal taxes in 2003 and voted Republican in 2004: Arkansas, Idaho, Iowa, Kansas, Kentucky, Louisiana, Mississippi, Missouri, Montana, Nebraska, New Mexico, North Carolina, North Dakota, Oklahoma, South Dakota, South Carolina, Tennessee, Utah, Virginia, and Wyoming. If we assume that voting Republican is correlated with accepting the myth of the rugged, individualistic, self-sufficient ethos of the South and West (and it's a good assumption, since Republican ideology and individual Republicans often make this point), then there is a serious disconnect between ideology and reality for many of the voters in these twenty states. They really ought to admit that they are parasites on the liberal northeastern states (and a few fellow central, southern, and western states) or else accept less federal tax money. It's something for them to think about, anyway, as they ride on their roads and bridges, use electricity, and rely on law enforcement that is to a great extent paid for by the citizens of those northeastern liberal states toward whom these westerners and southerners feel so superior.

2. Dominique Dhombres, "Michael Moore Est un Clown Qui Dit la Vérité" (Michael Moore Is a Clown Who Speaks the Truth), *Le Monde*, May 25, 2004 (translation by the author).

3. "Teaming Up," *Newsweek*, November 15, 2004. This election wrap-up story was reported by Eleanor Clift, Kevin Peraino, Jonathan Darman, Peter Goldman, Holly Bailey, Tamara Lipper, and Suzanne Smalley, and written by Evan Thomas.

4. For example, on *The Charlie Rose Show*, July 1, 2004.

5. Jim Rutenberg, "Disney Is Blocking Distribution of Film That Criticizes Bush," *New York Times*, May 5, 2004.

6. See Andrew Gumbel's "Moore Accused of Publicity Stunt over Disney 'Ban,'" *Independent* (U.K.), May 7, 2004.

7. Seeing this clip of Bush displaying his self-regard, one is painfully reminded that this is the man who, when questioned about what he has done to address racial problems and to win the allegiance of black voters, responded that he was "disappointed, frankly, in the vote I got in the African-American community." Richard W. Stevenson, "Bush Says He Will Press Ahead with Broad Political Agenda," *New York Times*, October 5, 2005.

8. Louis Menand, "Nanook and Me," *New Yorker*, August 9, 2004.

9. Mary Ann Poust, *Catholic New York*, October 26, 2000.

10. For a detailed overview of the failed negotiations involving Unocal, the Taliban, and the U.S. State Department, see Ahmed Rashid's fascinating book *Taliban: Militant Islam, Oil and Fundamentalism in Central Asia* (New Haven, CT: Yale University Press, 2001), especially chapter 13, "Romancing the Taliban 2, the Battle for Pipelines 1997–99: The USA and the Taliban."

11. Teresa Watanabe, "Overture by Taliban Hits Resistance," *Los Angeles Times*, March 16, 2001.

12. Robin Wright, "Taliban Asks US to Lift Its Economic Sanctions," *Los Angeles Times*, March 20, 2001.

13. Watanabe, "Overture by Taliban."

14. To his credit, Moore does reprint material mentioning Clarke's role in the bin Ladens' departure in *The Official Fahrenheit 9/11 Reader* (New York: Simon and Schuster, 2004). At a public lecture, I once heard Moore insist that the jet that was commandeered for this purpose was the plane that was usually used to fly the Washington press corps around, and that that decision was made by Karl Rove, just to show that he could do something outrageous and tweak the press at the same time and that the incompetent, sycophantic press would never even catch on. This story seems to combine paranoia and a wildly distorted view of Karl Rove's decision-making powers.

15. Again, Moore included an article on this subject in *The Official Fahrenheit 9/11 Reader*.

16. See *Fahrenheit 9/11* ("Was it the guy my daddy's friends delivered a lot of weapons to?") and also Moore's use of sources to "prove"—was it ever in dispute?—that the Reagan administration sold arms to Iraq during the Iran-Iraq war, in *The Official Fahrenheit 9/11 Reader*, pp. 144–45.

17. See Christopher Hitchens, "Unfairenheit 9/11," *Slate*, June 21, 2004 (http://slate.msn.com/id/2102723/; active as of August 2005).

18. John Berger, "The Beginning of History," *Guardian* (U.K.), August 31, 2004, and as reprinted in the introduction to Moore's *The Official Fahrenheit 9/11*

Reader. Berger also approvingly found in the film the conclusion—worthy of an idealistic high school student—that "a political economy which creates colossally increasing wealth surrounded by disastrously increasing poverty, needs—in order to survive—a continual war with some invented foreign enemy to maintain its own internal order and security. It requires ceaseless war."

19. See Lowry's comments on *National Review Online*'s "The Corner," November 22, 2004 (www.nationalreview.com/thecorner/04_11_22_corner-archive .asp#046444; active as of October 2005).

8 New York 2004: Among the Republicans

1. Ann Coulter, "Put the Speakers in a Cage" (http://anncoulter.com/columns/2004/072604.htm; active as of August 2005).

2. Ann Coulter, "This Is War," *National Review Online*, September 13, 2001 (no longer posted).

3. Unpublished fragment quoted in *Washington Monthly Online* (www .washingtonmonthly.com/features/2001/0111.coulterwisdom.html; active as of August 2005).

4. Jonah Goldberg, "L'Affaire Coulter," *National Review Online*, October 3, 2001 (www.nationalreview.com/nr_comment/nr_comment100301.shtml; active as of August 2005).

5. See www.nationalreview.com/thecorner/2002_10_20_corner-archive.asp; active as of August 2005. As it turns out, John Muhammad is not gay, as far as anyone knows.

6. See Richard H. Davis, "Anatomy of a Smear Campaign," *Boston Globe*, March 21, 2004.

7. Michael Moore, *USA Today*, September 1, 2004.

8. For a description of this party, see Thomas Frank, "What's the Matter with Liberals?" *New York Review of Books*, May 12, 2005.

9. From a transcript of Giuliani's speech to the convention posted on CNN's Web site (www.cnn.com/2004/ALLPOLITICS/08/30/giuliani.transcript/; active as of August 2005).

9 Fahrenheit versus Celsius

1. Those who stand to lose out due to this arrangement are never idle, however. It is worth mentioning that the first reaction of Donald Rumsfeld and George W. Bush to the Abu Ghraib pictures was to blame those who took them; the problem was not the abuse, it was the pictures of the abuse. In memos and orders, Bush and Rumsfeld immediately set about confiscating as many pictures as they could find rather than addressing the genesis of this shameful crisis.

2. David Bossie, interviewed on CNBC's *Capital Report*, September 29, 2004.

3. The *Washington Times* is published by the Korean billionaire Sun Myung Moon, of Moonie cult fame, who is a major contributor to right-wing causes and who wields such influence in the capitol that he was crowned the new Messiah in a ceremony in the Dirksen Senate Office Building on March 23, 2004, with Congressmen Tom Davis III, Philip Crane, Eddie Johnson, Curt Weldon, Danny Davis, Harold Ford Jr., Roscoe Bartlett, Sanford Bishop, and Chris Cannon attending, along with Senator Lindsey Graham and former senator Larry Pressler. Moon somehow got a shofar-blowing rabbi to declare him "possibly the Messiah." Who says politics is boring? (See John Gorenfeld, "Hail to the Moon King," *Salon*, June 21, 2004,

http://archive.salon.com/news/feature/2004/06/21/moon/index_np.html; active as of August 2005.)

4. For his role in the Iran-Contra scandal of the mid-1980s, Oliver North was convicted of accepting an illegal payment, obstructing a congressional investigation, and illegally destroying documents. His conviction was overturned on a technicality; a court ruled that it was derived from North's own testimony, for which he had been offered immunity. North was later granted a full pardon by outgoing president George H. W. Bush in 1992.

5. David N. Bossie and Christopher M. Gray, "Bin Laden's Rage: Why He and His Followers Hate the United States," policy paper posted on www.citizensunited.com and published in Citizens United's own journal, *Citizens United Public Policy Review* 1 (no. 2). For an excellent discussion of the European democracies' role in suppressing democracy in the Arab world, see Rashid Khalidi, *Resurrecting Empire: Western Footprints and America's Perilous Path in the Middle East* (Boston: Beacon Press, 2004).

6. David N. Bossie, "Blame America First: College Campuses Respond to the War on Terror," policy paper posted on www.citizensunited.com and published in *Citizens United Public Policy Review* (no. 6).

7. In 1954, the CIA commissioned a secret report, since declassified, that was written by Dr. Donald N. Wilber, a participant in the coup; the report is titled "Clandestine Service History: Overthrow of Premier Moussadeq of Iran, November 1952–August 1953." The table of contents of the original report, with links to every chapter, can be found at www.nytimes.com/library/world/mideast/iran-cia-intro.pdf; there is extensive commentary at www.nytimes.com/library/world/mideast/041600iran-cia-index.html. A different version of the report, one that restores some passages that were deleted prior to release, can be found at Iran Online, www.iranonline.com/newsroom/Archive/Mossadeq/index.html. Links were active as of August 2005.

8. See David B. Ottaway, "Democratic Fundraiser Pursues Agenda on Sudan," *Washington Post*, April 29, 1997.

9. For a more convincing survey of the forces in the Middle East that fed the terrorist ideology, see Kanan Makiya, "Arab Demons, Arab Dreams," in *The Fight Is for Democracy: Winning the War of Ideas in America and the World*, George Packer, ed. (New York: HarperPerennial, 2003).

10. For a thorough debunking of Emerson's work even before September 11, see John F. Sugg, "Steven Emerson's Crusade," December 4, 2000, at www.mediamonitors.net/whoisemerson.html; active as of August 2005.

11. Moore has this on film in *Fahrenheit 9/11* in a scene that cannot be taken out of context.

12. An article in the *Washington Post* reported:

A week before George W. Bush's [late June] 1990 sale of stock in Harken Energy Co., the firm's outside lawyers cautioned Bush and other directors against selling shares if they had significant negative information about the company's prospects. [Harken President Mikel D. Faulkner had told company directors in April that the company was facing a grave financial crisis.] The sale came a few months before Harken reported significant losses [$23.2 million], leading to an investigation by the Securities and Exchange Commission. The June 15, 1990, letter from the Haynes and Boone law firm wasn't sent to the SEC by Bush's attorney Robert W.

Jordan until August 22, 1991, according to a letter by Jordan. That was one day after SEC staff members investigating the stock sale concluded there was insufficient evidence to recommend an enforcement action against Bush for insider trading. . . . The delay in delivering the law firm's report to the SEC—Harken executives had previously withheld it citing attorney-client privilege—indicates that regulators did not have a full picture of the Bush transaction when they finished their investigation, said Michael Aguirre, a securities lawyer in San Diego, who obtained the documents in the case last summer after filing a Freedom of Information request. "There was a failure to deal with the most important piece of evidence," he said.

Peter Behr, "Bush Sold Stock after Lawyers' Warning," *Washington Post*, November 1, 2002. Action against George W. Bush was later dropped. Richard Breeden, the chairman of the Securities and Exchange Commission at the time, was a good friend of George H. W. Bush, had served as Bush Sr.'s deputy counsel when Bush was vice president, and had been appointed by Bush Sr. to the SEC position when he became president. James R. Doty, the SEC's general counsel, had advised George W. Bush on matters relating to the Texas Rangers. The SEC investigators, however, explicitly said that although the agency declined to take action, this should not be taken as an absolution of George W. Bush in the matter. Bruce Hiler, the agency's associate director for enforcement, wrote in a memo of October 18, 1993, that "the investigation has been terminated as to the conduct of Mr. Bush, and that, at this time, no enforcement action is contemplated with respect to him. . . . [This] must in no way be construed as indicating that the party has been exonerated or that no action may ultimately result."

13. Perhaps this is due to a technicality—Hawaii was a U.S. territory but not a state in 1941—but it seems to be a technicality employed to reduce the status of one of America's greatest wartime leaders, a man who rarely invoked religion.

14. As someone who tried very hard to get an interview with Moore, I have a great deal of sympathy for Wilson's frustration.

15. Jim and Ellen Hubbard, interview with Liane Hansen on "Weekend Edition," National Public Radio, September 5, 2004.

16. Michael Wilson's film is an exception in this regard; Wilson does seem less focused on partisan politics than the other anti-Moore movies, and more concerned with human truths, however banal.

17. Comments from Drudge and Cutler in Joe Hagan, "Amanpour Says Saddam TV Was Distorted . . . Drudge Says Moore's 9/11 Is Pure—Drudge!" *New York Observer*, July 12, 2004.

18. In July 2005, there were no less than fourteen books for sale on Amazon.com that were dedicated to debunking Limbaugh's bizarre misstatements of fact. A search of the Web site of Fairness and Accuracy in Media (www.fair.org) will return an enormous list of Rush statements that are simply not true.

10 Moore Abroad

1. The question of why the British, who also have Middle Eastern colonial experience, did not realize this is an interesting one. It is true, however, that the British occupying forces in Iraq have had significantly more success than the American forces in navigating the cultural perils, in spite of their truly disastrous episode of colonialism in twentieth-century Iraq (it may also have to do with their assignment

to the Shi'ite south of the country, where Saddam had few adherents and where the invasion was more widely viewed as a liberation). It might simply be that the pull of the "special relationship" with their cousins across the Atlantic is more powerful than their former colonial relationships and colonial knowledge.

Then again, British and French colonial patterns were always different. While the British system of indirect rule might have given many colonial subjects more day-to-day control of their own lives—and kept the British out of sight in many colonial matters—the French were more willing to assimilate their subjects, in the process perhaps getting to know them better. Starting in 1834, French colonial subjects under certain circumstances could acquire French citizenship, and in 1848, when universal male suffrage was introduced, colonial men who had citizenship could vote and sit in the French parliament as representatives of their native districts. It's hard to imagine Indians representing Indian districts in the Parliament of Victoria, or that of George VI in 1947 (although a few ethnic Indians did represent British districts, as naturalized British citizens resident in Britain). In many ways, French colonialism was more intimate than the British version, if no more legitimate.

2. Christopher Hitchens, in a comment on MSNBC's *Scarborough Country*, May 18, 2004.

3. John Berger, "The Beginning of History," *Guardian* (U.K.), August 24, 2004.

4. Jean-Luc Douin, "La croisade anti-Bush d'un justicier cineaste" (The anti-Bush crusade of a justice-seeking filmmaker), *Le Monde*, July 7, 2004 (translation by the author).

5. Pascal Bruckner, "Paris Dispatch: Tour de Farce," *New Republic*, July 19, 2004.

6. Ibid.

7. William Karel, interview in *Le Monde*, June 12, 2004 (translation by the author).

8. Hussein Ibish, "Fahrenheit 9/11 Misses Mark on Conspiracies," *Daily Star* (Lebanon), July 12, 2004.

9. Comment posted on the Web site of the Polish film society Stopklatka, July 25, 2004 (translation by the author).

10. Stephen Zeitchik, "Michael Moore in Germany: Better Known than JFK?" *Publishers Weekly*, October 22, 2003.

11. Die Zeit, "Nicht Ganz Amerika Ist Verrückt" (Not All Americans Are Crazy), www.zeit.de/2003/46/AbdruckMoor, November 6, 2003 (translation by the author).

11 Populism

1. Moore had taken *Fahrenheit 9/11* out of contention in the documentary category so as to be able to show it on television just prior to the 2004 election; films that have appeared on television prior to the awards are not eligible in the documentary category. Had *Fahrenheit* been nominated for Best Picture, it would have been competing in this category against an unusually strong field that included *Sideways, Hotel Rwanda, Million Dollar Baby,* and *Ray*.

2. Michael Moore, interviewed on CNN's *Lou Dobbs Moneyline*, April 12, 2002.

3. Michael Kazin, *The Populist Persuasion*, rev. ed. (Ithaca, NY: Cornell University Press, 1998), p. 11.

4. In a time of war in the Middle East, unstable oil supplies, and terrorism that derives some of its funding from oil profits, one could make the argument that wasting fuel is unpatriotic, but you won't hear this from a Republican elite firmly allied with the U.S. energy industry.

5. Think, for example, of Newt Gingrich's new book, *Winning the Future: A 21st-Century Contract with America* (Washington, DC: Regnery Publishing, 2005), in which this man who has never shown much personal religious devotion urges even greater penetration of the institutions of state by the religious agenda of "people of faith."

6. *New York Times*, October 29, 2000.

7. Maureen Dowd, "G.O.P.'s Rising Star Pledges to Right Wrongs of the Left," *New York Times*, November 10, 1994.

8. Peggy Noonan, in an online question-and-answer session for the *Washington Post*, February 17, 2004.

9. Susan Threadgill, "Who's Who," *Washington Monthly*, October 2000.

10. Kevin Phillips, "The Future of American Politics," *National Review*, December 22, 1972.

11. Richard Hofstadter, *The American Political Tradition* (New York: Vintage Books, 1989), p. 62.

12. Kazin, *The Populist Persuasion*, p. 22.

13. Robert Warshow, "The Gangster as Tragic Hero" (1949), in *The Immediate Experience: Movies, Comics, Theater, and Other Aspects of Popular Culture* (Cambridge, MA: Harvard University Press, 2001), p. 97.

14. Nikita Khrushchev, in *Khrushchev Remembers: The Glasnost Tapes*, Jerrold L. Schecter and Vyacheslav V. Luchkow, eds. (Boston: Little, Brown, 1991), p. 194.

15. Robert Warshow, "The 'Idealism' of Julius and Ethel Rosenberg" (1953), in *The Immediate Experience*, p. 47.

16. Range also contributed an article to the harshly partisan *Michael Moore Is a Big Fat Stupid White Man*.

17. For example, "Michael Moore's Truth Problem," *Blueprint* (www.dlc.org/ndol_ci.cfm?contentid=252483; active as of August 2005).

12 Terrorism

1. George Galloway, interview on Abu Dhabi television, March 28, 2003.

2. John Deane, "Galloway Urges British Troops to Disobey Orders," *Press Association*, April 1, 2003.

3. The issue of the effects of sanctions is nowhere near as simple as those who have joined the chorus of absolutist protest would have it. The number of 500,000 dead children, which has entered the public consciousness as common knowledge, is highly vexed. This number apparently arose twice, independently: once from a post-1991 study performed under UN auspices by Saddam's health ministry, which used a very limited sample and had every motivation to inflate the number of dead, and once from a more respectable UNICEF study that found that if the reduction in infant mortality that Iraq saw in the 1980s had continued in the 1990s, there might have been a total of 500,000 fewer under-five deaths. Certainly sanctions played a part here, but that's a subtly yet importantly different statement than saying that the sanctions caused 500,000 child deaths. It's also a huge hypothetical that encompasses a great many things—like three wars (Iran-Iraq, the 1990 Gulf War, and the 2003 invasion of Iraq), two uprisings and their repression, an enormous deterioration in social services, and a period (1991–1996) in which Saddam was refusing the oil-for-food program—in addition to the sanctions.

There is no question that the Iraqi government under Saddam Hussein greatly contributed to the deaths. The Republican Guard and Saddam's elite were well fed, and palace construction went on apace during the period of the sanctions. Perversely, the regime had an incentive not to look after its people; the more dead children, the easier the propaganda victories. Life expectancy in the Kurdish-administered north of Iraq, where there were leaders who actually had an interest in public health rather than in brutalizing their constituents, went up during the period of the sanctions (although this comparison isn't quite fair, since there were many more humanitarian organizations operating there, the north received proportionately more money from the oil-for-food program, and the borders were much more porous, which encouraged smuggling). Still, it is true that a de facto Kurdish government that was actually concerned with its people's well-being made an enormous difference compared to areas under Saddam's control.

Richard Garfield, a professor of clinical international nursing at Columbia and one of the foremost experts on Iraq's multidimensional public health crisis, has estimated 350,000 excess under-five deaths between 1991 and 2002. This is an enormous number and an enormous tragedy, one that has been shown no respect by its shameless politicization by interest groups on both sides of the sanctions question. Garfield's analysis suggests a complex matrix of causes, some of which were directly or indirectly related to sanctions, some of which have to do with the lingering primary, secondary, and tertiary affects of the 1991 Gulf War, and some of which have to do with really bad public health practices under the government of Iraq post-1991. This clearly does not mean that all of those deaths can be attributed to sanctions, nor that the numbers given by the Iraqi government and its activist sympathizers can be accepted without skepticism. I myself once spoke to a former administrator of the oil-for-food program who told me, "The Iraqis act as if no one ever died before the sanctions; every death is counted as sanctions-related." (For a very interesting discussion of the political uses of sanctions, both for and against, see Matt Welch, "The Politics of Dead Children," *Reason Online*, March 2002, www.reason.com/0203/fe.mw.the.shtml. For more detailed information, see Richard Garfield's study, "Morbidity and Mortality among Iraqi Children from 1990 through 1998: Assessing the Impact of the Gulf War and Economic Sanctions," July 1999, www.casi.org.uk/info/garfield/dr-garfield.html; active as of August 2005.)

There is also the uncomfortable fact that in the absence of any sanctions, Saddam Hussein very likely would have been working on his weapons programs. There was a very powerful argument for reforming the sanctions while Saddam was in power, so that they would more effectively target the regime rather than the Iraqi people. However, a considerable part of the anti-sanctions movement was focused on dropping them entirely, opposing even "smart sanctions." The complete opposition to sanctions, with the implication that their official intent of blocking weapons development was a sham, conveniently supported the thesis that the United States and the United Nations were inflicting misery on Iraq out of some irrational neocolonial sadism. Iraq was, in fact, for much of the world, an enormous problem without any painless solutions between 1991 and 2003.

4. Galloway, interviewed on Abu Dhabi television, November 20, 2004.

5. Details of Galloway's office and his statements about Castro and North Korea can be found in Andrew Mueller's interview with Galloway in the *Independent on Sunday*, October 26, 2003.

6. Simon Hattenstone, "Saddam and Me," *Guardian*, September 16, 2002.

7. *Times* (London), January 20, 1994, as transcribed from the BBC Monitoring Service's record of the speech on Baghdad Radio. Galloway spoke in English and was followed by an Arabic translation.

8. Although Chait's and Pollack's arguments rested primarily on the threat of Saddam's weapons of mass destruction, they worked from the best information available to them at the time, and they did so honestly (unlike the Bush administration, which let it be known what kind of information it wanted), and both have made other arguments, too.

Furthermore, it would be shallow and callow to suggest that the WMD argument has been completely discredited. An important part of Pollack's thesis was that the post-1991 sanctions regime on Iraq was falling apart and that it could not be sustained much longer. In the absence of sanctions, there would have been no effective way of keeping Saddam from fulfilling his long-held ambition of acquiring these weapons. Would this have been an acceptable scenario? There were legitimate arguments against going to war with Iraq, and there were legitimate arguments for lifting sanctions, which were clearly hurting the Iraqi people more than they were hurting Saddam's power structure. But liberals who argued at the time—as, unfortunately, many did—both against war and against sanctions were indulging in irresponsible moral grandstanding.

9. Patrick D. Healy, "Rove Criticizes Liberals on 9/11," *New York Times*, June 23, 2005.

10. Shelby Steele, "Radical Sheik," op-ed, *Wall Street Journal*, December 10, 2001.

11. Michael Moore, *Downsize This!* (New York: HarperPerennial, 1997), p. 18. In Moore's film *The Big One*, he makes a particularly silly exposition on this comparison. He points out that many of the people laid off by large, profitable corporations will eventually die from various causes, some of which, he speculates, would be related to getting laid off. "What do you call that?" he asks rhetorically.

12. From www.michaelmoore.com (no longer posted).

13. "Mike's Letter," on www.michaelmoore.com, April 14, 2004 (www.michaelmoore.com/words/message/index.php?messageDate=2004-04-14; active as of August 2005).

14. The preceding remarks were made by Cindy Sheehan at a rally at San Francisco State University on April 27, 2005 (transcript available at www.discoverthenetwork.org/Articles/Stewartrally.htm; active as of September 2005).

15. "Mike's Letter," on www.michaelmoore.com, September 14, 2001. Postings from Moore's road trip in the aftermath of September 11 are available through the Internet's "wayback machine" at www.archive.org.

16. "Mike's Letter," on www.michaelmoore.com, September 15, 2001.

17. Michael Moore, interview with Kazumoto Ono for the *Shukan Post*, April 21, 2003.

18. Michael Moore, *Dude, Where's My Country?* (New York: Warner Books, 2003), p. 101.

19. See Nancy Tartaglione, "Fahrenheit to Be First Doc Released Theatrically in Middle East," *Screen Daily*, June 9, 2004.

20. Osama bin Laden's videotape, as translated and broadcast by CNN, October 24, 2004. Of all the things one can criticize about Bush's reaction to September 11 and his conduct of the war on terror, that seven minutes surely should not be one of them. As conservatives have rightly pointed out, how would it have helped to jump up in a panic and run from the room before he could have had any solid information about the situation? The Secret Service was arranging a secure route back to Air Force One while Bush sat in the classroom. Whatever one thinks of Bush's character and his competence, his calm at that moment does not reflect badly on either

one. Also, Moore got a minor detail wrong. It was *The Pet Goat*, not *My Pet Goat*, and it was a calibrated reading exercise, not a children's story as such.

21. Peter Beinart, "A Fighting Faith: An Argument for a New Liberalism," *New Republic*, December 13, 2004.

22. John B. Judis, "Purpose Driven," *New Republic Online*, December 8, 2004.

23. Eric Alterman, "A Reply to Peter Beinart," *Nation*, January 10, 2005.

24. During the 2000 presidential campaign, dogged by rumors of cocaine use, Bush finessed the question in a way that presumably could not lead to charges that he had lied about his past. He said that he could have legitimately obtained a National Security clearance at the time of his father's presidential administration, which began in 1989. Since the standard for a clearance at that time required no illegal drug use for the last fifteen years, this was interpreted as a statement that he had not used any illegal drugs since 1974. (See Andrew Miga, "Bush Maintains He's 25 Years Drug-Free," *Boston Herald*, August 20, 1999.) In 1994, when asked about cocaine use, he replied, "Maybe I did, maybe I didn't. What's the relevance? How I behaved as an irresponsible youth is irrelevant to this campaign. It does not matter what I did, nor [what] Ann Richards did. What matters is how I behave as an adult." ("Drugs 'irrelevant to race,' Bush says," *Houston Chronicle*, May 3, 1994.) This is less than an absolute denial, and a particularly hypocritical evasion, since, when Bush was the governor of Texas, he signed a 1997 law that mandated increased penalties for anyone, "irresponsible youth" or not, caught with less than a gram of cocaine. Clearly, different rules apply to members of Bush's social class. On the day that Bush categorically denies that he has ever used cocaine, I will withdraw my statement that he used the drug and got away with it. I'll take his word for it.

25. Michael Moore, *Stupid White Men* (New York: Regan Books, 2002), p. 195.

26. Larissa MacFarquhar, "The Populist," *New Yorker*, February 16 and 23, 2004.

27. See Steven Erlanger, "In Europe, Some Say the Attacks Stemmed from American Failings," *New York Times*, September 22, 2001.

28. David Boaz, "Attacks on American Values," October 1, 2001, Cato Institute Web site (www.cato.org/dailys/10-01-01.html; active as of August 2005).

29. John Derbyshire, "May Diary," *National Review Online*, May 28, 2004.

13 Prospects

1. "Mike's Letter," September 7, 2005 (www.michaelmoore.com/words/message/index.php?messageDate=2005-09-07; active as of October 2005).

2. See Michael Moore, *Stupid White Men* (New York: Regan Books, 2002), pp. 252–53.

3. Harry Levine, "Ralph Nader, Suicide Bomber: How the Great Crusader Used the Green Party to Get His Revenge," *Village Voice*, May 3, 2004. Levine also recounts a conversation with Tarek Milleron, Nader's 2000 campaign manager, in which Milleron explains the reason that the Nader campaign was not going to engage in vote-swapping with Gore: "[W]e want to punish the Democrats, we want to hurt them, wound them." It's this kind of attitude that has made Nader very unwelcome among many on the American left since 2000.

4. Goldberg's list is a weird one. I can't follow his reasoning as to why the mild-mannered, sincere Al Franken is one of the people who is doing the most harm to American political discourse. Why is the serious sociology and policy writer Jonathan Kozol on the list? Does Gloria Steinem really deserve a place? Eve Ensler? Lee Bollinger, president of Columbia University and former president of the University

of Michigan, makes the list because he took a nuanced position on affirmative action. Bill Moyers is there; Rush Limbaugh and Ann Coulter are not. To Goldberg's credit, his list does include a few figures from the lunatic hard right. Roy Moore of Alabama is on it, for example. Judge Moore is the former chief justice of the Alabama Supreme Court who refused to remove his two-and-a-half-ton stone Ten Commandments monument from the State Supreme Court building when a federal judge so ordered him. So is Michael Savage, the desperately vicious far-right radio host and political commentator. But the list is so heavily weighted toward the center-left that one suspects that the far-right characters who made the list are merely protective camouflage to make Goldberg's agenda look less partisan than it is.

5. *Saturday Night Live*, October 30, 2004.

6. Todd Gitlin, "Michael Moore, Alas," OpenDemocracy.net, July 1, 2004 (www.opendemocracy.net/themes/article-3-1988.jsp; active as of August 2005).

7. Naomi Klein, "Bring Najaf to New York," *Nation*, September 13, 2004.

8. Moore, *Stupid White Men*, p. xvii.

9. For a fuller description of Moore's stock portfolio, see *Peter Schweizer, Do as I Say (Not as I Do): Profiles in Liberal Hypocrisy* (New York: Doubleday, 2005), pp. 52–55.

10. Kathleen Antrim, "Moore Now Getting Less," *San Francisco Examiner*, February 25, 2005.

11. Laura Fraser, "In *Roger & Me*, Michael Moore Plays Fast and Loose with the Facts," *San Francisco Bay Guardian*, January 17, 1990.

12. Daniel Okrent, "The Public Editor: An Advocate for *Times* Readers Introduces Himself," *New York Times*, December 7, 2003.

13. Mark Dowie, "A Nation of Minds," unpublished, courtesy of Mr. Dowie.

Postscript: A Challenge for Conservatives

1. *Time*, cover, April 25, 2005.

2. Charles Krauthammer, "In Defense of Secret Tribunals," *Time*, November 19, 2001, and "The Truth About Torture," *Weekly Standard*, December 5, 2005. Krauthammer apparently believes that torture really can be invoked and controlled in restricted circumstances, without corrupting military practices and the society that sponsors those practices. He seems unaware that the abuse at Abu Ghraib, which he deplores, was exactly such a controlled circumstance. Krauthammer wants to believe that Abu Ghraib was a rogue operation. But as Seymour Hersh has shown in his important book, *Chain of Command: The Road from 9/11 to Abu Ghraib* (New York: HarperCollins, 2004), what took place in Abu Ghraib under American command was the result of policy decisions made at the very top, by Bush, Cheney, Rumsfeld, and Rumsfeld's aide Stephen Cambone, the undersecretary of defense for intelligence.

Krauthammer also seems to have no idea what a slippery slope he is on. He approvingly cites the use of torture by Israeli soldiers in a successful attempt to learn the whereabouts of a kidnapped colleague. Would he approve of Hezbollah torturing an Israeli soldier for urgent information about the where abouts of a captured Hezbollah operative, an operative who, in Krauthammer's grim world, might well be scheduled for torture by Israelis? If not—and, I think it's safe to say, this is a "not"—Krauthammer's position is by no means as rational and logical as he presents it to be.

3. Charles Krauthammer, "Gitmo Grovel: Enough Already," *Washington Post*, June 3, 2005. In this column, Krauthammer also makes the specious argument that "Koran abuse" as a tool of interrogation is a trifling thing compared to the attacks of

September 11. Of course it is; but—even leaving aside the obvious concern about how public knowledge of this practice helps terrorists win hearts and minds around the world—should American interrogators be limited in their techniques only by what is less bad than September 11? That leaves a great many things open, and this is consistent with Krauthammer's views. In focusing on "Koran abuse," he lets the Guantanamo jailers escape responsibility for much more serious crimes.

For a very different view of what goes on at Guantanamo, see Jane Mayer, "The Experiment," *New Yorker*, July 11, 2005. The deputy judge advocate general of the Air Force, Major General Jack Rives, the Navy's chief lawyer, Rear Admiral Michael Lohr, the senior Marine lawyer Brigadier General Kevin Sandkuhler, and the Army's top-ranking lawyer, Major General Thomas Romig, have all expressed grave doubts as to the legality of some of the interrogation practices in use at Guantanamo (Neil A. Lewis, "Military's Opposition to Harsh Interrogation Is Outlined," *New York Times*, July 28, 2005). The FBI at one point warned its agents not to participate in Guantanamo interrogations that could leave them open to criminal liability under international law.

The standards in effect at Guantanamo, and at many other U.S. detention facilities around the world, apparently reflect, perhaps informally if not by direct order, the legal conclusions of a memo that John Yoo prepared in August 2002 for Alberto Gonzales, under the signature of Yoo's supervisor, Jay Bybee. Yoo was at the time an attorney in the Justice Department's Office of Legal Counsel, and Gonzales was then counsel to the president, the chief White House legal adviser. This memo is an astonishing document. It is clearly designed to define torture in such a way as to make the word inapplicable to almost any act of brutality, and thereby to render torture legal in everything but name. Among other things, Yoo argues that for an act to be considered torture, there must be a specific intent on the part of the accused to inflict pain "even if the defendant knows that severe pain will result from his actions, if causing such harm is not his objective, he lacks the requisite specific intent even though the defendant did not act in good faith" (p. 4). This opens up an enormous field of action for creative lawyers. Yoo defines physical torture this way: "The victim must experience intense pain or suffering, of the kind that is equivalent to the pain that would be associated with serious physical injury so severe that death, organ failure, or permanent damage resulting in a loss of significant body function will likely result" (p. 13). (Memo from Jay S. Bybee to Alberto Gonzales, August 1, 2002. The memo can be found at www.washingtonpost.com/wp-srv/nation/documents/dojinterrogationmemo20020801.pdf, active as of August 2005.) Note that Yoo's view of what constitutes torture is by no means identical to that of the Geneva Conventions (or the eighth amendment of the U.S. constitution, as interpreted by the courts). Apparently Krauthammer had not read this memo or heard of its consequences when he pronounced the treatment of prisoners at Guantanamo to be "remarkably humane and tolerant," as cited previously.

There is an interesting discussion of this memo and its importance in Mark Danner's book *Torture and Truth: America, Abu Ghraib, and the War on Terror* (New York: New York Review of Books, 2004). Dana Priest of the *Washington Post* has recently reported on a clandestine system of CIA prisons all over the world, in which suspected terrorists are held without charge and without anyone outside the system having knowledge of their identities, status, or even existence. This is a system designed to defeat transparency and accountability, and thus might as well have been designed to encourage human rights abuses. It is fundamentally antidemocratic, a betrayal of everything the United States is supposed to stand for, everything

American conservatives and American liberals are supposed to stand for, and it corrupts the U.S. government at home. See Dana Priest, "CIA Holds Terror Suspects in Secret Prison," *Washington Post*, November 2, 2005. Krauthammer thinks these prisons are just fine; see Charles Krauthammer, "The Truth about Torture," *Weekly Standard*, December 5, 2005.

4. Ann Coulter, "Live and Let Spy," www.anncoulter.com, December 21, 2005. This article was no longer posted as of January 2006 but is in syndication at www.townhall.com.

5. Michael Savage, *Liberalism Is a Mental Disorder: Savage Solutions* (Nashville, TN: Nelson Current, 2005).

6. Michael Savage, as host of *Savage Nation* on MSNBC, July 5, 2003.

SOURCES

Books and Periodicals

Ali, Tariq. *The Clash of Fundamentalisms: Crusades, Jihads, and Modernity*. London: Verso, 2002.

Anderson, Jack. *Inside the NRA: Armed and Dangerous*. New York: Dove Books, 1996.

Barnard, John. *Walter Reuther and the Rise of the Auto Workers*. Boston: Little, Brown & Co., 1983.

Bossie, David, and Christopher M. Gray. "Bin Laden's Rage: Why He and His Followers Hate the United States." *Citizens United Public Policy Review* 2 (no. 1).

———."Blame America First, Again: The Campus Left Responds to the War on Terror." *Citizens United Public Policy Review* 2 (no. 6).

Brody, Reed. *Contra Terror in Nicaragua: Report of a Fact-Finding Mission, September 1984–January 1985*. Boston: South End Press, 1985.

Brown, Timothy C. *The Real Contra War: Highlander Peasant Resistance in Nicaragua*. Norman: University of Oklahoma Press, 2001.

Bugliosi, Vincent. *The Betrayal of America: How the Supreme Court Undermined the Constitution and Chose Our President*. New York: Nation Books/ Thunder's Mouth Press, 2001.

Coulter, Ann. *Slander: Liberal Lies about the American Right*. New York: Crown, 2002.

———. *Treason: Liberal Treachery from the Cold War to the War on Terrorism*. New York: Crown Forum, 2003.

Danner, Mark. *Torture and Truth: America, Abu Ghraib, and the War on Terror*. New York: New York Review of Books, 2004.

Dershowitz, Alan. *Supreme Injustice: How the High Court Hijacked the Election of 2000*. New York: Oxford University Press, 2001.

Dizard, Jan E., Robert Merrill Muth, and Stephen P. Andrews Jr., eds. *Guns in America: A Reader*. New York: New York University Press, 1999.

Dowie, Mark. "A Nation of Minds." Unpublished, courtesy of Mr. Dowie.

Frank, Thomas. *What's the Matter with Kansas? How Conservatives Won the Heart of America*. New York: Metropolitan Books, 2004. (Published in the U.K. as *What's the Matter with America?*)

Franken, Al. *Lies and the Lying Liars Who Tell Them: A Fair and Balanced Look at the Right*. New York: Dutton Adult Books, 2003.

Friedlander, Peter. *The Emergence of a UAW Local, 1936–1939*. Pittsburgh: University of Pittsburgh Press, 1975.

Garfield, Richard. "Morbidity and Mortality among Iraqi Children from 1990 through 1998: Assessing the Impact of the Gulf War and Economic Sanctions." www.casi.org.uk/info/garfield/dr-garfield.html, July 1999.

Gingrich, Newt. *Winning the Future: A 21st-Century Contract with America*. Washington, DC: Regnery Publishing, 2005.

Glassner, Barry. *The Culture of Fear: Why Americans Are Afraid of the Wrong Things*. New York: Basic Books, 2000.

Goldberg, Bernard. *100 People Who Are Screwing Up America (And Al Franken Is #37)*. New York: HarperCollins, 2005.

Gray Davidson, Osha. *Under Fire: The NRA and the Battle for Gun Control*. Iowa City: University of Iowa Press, 1998.

Haggerty, Richard A., ed. *El Salvador: A Country Study*. Washington, DC: Federal Research Division, Library of Congress, 1990.

Hamper, Ben. *Rivethead: Tales from the Assembly Line*. New York: Warner Books, 1992.

Hardy, David T., and Jason Clarke. *Michael Moore Is a Big Fat Stupid White Man*. New York: Regan Books, 2004.

Heath, Joseph, and Andrew Potter. *Nation of Rebels: Why Counterculture Became Consumer Culture*. New York: HarperBusiness, 2005.

Hersh, Seymour. *Chain of Command: The Road from 9/11 to Abu Ghraib*. New York: HarperCollins, 2004.

Hitchens, Christopher. *A Long Short War: The Postponed Liberation of Iraq*. New York: Penguin Slate Books/Plume Books, 1998.

Hofstadter, Richard. *The American Political Tradition*. New York: Vintage Books, 1989.

―――. *The Paranoid Style in American Politics and Other Essays*. Cambridge, MA: Harvard University Press, 1996.

Kagan, Robert. *A Twilight Struggle: American Power and Nicaragua, 1977–1990*. New York: Free Press, 1996.

Kazin, Michael. *The Populist Persuasion: An American History*, rev. ed. Ithaca, NY: Cornell University Press, 1998.

Keller, Maryann. *Rude Awakening: The Rise, Fall, and Struggle for Recovery of General Motors*. New York: HarperCollins, 1990.

Khalidi, Rashid. *Resurrecting Empire: Western Footprints and America's Perilous Path in the Middle East*. Boston: Beacon Press, 2004.

Konrád, György. *Antipolitics: An Essay*. San Diego: Harcourt Brace Jovanovich, 1984.

Korten, David C. *When Corporations Rule the World*. San Francisco: Berrett-Koehler Publishers/Kumarian Press, 2001.

Lawrence, Ken, ed. *The World According to Michael Moore*. Kansas City, MO: Andrews McMeel Publishing, 2004.

MacFarquhar, Larissa, "The Populist." *New Yorker*, February16 and 23, 2004.

Menand, Louis: "Nanook and Me." *New Yorker*, August 9, 2004.

Merrill, Tim R., ed. *Nicaragua: A Country Study*. Washington, DC: Federal Research Division, Library of Congress, 1994.

Meyssan, Thierry. *9/11: The Big Lie*. London: Carnot USA, 2003. (Original French title: *11 Septembre 2001: L'effroyable imposture*. Editions Carnot, 2002.)

Micklethwait, John, and Adrian Wooldridge. *The Right Nation: Conservative Power in America.* New York: Penguin Press, 2004.

Moore, Michael. *Downsize This!* New York: HarperPerennial, 1997.

———. *Dude, Where's My Country?* New York: Warner Books, 2003.

———. *Stupid White Men . . . and Other Sorry Excuses for the State of the Nation.* New York: Regan Books, 2002.

Moore, Michael, ed. *The Official Fahrenheit 9/11 Reader.* New York: Simon and Schuster, 2004.

———. *Will They Ever Trust Us Again? Letters from the War Zone.* New York: Simon and Schuster, 2004.

Moore, Michael, and Kathleen Glynn. *Adventures in a TV Nation.* New York: HarperPerennial, 1998.

Nichols, John, and David Deschamps. *Jews for Buchanan: Did You Hear the One about the Theft of the American Presidency?* New York: New Press, 2001.

Noble, Charles. *The Collapse of Liberalism: Why America Needs a New Left.* Lanham, MD: Rowman and Littlefield Publishers, 2004.

O'Neill, William L. *American High: The Years of Confidence, 1945–1960.* New York: Free Press, 1989.

Packer, George, ed. *The Fight Is for Democracy: Winning the War of Ideas in America and the World.* New York: HarperPerennial, 2003.

Palast, Greg. *The Best Democracy Money Can Buy: An Investigative Reporter Exposes the Truth about Globalization, Corporate Cons, and High-Finance Fraudsters.* New York: Plume Books, 2004.

Patterson, Kelly D., and Matthew M. Singer. "The National Rifle Association in the Face of the Clinton Challenge." In Alan Cigler and Burdett Loomis, eds., *Interest Group Politics,* 6th ed. Washington, DC: Congressional Quarterly Press, 2002.

Phillips, Kevin. *The Emerging Republican Majority.* New Rochelle, NY: Arlington House, 1969.

Pierson, John. *Spike, Mike, Slackers and Dykes: A Guided Tour across a Decade of American Independent Cinema.* New York: Hyperion/Miramax Books, 1997.

Pollack, Kenneth. *The Threatening Storm: The Case for Invading Iraq.* New York: Random House, 2002.

Ramirez, Sergio. *Adios, Muchachos: Una Memoria de la Revolucion Sandinista.* Miami, FL: Santillana USA Publishing, 2000.

Rashid, Ahmed. *Taliban: Militant Islam, Oil and Fundamentalism in Central Asia.* New Haven, CT: Yale University Press, 2000.

Reed, John. *Snowball's Chance.* New York: Roof Books, 2002.

Sammon, Bill. *At Any Cost: How Al Gore Tried to Steal the Election.* Washington, DC: Regnery Publishing, 2001.

Saperstein, Guy T. *Civil Warrior: Memoirs of a Civil Rights Attorney.* Berkeley, CA: Berkeley Hills Books, 2003.

Schecter, Jerrold L., and Vyacheslav V. Luchkow, eds. *Khrushchev Remembers: The Glasnost Tapes.* Boston: Little, Brown & Co, 1991.

Schultz, Emily. *Michael Moore: A Biography.* Toronto: ECW Press, 2005.

Schweizer, Peter. *Do as I Say (Not as I Do): Profiles in Liberal Hypocrisy.* New York: Doubleday, 2005.

Strauss, David A. "Bush v. Gore: What Were They Thinking?" In Cass R. Sunstein and Richard A. Epstein, eds., *The Vote: Bush, Gore and the Supreme Court.* Chicago: University of Chicago Press, 2001.

Stuart, Guy. "Databases, Felons, and Voting: Bias and Partisanship of the Florida Felons List in the 2000 Elections." *Political Science Quarterly* 119 (Fall 2004).

Sugarman, Josh. *National Rifle Association: Money, Firepower and Fear.* Washington, DC: National Press Books, 1992.

Tapper, Jake. *Down and Dirty: The Plot to Steal the Presidency.* Boston: Little, Brown & Co., 2001.

Tax Foundation. "Federal Spending in Each State per Dollar of Federal Taxes, FY 2003." Tax Foundation, 2005.

Thernstrom, Abigail, and Russell G. Redenbaugh. "The Florida Election Report: Dissenting Statement by Commissioner Abigail Thernstrom and Commissioner Russell G. Redenbaugh." 2001.

Toobin, Jeffrey. *Too Close to Call: The 36-Day Battle to Decide the 2000 Election.* New York: Random House, 2001.

Warren, Donald I. *Radio Priest: Charles Coughlin, the Father of Hate Radio.* New York: Free Press, 1996.

Warshow, Robert. *The Immediate Experience: Movies, Comics, Theater, and Other Aspects of Popular Culture.* Cambridge, MA: Harvard University Press, 2001.

Woodward, Bob. *Plan of Attack.* New York: Simon and Schuster, 2004.

Film and Television

Abbott, Jennifer, and Mark Achbar, dirs. *The Corporation* (2005).

Elder, Larry, dir. *Michael & Me* (2005).

Greenwald, Robert, dir. *Outfoxed: Rupert Murdoch's War on Journalism* (2004).

Karel, William, dir. *Le Monde Selon Bush* (2004).

Knoblock, Kevin, dir. *Celsius 41.11: The Temperature at Which the Brain Begins to Die* (2004).

Moore, Michael, dir. *The Big One* (1998).

———. *Bowling for Columbine* (2002).

———. *Canadian Bacon* (1995).

———. *Fahrenheit 9/11* (2004).

———. *Roger & Me* (1989).

Moore, Michael, producer: The *Awful Truth* (television show, 1998, 1999).

———. *TV Nation* (television show, 1993, 1994).

Olds, Ian, and Garrett Scott, dirs. *Occupation: Dreamland* (2005).

Parker, Trey, dir. *Team America: World Police* (2004).

Perez, Richard R., and Joan Sekler, dirs. *Unprecedented: The 2000 Presidential Election* (2002).

Peterson, Alan, dir. *FahrenHYPE 9/11* (2004).

Ridgway, James, dir. *Blood in the Face* (1991).

Sellier, Charles, dir. *Faith in the White House* (2004).

Stone, Oliver, dir. *JFK* (1991).

Wilson, Michael, dir. *Michael Moore Hates America* (2004).

Television news: ABC, Abu Dhabi television, BBC, CBS, CNN, FOX News, MSNBC, NBC, PBS.

Other television: *Saturday Night Live* (NBC).

Internet

See footnotes for exact articles referenced, where applicable.

American Enterprise Institute (www.aei.org)

Blueprint (www.ndol.org)
Cato Institute (www.cato.org)
Citylink Magazine (www.citylinkmagazine.com)
Citizens United (www.citizensunited.com)
Conservative Petitions (www.conservativepetitions.com)
Coulter, Ann (www.anncoulter.com)
Deutsche Welle (www.dw-world.de)
Education for Peace in Iraq Center (www.epic-usa.org)
Fairness and Accuracy in Reporting (FAIR) (www.fair.org)
Free Republic (www.freerepublic.com)
Gun Cite (www.guncite.com)
Heritage Foundation (www.heritage.org)
Journalism Jobs (www.journalismjobs.com)
Kopel, Dave: "59 Deceits in Fahrenheit 9/11" (www.davekopel.com/Terror/
    Fiftysix-Deceits-in-Fahrenheit-911.htm)
Manhattan Institute (www.manhattan-institute.org)
Media Transparency (www.mediatransparency.org)
Moore Exposed (www.mooreexposed.com)
Moore Lies (www.moorelies.com)
Moore, Michael (www.michaelmoore.com)
Moore Watch (www.moorewatch.com)
Move America Forward (www.moveamericaforward.org)
National Review Online (www.nationalreview.com)
Newsmax (www.newsmax.com)
Open Democracy (www.opendemocracy.net)
Palast, Greg (www.gregpalast.com)
Reason Online (www.reason.com)
Salon (www.salon.com)
Screen Daily (www.screendaily.com)
Slate (www.slate.com)
Stopklatka (Poland) (www.stopklatka.pl)
Thernstrom, Abigail and Stephan (www.thernstrom.com)
Townhall (www.townhall.com)
United States Federal Elections Commission (www.fec.gov)
Variety Online (www.variety.com)

Government

Office of the Independent Counsel (Kenneth Starr). *The Starr Report: The Official Report of the Independent Counsel's Investigation of the President* (Official title: *Referral to the United States House of Representatives pursuant to Title 28, United States Code, § 595(c) Submitted*) (Library of Congress, 1998).
U.S. Census Bureau.
U.S. Commission on Civil Rights. *Voting Irregularities in Florida during the 2000 Presidential Election.*
U.S. Government Printing Office. *The Congressional Record.*
U.S. Federal Election Commission. *Database of Individual Electoral Contributions.*
Wilber, Donald N. "Clandestine Service History: Overthrow of Premier Moussadeq of Iran, November 1952–August 1953." U.S. Central Intelligence Agency, 1954.

INDEX